The Islamic Republic of Iran

The Islamic Republic of Iran: Reflections on an Emerging Economy provides an in-depth study of Iran's post-1979 Revolution economy under the Islamic Republic, with new material and related journal articles combined in one volume in a reader-friendly style.

The volume starts with an overview summarizing the development of the Iranian economy under five successive administrations in five distinct phases. This is followed by 15 articles providing detailed information which expands on, and complements, the discussion in the introductory overview. Appropriate references on specific topics are made in the overview to each relevant article, ensuring that the material is easily accessible to the reader.

Topics discussed include public finance, employment, banking, petroleum, privatization and the exchange rate. Full references are also made to US and universal economic sanctions and their effects, and to the legacies of the Khatami and Ahmadinejad administrations.

This versatile title is designed to appeal to a wide readership, including students, academics, business people, researchers and professionals. Some readers, interested in a quick review of the subject matter, may simply read the original text, while others can take the time to read the supplementary articles and review what is related to the topic of their choosing.

Jahangir Amuzegar, an international economic consultant, received his PhD in economics from the University of California after studying at the University of Tehran and the University of Washington. He was Iran's Minister of Commerce in 1962–63, Minister of Finance in 1963 and Ambassador-at-Large from 1963–79. He was also an executive director of the International Monetary Fund from 1974-80. Dr Amuzegar's many publications include *Managing the Oil Wealth: OPEC's Windfalls and Pitfalls* (1999).

Europa Emerging Economies
Editor Robert E. Looney

The Europa Emerging Economies series from Routledge, edited by Robert E. Looney, examines a wide range of contemporary economic, political, developmental and social issues as they affect emerging economies throughout the world. Complementing the Europa Regional Surveys of the World series and the *Handbook of Emerging Economies*, which was also edited by Professor Looney, the volumes in the Europa Emerging Economies series are a valuable resource for academics, students, researchers, policy-makers, professionals, and anyone with an interest in issues regarding emerging economies in the wider context of current world affairs.

Some of the volumes in the series provide in-depth country studies, while others examine issues and concepts; all are written or edited by specialists in their field. Volumes in the series are not constrained by any particular template, but may explore economic, political, governance, international relations, defence, or other issues in order to increase the understanding of emerging economies and their importance to the world economy.

Robert E. Looney is a Distinguished Professor at the Naval Postgraduate School, Monterey, USA, who specializes in issues relating to economic development in the Middle East, East Asia, South Asia and Latin America. He has published over 20 books and 250 journal articles, and has worked widely as a consultant to national governments and international agencies.

The Islamic Republic of Iran
Reflections on an emerging economy

Jahangir Amuzegar

Routledge
Taylor & Francis Group
LONDON AND NEW YORK

First edition published 2014 by Routledge

2 Park Square, Milton Park, Abingdon, Oxfordshire OX14 4RN
52 Vanderbilt Avenue, New York, NY 10017

Routledge is an imprint of the Taylor & Francis Group, an informa business

First issued in paperback 2020

British Library Cataloguing in Publication Data
A catalogue record for this book is available from the British Library

Library of Congress Cataloging in Publication Data
Amuzegar, Jahangir.
The Islamic Republic of Iran : reflections on an emerging economy / Jahangir Amuzegar.
pages cm. -- (Europa emerging economies)
Summary: "This title provides an in depth study of Iran's post 1979 Revolution economy under the Islamic Republic, with new material and related journal articles combined under one roof in a novel and reader friendly style. The volume starts with an original text, summarizing the development of the Iranian economy under five successive administrations, in five distinct phases. Following this are fifteen accompanying articles providing detailed information that expands on, and compliments, the discussion in the original material. Appropriate references on specific topics are made to each relevant article, ensuring the material is easily accessible to the reader. Topics discussed include public finance, employment, banking, petroleum, privatization, and the exchange rate. Full references are also made to US and universal economic sanctions and their effects, with the legacies of the Khatami and Ahmadinejad administrations also covered. This versatile title is designed to appeal to a vast readership. The hurried business executive or high government official, interested in a quick review of the subject matter may simply read the original text while think tank researchers, research fellows and students can take the time to read the supplementary articles and review what is related to the topic of their choosing"--Provided by publisher.
Includes bibliographical references and index.
ISBN 978-1-85743-748-5 (hardback) -- ISBN 978-1-315-75487-1 (ebook) 1. Iran--Economic conditions--1979-1997. 2. Iran--Economic conditions--1997- 3. Iran--Economic policy. I. Title.
HC475.A646 2014
330.955--dc23

2014016189

ISBN 13: 978-1-85743-748-5 (hbk)
ISBN 13: 978-0-367-66921-8 (pbk)

Typeset in Times New Roman
by Taylor & Francis Books

Europa Commissioning Editor: Cathy Hartley
Editorial Assistant: Lydia de Cruz

Contents

Foreword

In the standard published texts on the market, whenever additional information and awareness are required, the reader is directed by means of footnotes to the supplementary sources – a process which is distant, cumbersome, and often out of reach of a typical reader, or beyond the reader's time and patience for the search. In an overwhelming number of cases, therefore, the distant information which is referred to in the footnote is neglected, and the source is never consulted.

In this volume, the text and additional information are combined in a simple and accessible manner. Thus, whenever the discussion in the main text requires further clarification, the material is immediately available to the reader and does not require a distant and tedious search.

The volume starts with a succinct summary chronicling the post-1979 revolution Iranian economy under five successive Islamic administrations in five distinct phases. Standing by itself, this summary offers the hurried and busy reader a thorough account of the economy in the last three-and-a-half decades. For the more interested and leisurely reader related published articles on the subject provide further information and clarification. Thus, in the course of the introductory narrative, special references will be made to 15 articles published in different US journals on Iran's public finances, employment, banking, petroleum, privatization, exchange rates and imposed sanctions.

This book will be of interest to a wide spectrum of readers. The busy business executive or high-ranking government official interested in a quick review of the subject matter may simply read the introductory summary, and forego the supplementary articles. Researchers at think tanks, and students in various programmes of Iranian studies, however, may take their time and review their chosen topic in the related articles.

About the author

Dr Jahangir Amuzegar, an international economic consultant, received his PhD in economics from the University of California, USA, after studying law at the University of Tehran, Iran, and economics at the University of Washington, USA. He was Iran's Minister of Commerce in 1962–63, Minister of Finance in 1963 and Ambassador-at-Large from 1963–79. He was also an executive director of the International Monetary Fund from 1974–80. Dr Amuzegar has held a number of academic positions, including at the University of California at Los Angeles, Occidental College, University of Michigan, Michigan State University, American University and the Johns Hopkins School of Advanced International Studies. Dr Amuzegar's many publications include more than 100 articles published in, among others, *Foreign Affairs*, *Foreign Policy*, *Middle East Journal*, *Middle East Policy*, *Middle East Economic Survey SAIS Review*, *Oil and Gas Journal*, *Washington Quarterly*, *PROSPECT* and *Third World Quarterly*. He is also the author of several books on Iran, its oil and the country's economic development, including *Iran: Economic Development under Dualistic Conditions* (1971), *Iran: An Economic Profile* (1977), *Comparative Economics* (1981), *The Dynamics of the Iranian Revolution* (1991), *Iran's Economy under the Islamic Republic* (1993/1997) and *Managing the Oil Wealth: OPEC's Windfalls and Pitfalls* (I.B. Tauris, 1999), which was awarded *Choice*'s Outstanding Academic Title.

Acknowledgements

This book is an attempted response to the frequent urgings of my close friends and supportive readers to bring together some of my articles on the Iranian economy published in the last few years in a single volume in order to produce a more comprehensive picture of economic conditions in the Islamic Republic of Iran.

Encouraged by such sentiments, this volume starts with a short, original essay discussing the development of the post-1979 revolution Iranian economy under five successive Islamic administrations. Standing by itself, the essay offers the hurried and busy reader an informative and concise account of the economy in the last three-and-a-half decades. The subsequent 15 selected published articles, in turn, elaborate and expand the themes and topics covered in the essay for those with more time and further interest.

Many words of appreciation are due to those who made the publication of this volume possible. Special gratitude goes to the editors and publishers who graciously permitted the articles contained within this volume to be reproduced—Anne Joyce of *Middle East Policy*, Dr Saleh Jallad and Walid Khadduri of the *Middle East Economic Survey*, and Michael Dunn and Jacob Passel of the *Middle East Journal*. At Routledge, special thanks should go to Cathy Hartley, Europa Commissioning Editor; Lydia de Cruz, Editorial Assistant; Ruth Bradley, Production Editor; Alison Phillips, Copyeditor and Alison Neale, Proofreader, who went out of their way to be co-operative and accommodating. Zachary Vono at the Middle East Council and Garbis Kiremidjian at the *Middle East Economic Survey* provided invaluable technical support. Susan Englebreacht painstakingly typed up all the articles from nearly illegible script on yellow pages.

A final and distinct expression of gratitude is owed to Professor Robert Looney, who welcomed my initial inquiry, encouraged me to go ahead with the study, got the publisher interested in the project, and selflessly followed the task to fruition.

Jahangir Amuzegar

A word of caution

Speaking confidently about the behaviour and performance of the Iranian economy under the ayatollahs requires a good deal of professional courage. While more data on some basic economic indicators are officially published in Iran than in most other countries in the region, three essential elements continue to elude objective analysts: reliability, consistency and transparency. First, data published by the Central Bank on inflation, foreign reserves and external debt, the figures on unemployment published by various government agencies, and the Treasury's budget reports are frequently questioned by independent analysts who detect possible bias or inaccuracy. Second, statistics supplied by various official agencies on the same subject, such as population, employment, investment and economic growth, do not always tally. Furthermore, various data have been repeatedly revised, which may make the latest figures cited in this review somewhat divergent from those appearing in the articles. Finally, and most significantly, information about the balance sheets of public enterprises, the financial status of *bonyads* (charitable foundations), direct and indirect public subsidies, and capital flows in and out of the country, are missing, opaque, or deliberately camouflaged. There is virtually no consensus estimate on the size and functioning of the informal or 'underground' economy. The financial and operational accounts of the gargantuan Islamic Revolutionary Guard Corps—the *Pasdaran*—or the Supreme Leader's supervised trusts are never published. The concurrence of multiple exchange rates makes the conversion of the local currency into dollars for the purpose of international comparisons virtually meaningless, if not actually impossible.

For these and other reasons, the conclusions reached in this study should be treated with caution and are subject to correction and clarification as more information becomes available.

Abbreviations

CBI	Central Bank of Iran
CTJS	Corporation for Transfer of Justice Shares
EU	European Union
GDP	gross domestic product
IAEA	International Atomic Energy Agency
IMF	International Monetary Fund
IR	Iranian rial
IRGC	Islamic Revolutionary Guard Corps
JSC	Justice Shares Cooperative
MPO	Management and Planning Organization
NGO	nongovernmental organizations
NIOC	National Iranian Oil Company
NPT	Nuclear Non-Proliferation Treaty
OIC	Organization of the Islamic Conference
OPEC	Organization of Petroleum Exporting Countries
OSF	Oil Stabilization Fund
QH	*qar-zol-hassaneh*
UNDP	United Nations Development Programme
UNSC	United Nations Security Council

Overview

The unforeseen upheaval

In February 1979 a seemingly secure, militarily powerful, internationally respected, economically viable and relatively prosperous monarchy in the Middle East was overthrown by a frail and ageing Shi'ite cleric with no troops, no weapons, no visible source of finance and no credible foreign support. Even in a century marked by frequent and ferocious outbursts of violence—revolutions in Russia, China and Cuba, accompanied by a series of military coups in Africa, Asia and Latin America—Iran's Islamic Revolution stands out to this day as an epochal event.

At the time, however, the portent, pitfalls and potential of this unique event were missed by most Iran pundits. Ominously, in its 'Man of the Year' issue of 1980 *Time* magazine portrayed Ayatollah Ruhollah Khomeini's victory as a threat to 'the world balance of power more than any political event since Hitler's conquest of Europe'. It called it a 'model for the future uprisings throughout the Third World'. Meanwhile, a group of academics respected for their knowledge of Iranian affairs, argued that the Shi'ite clergy was mentally and emotionally unprepared for the challenge of running Iran, and that the Khomeini revolution would end up as an authoritarian leftist regime, a right-wing military junta, or a Western-style liberal democracy. Some left-leaning Iranian scholars foresaw a quick defeat for Khomeini at the hands of the labour movement and the masses. The collective wisdom was that Khomeini's Government would be makeshift, and that he himself would be unlikely to play a central part in governing the new Iran.

Pronouncements made by the Ayatollah in late 1978 while he was exiled in France gave solid credence to these prognostications. In an interview with Reuters on 26 October 1978 he said: 'In Islamic Iran, the clerics will not govern, but only supervise the Government's actions. I myself will have no leadership role, and will go back to my lecture class in Qom.' Speaking on Austrian television on 16 November 1978 he said: 'I do not wish to be a leader of the future Islamic Republic, or to take the Government's power in my own hands.' On the following day, 17 November, he reiterated this stance in an interview with the Associated Press: 'Neither my own inclination, nor my physical health, permits me to take a personal role in the Government after the Shah's regime is overthrown.' Finally, in an interview on 9 January 1979 with the French newspaper *Le Monde* he stated: 'After the Shah's departure, I will not become the President of the republic, nor will I accept any other leadership position.' It transpired that these statements were all *taqieh*—the Shi'ism practice of intentionally falsifying discourse in order to deceive the enemy.

As it turned out, not only did expert speculations about the short life, and early demise, of the Khomeini rule prove to be premature, the outcome was neither a leftist dictatorship, nor a military junta, and certainly not a Western democracy. Instead, the revolution metamorphosed into a special regime with its own bizarre characteristics. The post-revolution Islamic Government that was established following a speedily held referendum not only disproved the pundits' predictions, but astounded all the experts. Ayatollah Khomeini, now known as the imam, assumed absolute political power, and within a year or so methodically eliminated nearly all of his co-revolutionaries. Contrary to his earlier anti-Shah protestations made under the banners of Persian nationalism and economic populism, he managed to establish his vision of Islamic governance, the *velayat-e faqih* (rule by a religious jurist), in exactly the same way that he had outlined extensively during his earlier lectures in Qom—propositions that few regime supporters had bothered to read, or refused to believe.

The Khomeini model, however, was not followed in the region's other Muslim monarchies (or hereditary governments) as predicted by *Time* and others. Nor did it spawn similar tendencies in other countries with sizeable Shi'a contingents such as Iraq, Lebanon, Pakistan, Bahrain or Azerbaijan. Instead, it encouraged and spread a new cult of martyrdom in the form of state terrorism, political assassinations and public sabotage among its fervent followers. Furthermore, Imam Khomeini's unique, albeit flawed, system of *velayat-e faqih*, displayed an extraordinary instinct for survival. Despite violent early revolutionary turmoil, the loss of a large number of its top religious, political and military commanders at the hands of domestic opposition groups, a long, bloody and disastrous war with Iraq in the 1980s, ethnic separatist insurrections, international sanctions, a burgeoning population, and frequent natural disasters, the clerical establishment managed to survive.

In spite of its inherent capriciousness, political repression, human rights violations, and an anachronistic moral code, the Islamic Republic has been successful so far in eliciting support and loyalty from a large part of the population. The regime has also rebuilt its military power following the 1989 cease-fire with Iraq, enhanced its defence systems on land and sea, successfully developed medium- and long-range ballistic missiles, and sought to obtain capabilities for eventual nuclear defence.

The Government, however, has shown a curious dualism manifested in its internal weaknesses and external strength. The Iranian economy has been stagnant for the past three and a half decades due to the regime's inherent constitutional contradictions, faulty and unrealistic national goals, shifting politico-economic models, considerable bureaucratic incompetence, an anachronistic domestic moral code, and a distorted world view. Externally, however, three fortuitous factors—none of the regime's own making—have helped the Islamic Republic to gain a new-found power, prestige and confidence in the region and within the world community. First, the Union of Soviet Socialist Republics (USSR)—historically an enemy of Iran—was dismantled in 1991, and has now become the regime's closest and most powerful ally. Second, Iran's post-revolution adversaries—President Saddam Hussain of Iraq and the Taliban in Afghanistan—were crushed by allied forces, making the clerical regime a regional superpower. Third, a decade-long increase in income from exports of crude oil—up to 2011 and before the impact of crippling universal economic sanctions—has enabled the country to strengthen its defences, to build a considerable arsenal of modern weapons, and to make significant progress in the development of atomic energy and enrichment of uranium.

The anti-monarchy manifesto

The clerical elements that formed a coalition with other secular dissidents against the Pahlavi monarchy under Khomeini's leadership, and which ultimately succeeded in eliminating other revolutionary contingents, admittedly had no concrete agenda beyond repudiating the old regime's policies and programmes. The Shah's Government was denounced for having surrendered Iran's political independence to the USA, denied its citizens basic human freedoms, and failed to follow the Islamic creed. In particular, the regime was chastised for adopting a Western development model that neglected 'the national interest', and made the country's economic growth and prosperity dependent upon foreign technology, management know-how, industrial materials, and trade. The Pahlavi Government was castigated further for the excessive exploitation of endowed oil reserves far beyond domestic needs, inattention to agricultural self-sufficiency, an industrial policy geared at assembly plant operations, undue reliance on oil export receipts to finance the public budget, scant regard for non-oil exports, widening gaps between income strata, classes and regions, and altogether a strategy devoted to the promotion of a consumerist society. In short, the monarchy's legacy was depicted as a country that was dependent on capitalist economies, Western technology, industrial inputs, and imported food, and which was developing unevenly in the interests of certain privileged groups, regions and classes. Its alleged strategy of 'growth first, distribution later', it was argued, had resulted in the advancement of industry and urban centres at the expense of the agricultural sector and rural areas. Finally, the former Government was accused of detracting the populace from the path of spirituality, virtue and contentment.

The Shah's own complex and enigmatic character was portrayed by his triumphant enemies as autocratic, self-centred, imperious, megalomaniac and corrupt. More generous characterizations ranged from an insecure, aloof, edgy and self-indulgent man, to a fair-weather hero, risk averse and intolerant of criticism.

Contrary to these accusations, however, reams of official documents and data show that on the eve of the 1979 revolution, Iran had just completed nearly two decades of rapid growth and impressive social progress. By any criteria, the country was thriving, vibrant, prospering and expanding—with impressive rates of growth in savings, investments, consumption, employment and per head income. The Iranian rial was effectively a convertible currency towards the end of the period. All sectors of the economy showed significant expansion, though with variations in pace. Data published by the World Bank show that during 1960–77 Iran's annual real growth rate of 9.6% was about double the average for countries in its income category, and higher than the average for countries in any other categories. During these two decades Iran was transformed systematically from a largely agrarian and stagnant economy into a modern, progressive society as a result of profound structural changes in the tradition-bound socio-economic order. Through public guidance and assistance, the economy was directed onto a path towards modernization, diversification, industrialization, urbanization and integration into the global economy. The Government had sizeable foreign investments in German, French and British firms among others; it had lent money to the International Monetary Fund (IMF), the World Bank and several developing countries. Iranian citizens could travel to many parts of the world without a visa. In short, unlike many Third World nations whose economic growth and prosperity were curbed owing to insufficient physical and human capital, Iran enjoyed both in relative abundance.

Astonishingly enough, most of the policies and programmes for which the Pahlavi Government was criticized strongly have been equally, if not more vigorously pursued by the Islamic regime. Over the past 20 years the Government has sought to achieve again an oil output of around 6m. barrels per day (b/d), which actually had been reached in the late 1970s, but without success. Iran's agricultural sector, according to a former Islamic government minister, is now in a worse shape than ever before, with an unprecedented national dependence on food imports. There are more assembly plants in Iran than ever. The annual budget relies more heavily on oil receipts than at any time during the Pahlavi reign. As will be shown below, the post-revolution generation currently enjoys neither true political independence, nor true political democracy, nor real economic security based on social justice, and not even the minimum freedoms guaranteed by the regime's own Islamic Constitution.[1]

Velayat-e faqih in theory and practice

The banners under which the anti-Shah revolutionary victors established the new regime bore three simple slogans: independence, freedom and the Islamic Republic—but there was no clear definition of any of these. In practice, independence turned out to mean hostility towards the USA and Western culture, combined with respect and amity towards Russia and the People's Republic of China—this despite the motto over the Ministry of Foreign Affairs' portal in Tehran that reads 'Neither East nor West'. Freedom in effect meant a lack of reliance upon foreign countries, and an emphasis on economic self-sufficiency that was planned and carried out by the central Government. Moreover, the Islamic Republic was determined to find an 'Islamic economic model' which could put an end to what the revolutionaries called 'crass materialism' and 'consumerism'.

Pending the formulation of an ideal model, successive administrations have managed Iran's economy in an ad hoc, improvised and inconsistent manner. A curious mixture of capitalism, populism and pragmatism has served to anchor the economy. Lurching from one crisis to another, the regime has squandered valuable national resources, endured high opportunity costs of poor investment projects, and suffered as a result of colossal waste and inefficiency in public operations. At the same time, Iran has endured an intellectual vacuum through an unchecked brain drain, witnessed a gradual worsening of the environment for business enterprise, become mired in increasing rent-seeking activities and financial corruption, and, finally, paid dearly for its inexcusable blunders in major foreign policy decisions.

Not surprisingly, therefore, after more than three decades of absolute and uncontested rule, the Islamic Republic has been unable to shake off any of the 'horrors' of the old regime. The nirvana that the post-1979 generation was meant to have enjoyed has actually turned out increasingly to resemble a form of purgatory in five different phases and under the stewardship of five different politicians.[2]

Phase one: a legalized anarchy

The first phase, covering the years 1979–81, should be called a period of 'legalized anarchy'—devoted to post-revolution 'purification' and institutional reconstruction. During this chaotic period, the economy was poorly managed. For a while, the regime toyed with a doctrine called the 'economics of divine unity', whose basic premise was not the conventional economics assumption of scarcity, and the need for rational resource allocation, but the prevalence of material plenty and the task of income distribution. This somewhat counter-intuitive thesis was the brainchild of the Islamic Republic's first elected president, Abolhassan Bani-Sadr. The thesis was a poorly conceived and distorted version of Karl Marx's labour theory. Its immediate manifestations were to deny the sanctity of private property and to advocate the mass distribution of wealth and income. The slogan was 'distribution before growth'.

Meanwhile, a Revolutionary Council, appointed by Ayatollah Khomeini, embarked on a radical transformation of the economy from a basically Western-oriented, free enterprise system to a state-managed and anti-market system. More than 60 separate council decrees issued between February 1979 and

July 1980 ordered the confiscation without compensation of thousands of private properties and business firms belonging to the Shah's associates and supporters. Under a mixture of revolutionary ideology and Islamic orthodoxy, all major industries were taken over from private owners/managers. Thousands of firms working in agriculture, small industry, trade and tourism were confiscated and were randomly transferred to a number of newly established *bonyads* (charitable foundations). A series of further decisions, sanctioned by a new 1979 Islamic Constitution, involved the wholesale nationalization of 'basic' industries, private banks, insurance companies, major private industrial enterprises and agribusinesses. Experienced and knowledgeable private owners/managers were hastily replaced by young revolutionaries, 'committed Muslim' job seekers, and mullahs' friends and relatives. The result was a disastrous decline in national production and income, accompanied by inflation and unemployment.[3] Between 1978/79 and 1980/81 Iran's gross domestic product (GDP) decreased by 20% in real terms, the value of the Iranian rial plummeted from IR 70 = US $1 to IR 235 = US $1, and the consumer price index rose by 22% each year.

Phase two: monolithic theocracy

The second phase—to be called a monolithic theocracy—was dominated almost exclusively by Ayatollah Khomeini's diktat. Coinciding roughly with the Iran–Iraq war, this period was guided by a Soviet-Indian economic model characterized by widespread state intervention, wartime restrictions and 'Big Brother' controls where economic austerity, insularity and an emphasis on self-sufficiency were in vogue. This was a period marked by incalculable human suffering, heavy damage to oil installations, the devastation of basic infrastructures, incapacitated industrial facilities and ruined farmland. Meanwhile, the country confronted increased military expenditure, the loss of oil revenues and reduced access to external funds following the imposition of US and international sanctions as a result of the hostage crisis. The ideology pursued during this period was that of an ascetic, egalitarian and self-reliant life. At the same time, the economic strategy adopted by the regime, far beyond the exigencies of managing a wartime economy, was again the reflection of a pseudo-Marxist ideology followed by some leftist elements that were still active within the revolution's rainbow coalition. The period's official mantra was economic austerity, personal sacrifice and an emphasis on national self-sufficiency involving further state intervention in the economy, restrictions on private ownership and business transactions, and the rationing of consumer products. This short-sighted and expedient, but ultimately disastrous, paradigm was presided over by Mir Hossein Mousavi, a fanatical Islamic Marxist zealot and interventionist, who was openly hostile to 'American capitalism' and multinational corporations. Policies adopted during this period—strict wage and price controls, rationing, and heavy food and fuel subsidies—formed the basis of many of Iran's economic woes for the next 30 years.

During this difficult period, wartime exigencies and US economic sanctions were invoked to expand government ownership and operation. The official goal was presumably to achieve Islamic 'social justice'. One of the administration's signature strategies was, however, a pro-natalist policy designed to beget '20 million soldiers of Islam'—a policy that culminated in protracted and intractable levels of unemployment in Iran and abysmally low national productivity over the next two decades. At the same time, by keeping the official dollar value of the Iranian rial at the 1979 level while the wartime economy was experiencing rising inflation, and budget deficits were financed by the printing press, the weak economy was further exposed to serious cost/price distortions, a rent-seeking business culture, and a costly and unfair subsidy system. To cope with resulting stubborn inflation, a vast array of wage, price and exchange controls were imposed, the rationing of essential consumer goods was further intensified, and imports were compressed through strict foreign currency allocations and a raft of multiple exchange rates for various transactions.

The outcome was unsurprisingly calamitous. According to official figures, gross domestic investment fell by 6.6% per year on average, reaching only about 11% of GDP at the end of the period, and less than the capital depreciation rate. Some industries operated at only 30% of capacity due to shortages of raw materials. Iran's GDP in real terms during the eight-year period declined by 1.8% per year on average, with the result that the real national product in 1988/89 was only equal to that recorded 15 years earlier. With a rapidly increasing population, per head income fell to 55% of the 1977/78 level. Unemployment reached nearly 16%. Inflation climbed to nearly 30% in 1988—the highest level since the end of the Second World War. The budget deficit exceeded 44% of total expenditure, and 9% of GDP. The exchange value of the rial in the 'grey market' reached 20 times the official rate. Capital flight and the emigration of entrepreneurs and managers accelerated. Altogether, the average annual decline in GDP during the first two periods between 1978 and 1988 was 2.4%.

Phase three: clerical oligarchy

The third phase (1989–97), to be known as the clerical oligarchy, began with the Iran–Iraq cease-fire, and covered the first two Five-Year Development Plans. During this period political power was shared in an oligarchic manner by (1) the new Supreme Leader, Ayatollah Ali Khamenei, who was selected following the death of Ayatollah Khomeini in June 1989; (2) the newly elected President of the Republic, Ali Akbar Hashemi Rafsanjani—a businessman by profession and a clergyman by avocation; (3) the influential Council of Guardians; and (4) a more assertive Majlis (national assembly).

Under President Hashemi Rafsanjani the economy adopted the so-called structural adjustment model which placed greater emphasis on free market principles. It was dubbed Rafsanjani's perestroika. The massive devastation left by the revolution itself, and the enormous destruction wrought by the ruinous eight-year war with Iraq, had exhausted the people's patience and endurance. With the death of Ayatollah Khomeini in 1989, a number of young technocrats and progressive clerics began to realize that the early revolutionary slogan of 'Islam is the solution' was no longer applicable. A group loyal to President Rafsanjani spearheaded a movement to redirect the economy towards liberalization, privatization and global participation. The newly approved Five-Year Economic Development Plan (1989–93) adopted a multi-pronged strategy aimed at reconstructing war-torn areas, expanding basic infrastructure neglected during the war, and reviving the private sector under a structural adjustment programme called *ta'deel eqtesadi.* The Plan promised to transform the war economy into a market-oriented, investment-driven and more efficient system through trade liberalization, wage-price deregulation, privatization of state enterprises, and other economic reforms. Disregarding the earlier emphasis on self-sufficiency, the Government began actively to seek foreign credit from the World Bank and other international financial institutions. Earlier strategies that had reflected Bani-Sadr's economic dilettantism, and Mousavi's obsessive interventionism, were overtaken by Rafsanjani's liberal stance. Above all, Mousavi's disastrous pro-natalist policy was replaced by strict population controls.

Initially, the paradigm change was successful. The overall outcome of this phase was better than that of the first two phases, but still below the planned growth target. Large industrial excess capacity unused during the war, the release of soldiers from war duties, and particularly rising oil export receipts following Iraq's invasion of Kuwait helped to increase economic growth during the first three years of the Plan, thus overshooting the targets. The cost of a number of price-controlled items was cut drastically, and import restrictions were substantially removed. Under a limited but highly controversial programme, some 200 public enterprises were privatized.[4]

Advances on the liberalization and deregulation fronts, however, were short-lived as their social costs proved intolerable. In response to the removal of import and exchange restrictions, private consumption exceeded planned projections, rising by 19.5% in 1990 alone, compared to just 2.5% in 1989. Lack of discipline in the conduct of the Plan's mandates was equally responsible for a series of emerging bottlenecks. The first setback was triggered in March 1993 with a precipitous decision to unify the 12 different exchange rates into a single 'floating' rate at 1,600 rials to the US dollar—replacing the long-outdated basic parity rate of 70 rials. Without complementary monetary and fiscal policies, and accompanied by a series of other misguided decisions, the unification decision backfired badly. Imports rose from US $10,600m. in 1988–89 to $25,200m. in 1991–92 largely on short-term export credits. The country's balance of payments experienced huge deficits, exchange reserves were rapidly exhausted, and state banks were unable to meet their short-term foreign repayment obligations. The Central Bank had to engage in a series of excruciatingly difficult bilateral negotiations with Iran's trade partners. As a result, by mid-1993 not only did the structural adjustment strategy decelerate, but many restrictions in foreign trade and exchange transactions had to be reinstated. The unified exchange rate was finally abandoned in December 1993. Price controls were re-imposed, and severe new penalties (*taa'zeerat*) were imposed on violators. With the exception of energy, all the other sectors fell short of their planned targets. Both public and private consumption exceeded their set limits, and aggregate investment declined below its projected level. Despite strict new price controls and huge subsidies, the consumer price index in the last year of the Rafsanjani presidency registered 49.5%—the highest in the post-revolution era. The consumer price index for the period ended with an average of 24.5% per year. Iran's foreign debt reached 11.4% of GDP—a record high for the country.

Phase four: 'Islamic democracy'

The fourth phase, a self-proclaimed era of Islamic democracy under the newly elected President Mohammad Khatami (1997–2004), was yet another period of reform and liberalization. It was also a period of notable recovery from relative stagnation thanks to a record surge in oil prices. In approving the outlines of the country's 20-Year Economic Perspective[5] and the outlines of the new 2000–05 Five-Year Economic Development Plan, Supreme Leader Khamenei urged government officials to combat the country's three scourges of 'poverty, discrimination and corruption'. While the objectives of the new Third Plan were more realistic and rational than those of the previous two, they still reflected the same familiar populist clichés embedded in the country's Constitution, and the commitments promised under the original structural adjustment programme. Accordingly, *social justice*—a code phrase for controlled prices and broad subsidies—was to be combined with *progress*—a code word for rapid growth, high employment and pro-market reforms.

As in the past the Plan's 'wish list' included such promises as downsizing government bureaucracy through privatization; improving the management of public enterprises by emphasizing professional competence instead of religious commitment; replacing across-the-board subsidies with a social safety net; population control through stepped-up family planning; reducing unemployment through increased investment, attracting foreign investment; matching job requirements with the educational curriculum; eliminating private monopolies; allowing greater transparency in the national budget; instituting fiscal reforms through the establishment of a value-added tax system; reorganizing the financial sector through the rationalization of interest rates and reducing Central Bank financing of budget deficits; eventual convertibility of the rial in current accounts; and reforming the trade system by gradual deregulation, removal of non-tariff barriers, and elimination of private tariff exemptions.

A novel feature of the plan was the establishment of an Oil Stabilization Fund (OSF) to safeguard future annual budgets against volatile oil price fluctuations. Under OSF provisions, annual oil export revenues in excess of the budgeted amount had to be deposited in the Fund to be drawn upon during oil price slumps and budget shortfalls. A proportion of the deposits could also be lent to private entrepreneurs for domestic investment subject to specific conditions.[6]

The country's economic fortunes fared somewhat better under the Third Plan, mainly as a result of new and unexpected oil windfalls, favourable weather conditions and a series of economic reforms. Average annual GDP growth reached 5.4%. The official unemployment rate averaged 12.5% for the period. The official inflation rate, aided by massive subsidies, averaged 16% per year, while rises in liquidity, at nearly 29% per year, overshot the target by 66%. The increase in national productivity at 0.52% per year also lagged behind the projected 0.86%. It was claimed that the number of people living below the absolute and relative poverty lines had declined. Foreign reserves exceeded US $34,000m. thanks to continued annual surpluses in the current account. The Central Bank was successful in floating two fully subscribed foreign exchange government bonds totalling €625m. With the average price of Iranian oil ranging between $21 and $44 per barrel, monetary and fiscal policies were eased, and private investments surpassed the planned targets.

By far the most significant reform achieved during this period, however, was the final unification of the exchange rate in March 2002, placing the 'floating' value of the Iranian rial into a 'basket' of currencies. Exchange reforms also included acceptance of the obligations of the IMF's Article VIII, eliminating most foreign exchange restrictions on current transactions for the first time since Iran joined the Fund in 1945. As part of a new trade liberalization drive, most export restrictions were eliminated. Non-tariff barriers were replaced by a better-structured and simpler tariff regime. Import licensing procedures were streamlined. The decades-old law for the attraction of foreign investment was revised in 2002 with a clearer legal framework and enhanced incentives.

In the monetary and financial area, both the Treasury and the Central Bank were authorized to issue debt certificates—called Participation Papers—to cover the budget deficit, and mop up excess liquidity. State banks were given greater flexibility to set rates for both deposits and loans. Several private banks and insurance companies were licensed for the first time since the revolution, and legislatively mandated credits to various sectors were reduced. New legislation regarding capital markets, electronic commerce, money-laundering, transaction checking and stock exchange operations were proposed to the Majlis. Fiscal reforms, in addition to the establishment of the OSF, included the significant reduction of corporate and individual income tax rates, and the consolidation of scores of different fees and levies on various goods and services into a new single transaction tax.

On the flip side, the budget-to-GDP ratio turned negative with the shortfall equal to 3% of GDP; the non-oil fiscal deficit rose from 13.5% of GDP to 18% during the period. The nominal exchange rate—Iranian rial per US dollar—rose from about 6,000 to nearly 9,000. Public external debt increased from US $8,000m. to $15,700m., with 'potential' liabilities reaching $33,000m. The privatization of state enterprises fell far short of the target. The Government's debt to the Central Bank reached an all-time high of IR 112,000,000m. Moreover, the OSF that was supposed to be drawn upon if oil revenues fell below target was used frequently to cover budget deficits—at a time when oil revenues exceeded the target every year.

Furthermore, the three crucial promises regarding the replacement of current unfair subsidies with an effective safety net, the conversion of current inefficient taxes into a value-added tax regime, and the greater transparency in programme budgeting still remained elusive goals. The Government's privatization efforts also were largely unsuccessful because the essential preconditions for such structural change—an open trading system; an effective regulatory framework; an active capital market; a competitive banking system; an impartial judiciary; and a predictable political environment for private investment—did not exist or were deficient. Furthermore, the country's relatively fair economic record was marred by publicly acknowledged significant air and water pollution, considerable soil erosion, and an alarming rate of desertification and deforestation. Added to these woes were the closely related social scourges of endemic corruption, widespread drug addiction, child labour employment, younger-age prostitution, violent urban crimes and increased underground economic activities.

In sum, despite President Khatami's best intentions and efforts, the Third Plan's quantitative and reform targets deviated from the targets by considerable margins—indicating once again the irrelevance of central planning to Iran's economic behaviour and performance, and the crucial difference that an honest and devoted administration might make in managing the economy.[7]

Phase five: messianic/populist autocracy

The fifth phase (2005–13), a tumultuous eight-year period, could be described as a messianic/populist/para-military autocracy under the leadership of Mahmoud Ahmadinejad—a fanatical religious zealot who claimed to be in daily contact with the Shi'ite occult imam; a populist demagogue who championed the cause of the poor and the disenfranchised against the rich and the 'oil mafia'; and a self-appointed agent provocateur against the West's domination of the world. Following Ahmadinejad's surprise election as the sixth President of the Islamic Republic in mid-2005, Iran began a period of internal political turmoil, economic stagflation and diplomatic isolation.

The two distinctive features of the Ahmadinejad administration, which were mainly responsible for the disastrous outcome of his stewardship, were (1) military and security dominance over the economy similar to that perpetrated in Indonesia and Egypt, resulting in unusually poor economic performance; and (2) hostility towards the West and the state of Israel, resulting in crippling universal economic sanctions.[8] The militarization of Iran's economy manifested itself in many ways. During Ahmadinejad's presidency, a considerable number of cabinet ministers, for example, were, like himself, former commanders of the Islamic Revolutionary Guard Corps (IRGC). Two engineering and construction firms controlled by the IRGC, Khatam ol-Anbia and its sister company, Khatam ol-Ossia, became the country's largest and richest domestic contractors during Ahmadinejad's tenure, winning government contracts in no-bid procedures, and exerting their influence over such sectors as oil, gas, petrochemicals, mines, road building, irrigation and dam construction. By 2013, IRCG reportedly controlled 21% of the Tehran Stock Exchange and 28 publicly traded companies.

Hostility towards the West manifested itself in a wholesale dismissal of Western-educated technocrats from sensitive economic and financial positions. Ahmadinejad not only refused to endorse the Fourth Development Plan (2005–10) that had been prepared meticulously under the Khatami administration, he actually undermined its operation through a series of countermeasures. A stunning manifestation of his antipathy was the abrupt closure of the 60-year-old Plan Organization (which was responsible for Iran's Five-Year Economic Development Plans) on the pretext that it was an 'American creation', staffed by Western-trained economists. As a result, the latest Five-Year Plan was the least successful of all the post-revolution economic plans, with growth, employment, inflation, investment and productivity all missing their targets by wide margins. A fifth plan for 2010–15 was prepared by Ahmadinejad's Government and approved by the Majlis. However, in the circumstances it remained mostly at the planning stage.

Ahmadinejad's economic record actually epitomizes his presidency. A self-confessed economic illiterate, he relied upon his own raw instincts and personal ideological inclination, ignoring all economic realities, embarking on a number of misguided economic policies and rejecting advice from independent economists. Influenced perhaps by his austere childhood, and regarding money as the key to every economic problem, he began his term in office with a highly expansionary programme—increasing the fiscal budget, revving up the Central Bank's printing press and expanding bank lending. The annual budget escalated by 5% above the annual inflation rate each year from IR 1,590,000,000m. in 2005 to IR 7,280,000,000m. in 2013—or by a factor of 4.5. Corresponding total liquidity increased from IR 92,000,000m. to IR 5,300,000m.—or by a factor of 5.75. During the same period, the state sector's debt to the banking system increased from IR 236,000,000m. to IR 1,152,000,000m.

Confronted by protracted double-digit inflation caused by perennial budget deficits and the banking system's increasing debt to the Central Bank (due to the financing of his pet projects), Ahmadinejad decided to combat this demand-caused economic disequilibrium by focusing on costs. Thus, instead of trying to raise revenues through taxes or to reduce excessive expenditure, he chose a crowd-pleasing, short-term economic policy of controlling costs—with scant regard for its harmful long-term implications. In order to curb household and business expenses, he proceeded to hold in check three vital cost factors—the exchange rate, interest rates and basic energy prices—through government diktats. The outcome was near disaster in all three areas.

Considering a strong national currency to be a symbol of affluence and prestige, President Ahmadinejad sought to keep the Iranian rial artificially high against the US dollar and other foreign exchanges when every economic indicator suggested that the precise opposite was necessary. This short-sighted policy of keeping the exchange rate artificially over-valued in order to hold down import costs led to a number of worrying consequences such as (1) reducing domestic producers' ability to compete with foreign suppliers; (2) constraining the domestic production capacity of import-competing industries by some 30%–40%; (3) rendering thousands of workers idle with every additional billion dollars' worth of imports; (4) worsening Iran's non-oil trade balance; and (5) awarding hefty subsidies to foreign farmers and manufacturers. The over-valued exchange rate also resulted in increased national dependence on the world economy (even for essential food items) and capital flight. Thus, with the imposition of new tough sanctions on Iran's oil exports and its Central Bank operations in late 2011, the rial lost two-thirds of its value against the US dollar and other foreign exchanges, and the long-dormant pressure on it blew up.[9] Strangely enough, towards the end of his tenure when the US dollar value of the Iranian rial was fixed by the Central Bank at approximately IR 10,000, and the inflation adjusted equilibrium rate would have warranted IR 24,000, the President still wished to reduce the rate to IR 5,000.

Extensive government regulation of interest rates and mandatory lending was Ahmadinejad's second policy mistake. Holding interest rates on savings deposits below the inflation rate, and keeping bank charges on commercial and investment loans below free market levels in the bazaar, inflicted incalculable damage on the economy. Low (and negative) returns on deposits discouraged individual savers, stifled productive investments, and compelled savers to move their funds from bank accounts to other outlets such as real estate, precious metals and US dollars. Losing savings deposits led the commercial banks to borrow steadily from the Central Bank in order to finance their voluntary as well as state-mandated loans. Government-dictated loans to favoured, but money-losing, projects became the main cause of the commercial banks' skyrocketing non-performing loans, estimated at IR 840,000,000m. in 2013 (excluding those already rescheduled).

Keeping energy prices artificially low for years resulted primarily in profligate energy use, with Iran's per head consumption estimated at six times the world average. Prior to the enactment of the Subsidies Targeting Act in 2010 Iran's energy prices were only 16% of the international norm. Low-priced gasoline and other forms of energy encouraged inefficiencies in homes, buildings and factories; the rise of energy-intensive (and labour-saving) industries contributed to unemployment and exposure to external shocks; an increased need for energy imports (both gasoline and natural gas); excessive air pollution and the rise of related diseases; and a marked acceleration in energy-smuggling to neighbouring countries. The Act initially caused energy prices to increase to 47% of global standards, but subsequent events and the devaluation of the US dollar reversed the situation by 2013.

The outcome of this blatant mismanagement was reflected in the behaviour of the main economic indicators. The growth of the gross national product to 6.9% in 2005 gradually tapered off year on year. During the last two years of Ahmadinejad's administration, 2011 and 2012, growth was –1.7% and –5.8%, respectively, while low or negative growth for the next two years was forecast. Such anaemic GDP growth was particularly unsatisfactory because it was accompanied by both unemployment and inflation.

Data on various aspects of employment and unemployment are among the least detailed, least informative, and least reliable published by the Government. The official unemployment rate reportedly rose from 11.5% in 2005 to 12.2% in 2013, with more than 3m. people out of work. In the same year figures for unemployment among the youth (aged 16–25 years) and women stood at more than 25%. Unofficial figures indicate that 20% of the total labour force were job seekers, including several thousand holders of advanced university degrees. With an additional 5m. youths entering the job market for the first time, the number of Iranian job seekers was set to reach 8m. Official figures by the Statistical Center of Iran show that labour force participation declined from 41% in 2005 to 37.3% in 2012. In short, despite the Ahmadinejad Government's claim to have created 'millions' of new jobs, recently published data show that only about 75,000 jobs were created each year during 2005–13, with approximately 34,000 individuals joining the unemployed total annually. In 2013 a deplorably small number of women (13.5%) participated in the labour force, while some 75% of college-educated women were housewives.

The official consumer price index, at 10.4% in 2005, began to rise steadily year on year, reaching 39.7% in mid-2013—the world's second highest level—when Ahmadinejad's term in office ended. Increases in the consumer price index for the whole period reached 22.6% per year, second only to levels achieved during the Rafsanjani era. With food prices increasing by almost 60% following the rial's massive loss of value during 2012–13, the bottom 20% of income receivers—whose daily expenses were concentrated on food items—lost more than 40% of their purchasing power. This represented the steepest loss since the revolution. In early 2014 Oxfam International ranked Iran at 80th place among 125 countries mainly because food items cost two-and-a-half times that of other consumer staples.

Runaway liquidity created to finance the President's three pet projects, which was almost entirely funded by the Central Bank's new money creation, was held responsible for the steady rise in consumer prices. The three projects were loans to the so-called quick-return enterprises to create 2m. jobs, low-cost housing constructed on the periphery of large cities (*maskan-e-mehr*), and the cash payment-based subsidies reform.[10] All three schemes are considered to have failed. The housing project alone, according to Abbas Ahmad Akhoundi, Minister of Transportation and Housing, was responsible for 40% of the increased liquidity. More than IR 1,200,000,000m. paid out as monthly subsidy cheques during the three years was itself equivalent to the country's two-year development budgets.

The Government's inability to control inflation through rational means was another failure of the Ahmadinejad administration. Instead of combating price increases through balancing the budget, reducing bank lending and controlling liquidity, the President relaxed import restrictions and allowed cheaper competing products in. A fortuitous rise in oil export receipts during Ahmadinejad's eight-year tenure awarded his administration some US $700,000m.—equivalent to 63% of all oil income in the last 108 years. The sum also compared to the $400,000m. received by all previous administrations since the revolution, and five times that earned between the oil discovery in 1906 and the end of the Pahlavi regime. Of the nearly $700,000m. of oil exports received during Ahmadinejad's tenure, some $440,000m. was spent on imports, raising yearly purchases from $36,000m. to $60,000m. The outcome, while benefiting low incomes through lower prices, was the destruction of competing domestic industries. At the same time, precious foreign exchange received from the export of a dwindling resource, oil, was squandered on the importation of consumer goods instead of being reinvested to produce new wealth.

By the time the new administration of Hassan Rouhani took office in August 2013, Iran was experiencing the worst combination of inflation and unemployment in nearly 25 years, with the consumer price index exceeding 40%, and youth unemployment exceeding 26%. According to the Cato Institute's 2013 annual report, the 'misery index' (a combination of inflation, unemployment and low consumer confidence) had risen from 21.9 in 2005 to 61.6—the second highest among 90 countries.

At the same time, despite its record oil revenues, the Ahmadinejad Government's debts to the Central Bank, the private and the public sectors reached an all-time high of IR 1,890,000,000m.—the largest of any Iranian government in history. As a result of economic recession, poor supervision, a lack of adequate guarantees, and blatant cronyism whereby loans were granted to some 100 individuals who were close to the Government, the extent of non-performing loans by the banking system in 2013 reached 15.6% of all bank loans—four times the global average. The loans in default reached more than IR 820,000,000m. (US $25,000m.) in 2013, up from IR 70,000,000m. in 2005.

In retrospect, the reasons for the failures recorded during the fifth phase can be attributed to three main factors: (1) Ahmadinejad's own personality; (2) rampant corruption among his military, security and civilian appointees; and (3) crippling economic sanctions imposed by the USA, the United Nations (UN) and the European Union (EU).

Ahmadinejad's personal values, his maverick management style, his misguided economic policies and his diplomatic incompetence were the fundamental cause of his widely recognized failures. As a child he experienced poverty and deprivation, and as an adult he regarded economics as a handbook for the distribution of wealth and income instead of a means of wealth creation. He rejected all non-Islamic systems as unjust and exploitive. He found the current distribution of income and wealth in Iran unfair, harboured an irrational grudge against banks and bankers, and distrusted big business. His governing style leaned towards ad hoc, dictatorial and micro-management, and shunned long-term preparation. His staff was chosen on the basis of loyalty and obedience instead of competence and expertise. His selected pet economic projects ostensibly based on 'compassion and fairness' defied careful economic cost/benefit analyses. Furthermore, he vowed to fight the West's 'geopolitical hegemony'.[11]

The prevalence of malfeasance among Ahmadinejad's officials, and the rise of corruption during his administration, were further factors responsible for the country's malaise. Transparency International's 2013 report, which ranked the Islamic Republic in 144th place among 177 countries, has termed the country 'highly corrupt'. It also shows that the situation has deteriorated over time. When Ahmadinejad came to power in 2005, only 55% of the countries observed by Transparency International were less corrupt than Iran. By the time he left office, this figure had increased to 81% of the world's nations.

Sanctions were the third aggravating factor. Earlier restrictions imposed by the US Administration in response to Iranian hostage taking, and those levied by the UN Security Council relating to the Islamic Republic's nuclear programme were mostly circumvented, and had an insignificant effect on the economy. However, the post-2011 sanctions imposed by the USA and the EU—particularly on oil exports and banking transactions (Iran's oil sales declined from 2.4m. b/d to fewer than 1m. b/d, while stiff restrictions were imposed on transferring the proceeds back to Iran)—have had devastating consequences particularly on the devaluation of the rial and consumer prices. As a result of the crippling universal economic sanctions imposed on Iran, oil revenues declined by over 50% to the lowest level in 25 years, causing Tehran to lose its coveted second place within the Organization of the Petroleum Exporting Countries.

An IMF team visiting Iran in February 2014 reached similar conclusions regarding Ahmadinejad's weak macroeconomic management, ambitious but inadequately funded social programmes, and a marked deterioration in the external environment caused by sanctions. Recently released data shows that between 2005 and 2013 the dollar/rial exchange rate in the free market rose 3.5 times; the economy's monetary base, 5.8 times; and the consumer price index, 4.5 times – while domestic output rose by only 20 percent.

A partisan assessment

The Islamic Republic's leadership, its surrogate Friday prayer imams, and its partisan supporters at home and abroad seize every opportunity to boast of the revolution's blessings and bounties. Reams of unsubstantiated official statistics are offered to show the expansion of basic infrastructures (highways, railways, rural roads, irrigation dams, airports and sea terminals); improvements in modern means of communications (radio and TV coverage, fax, mobile phones, internet connections, access to Facebook, Twitter); the extension of gas pipelines to hundreds of cities; eye-catching urban beautification and recreational facilities; and other bricks-and-mortar projects. Periodic self-sufficiency in some farm products, capacity increases in electric power generation and rural electrification, advances in industrial production and exports (basic metals, chemicals, oil and gas, automobiles), modern defence build-up (Iranian-constructed tanks, ships, submarines, drones and ballistic missiles), and notable progress in nuclear research are touted as Islamic achievements. Friday sermons and an abundance of selective data are presented to reflect notable feats in education evidenced by increases in adult literacy, student attendance at all levels of study, published professional papers and winners of scientific Olympiads. It is claimed that improvements in health care include higher life expectancy, lower infant mortality, a greater number of physicians and nurses per head, public access to safe water and sanitation, and progress in medical and health research. Equally strong emphasis has been placed on the way in which an 'adequate' standard of living was sustained for a growing population during the Iran–Iraq war, by successfully avoiding famine and prolonged shortages of essential goods and services, increasing the food intake and energy consumption per head, while combating foreign sanctions, and relying on only minimal financial and technical support from abroad.

Ignoring a plethora of reports that place Iran at the bottom of global rankings, government officials and their foreign apologists continue to boast about one particular document—the 2013 UN Human Development Report—which indicates that between 1980 and 2012 Iran's Human Development Index (HDI) rose from 0.443 to 0.742, an increase of 67%. What the celebration ignores, however, is that (1) the Report's rankings are based on information supplied by the country itself and are not independently obtained; (2) the HDI measures only three factors: health, education and per head gross national income (GNI); (3) the HDI of 0.742 is still below the average of 0.758 for countries at the high human development level; and (4) the publicized figures deal with only crude measures of life expectancy and years of schooling with no regard to the *content* of education, the *quality* of public health, or the *purchasing power* of the GNI.

Opposers of the regime—monarchists, secularists, democracy advocates, human rights activists and former Islamic Marxists—in turn point to a whole series of glaring economic shortcomings and deficiencies: (1) slow, sluggish growth of the national product and low per head income (despite a young labour force, favourable climate and unprecedentedly high oil reserves); (2) protracted unemployment particularly among the 16–25 age group, diploma-holding high school and university graduates, and women; (3) endemic double-digit inflation placing the heaviest burden on the poor; (4) small or even negative productivity of land, labour and capital; (5) an antiquated distribution system suffering from small and costly operations; and (6) increasingly widespread institutionalized corruption, fraud and malfeasance in both government and business—witnessed by sensational public trials, widening income gaps and prevailing poverty. The Legatum Institute's Prosperity Index, which ranks world nations in eight categoriess—wealth, education, health, employment opportunities, type of governance, personal freedoms, security, and social capitals—places Iran in 102nd place among 142 countries in its latest report.

Frequent references are also made by neutral observers to (1) an economy drained and undermined by grave environmental and social ills; (2) growing deforestation and desertification, the drying up of major lakes and water basins; (3) unbearable and suffocating air pollution in major cities resulting in frequent school closures; (4) extremely heavy city and highway traffic with the world's highest annual per head casualties; (5) widespread drug addiction, youth prostitution and high divorce rates; and (6) colossal annual brain drain. The opposition highlights airports opened despite having no air traffic; dams constructed with an inadequate water base; urban overpasses built at far greater cost than would be needed for underground transportation.

For their part, the old regime's sympathizers raise some legitimate questions regarding its claims to achievement. First, the raw quantitative data on specific social welfare indicators and infrastructural projects cited by state officials need to be adjusted and qualified for their content. For instance, the higher number of school admissions should be qualified by the quality of education and its suitability for the country's employment needs. The same goes for the actual skills of the greater number of teachers and health care providers versus the actual quality of health care. Second, an integral part of the success stories should include the invaluable contributions of assetss—both physical and humans—inherited from the previous regime: a nationwide modern infrastructure, sizeable industrial production capacity, a thriving oil industry, a strong defence capability, a vast cadre of talented and experienced public servants and business managers, and a thick stack of blueprints for potential projects. Without these facilities, for example, the clerical regime would hardly have been able to repel the well-equipped Iraqi army, or to withstand US sanctions and international arms embargoes. In fact, the Islamic regime is hard pressed to demonstrate that any of its showcase projects arise from its own initiative and are not built upon foundations already in place. The regime's much-vaunted nuclear research and development actually commenced during the Pahlavi era, and was actually originally denounced by the revolutionaries as a waste of resources.[12]

An objective evaluation

A non-partisan evaluation of Iran's post-revolution economic performance may be made in three different ways. First, the record may be dissected by the two standard criteria of (1) economic *efficiency* (called Islamic progress); and (2) *equity* (called Islamic social justice). Second, the results may be matched against the Islamic Republic's own revolutionary promises. Third, post-revolution achievements may be compared with those that occurred in a similar earlier period. Lack of reliable data permits no more than a partial, and somewhat rudimentary, assessment. A fourth yardstick—which requires a full study to itself and is not attempted here—is to compare Iran's economic development in the past 35 years with that of similar countries (e.g. South Korea and Turkey) since 1979.

The standard criteria are easiest to use. In terms of *efficiency*, official figures show that none of the universal indicators of development and progress has behaved satisfactorily after 1979. Real GDP growth in the last 35 years has risen by an anaemic 2% per year on average, somewhat below the 2.4% annual increase in population. Per head real GDP has declined by about 0.4% per year on average. Unemployment has been in the double-digit range during almost the entire post-revolution period, with yearly fluctuations officially put between 9% and 16%. Independent estimates have been almost double those figures for much of the period. The consumer price index has registered an average annual rate of about 20%. The fiscal budget—normally declared to be 'balanced'—actually has been in deficit for all but four years since the revolution. Generally, the balance of external payments also has been under pressure except during the recent oil boom.

This unenviable quantitative performance basically reflects the inherent growth-inhibiting features of the Iranian economy, including its outmoded, costly and ineffective central planning exercises. More significantly, Iran's modest economic growth rate of 4.7% per year since the end of the Iran–Iraq war has been due to high annual gross investments rather than from a more efficient use of resources. Iran's investment-to-GDP ratio has averaged about 19.5% per year during the period, matching those of high-growth Asian countries. Yet, GDP growth has been 50% lower due to the anaemic trends in labour and capital productivity. Labour productivity during the 35-year period is estimated to have increased by only about 1.5% a year, due mostly to a low level of workers' skills, and the mismatching of higher education curricula with the economy's job needs. Capital productivity has also been low, increasing by about 2% per year on average, due to the poor selection of investment projects, and their relatively long gestation period—estimated to be three times the global average. Iran's notably high capital-output ratio of 6.6% compares poorly with only about 4% among the Asian tigers.

Achievements in *equity* and social justice are harder to measure due to the lack of sufficient reliable data on domestic income distribution, shares of various social strata in free public services, extent of poverty and other social welfare indicators. Government officials claim that income distribution has improved slightly since the revolution from a Gini coefficient (a standard indicator of national income distribution) of 3.8 to that of 3.6. However, this is hard to confirm since the annual per head decline in GDP is unlikely to have affected all social strata uniformly. Furthermore, government data show that the bottom 10% of the population earn and consume only 2% of the national income, and the bottom 20% receive only 5.8%. By contrast, the top 10%

enjoy 34% of the total, and the top 20% enjoy close to 50%. The estimated number of people living below the national poverty line varies widely, according to officials from the Management and Plan Organization, the Social Welfare Organization and the Central Bank using various criteria, and are divided between the 'absolute', 'relative' and 'needy' categories. According to a statement by a former director-general of the Anti-Poverty Programme of the Ministry of Welfare and Social Security, 2% of the rural population and 4.5% of the urban population live under the absolute poverty line. Some 15% of the rural population and 17% of the urban population suffer from relative poverty. In 2013 it was estimated that 12m.–15m. people belonged to all three categories, and were being cared for by various charity organizations.

The second method of performance evaluation is a comparison between what the Islamic revolutionaries promised and what they have delivered so far. The Shah's regime was faulted by the revolutionaries, and particularly by the clerical elements within the rainbow coalition, on the grounds that it ignored vital national interests. The Shah, as mentioned previously, was chastised in particular for leading the nation towards the West's 'crass materialism' and 'consumerist culture', anchoring Iran's survival and prosperity to foreign goods, technology and managerial know-how. Agriculture was neglected. Industry was buttressed to assembly plant operations. Meanwhile, the banking system was oblivious to the needs of the poor. Oil export receipts were used to purchase sophisticated weapons, finance luxury imports and encourage profligate consumption. All these 'vices' were to be corrected once the Islamic regime came to power. Economic planning would then take place not for economic development alone, but also in the cause of social and cultural advancement. Agriculture would serve as the economy's pivot, and would eventually eliminate the nation's dependence on food imports. Industry would be freed from foreign dependence and assembly plant operations, and shift towards reliance on domestic resources and production for domestic needs. Foreign trade would be reconstructed with a view to curtailing reliance on the West and increasing relations with developing and Islamic countries. The banking system would be taken out of the sphere of foreign influence, and run on Islamic interest-free principles. Foreign borrowing would be limited to a bare minimum. Foreign investments would be permitted if accompanied by the transfer of technology. A frugal consumption model would be constructed to curb materialistic and consumerist instincts.

Now, evidence shows that none of the economic strategies and policies for which the Shah was taken to task has been fundamentally changed. Furthermore, none of the revolutionary promises has been delivered faithfully. Many promises have only partly been met, and some have been discarded totally. Khomeini's exhortations regarding the virtues of spirituality, frugality and disdain for material possessions have fallen on deaf ears. Even the Imam's initially devout followers now openly ignore his teachings. Clerical injunctions against crass materialism, wealth accumulation, profit making and greed have become a matter of derision among the younger generation. Citizens now openly boast of being millionaires and billionaires. President Khatami's Minister of Information went so far as to lecture the managers of a *bonyad* responsible for the welfare of the poor that the 'creation of wealth' should be regarded as a 'sacred' duty for the regime since the protection of liberty and provision of justice cannot be properly achieved without wealth. Reports about hoarding and speculation, money-lending at exorbitant interest rates in the bazaar, massive rent-seeking activities by people with access to the clerical power centres, special 'sweetheart' deals among related office holders, and blatant corruption fill the pages even of self-censored publications. Massive visual evidence now shows that despite 35 years of rejection of crass materialism, and the search for a frugal 'consumption model', the Islamic Republic now outshines all other countries of the same size and per head income with its multi-million-dollar penthouse apartments with indoor swimming pools and helipads; the US$500,000 European sports cars roaming Tehran's streets; its men's fashion boutiques where a complete outfit can cost $15,000; and its $250 per cover restaurants.

The economic self-reliance and self-sufficiency that the leaders of the revolution regarded as a *sine qua non* of political independence have also fallen by the wayside. In presenting his 1999 budget to the Majlis, President Khatami emphasized that no economy can develop without expanding its trade with the outside world, and that economic growth, high investment and full employment are all dependent upon foreign trade. Since 1996 the regime has applied for membership of the World Trade Organization a total of 22 times, only to be rebuffed on every occasion. The production of 6m. b/d of oil during the mid-1970s that was condemned by the anti-Shah groups as a betrayal of future generations' interest is now the most coveted goal of the regime, and the foremost investment priority of its '20-Year Economic Perspective'. Agriculture has never become the promised pivot for development, but actually continues to be shunned by domestic investors due to high production costs and government-controlled farm prices. The country's erstwhile celebrated self-sufficiency in wheat has been achieved at three times the average global cost per bushel and at the expense of cotton, oats, fruit, vegetables and other cash crops with which Iran has a clear comparative advantage. Near self-sufficiency in red meat and milk has been reached as a result of sharp decreases in demand due to their unaffordable prices for most wage earners. Non-oil exports that previously were considered to be badly neglected have increased in current dollar terms thanks to a number of government support measures, exchange rate guarantees and, particularly, the treatment of petrochemicals—the major item—as 'non-oil'. In addition, once they have been adjusted for inflation and stripped of their import contents, they still compare unfavourably with pre-revolution figures both as a percentage of the national product, and certainly in per head terms. Ironically enough, despite possessing 10% of the world's proven oil, and 15% of its natural gas reserves, the Islamic Republic is still a net importer of both—with annual payments for imported gasoline in some years consuming nearly one-half of all receipts from non-energy exports. Assembly plant operations developed in the Shah's period in office, which were denounced as a misguided industrialization policy and a waste of precious oil income, are now several times more prevalent than before not only in automobile manufacturing but in the making of many other consumer durable items. National expenditure on armaments and nuclear power that was denounced as profligate and wasteful is now being expanded both openly and discreetly despite pleas to the contrary by the world community.

In the financial sector, nationalized domestic and joint-venture banks have functioned as the GDP's most laggard sub-sector due to their inefficiency, poor investments and non-performing loans. Public energy and other large-scale projects have been routinely financed through foreign credit, buy-back deals and build-operate-transfer arrangements. Foreign direct investment that had to be shunned at all costs is now highest on the list of the regime's major foreign economic policy objectives. The Tehran Stock Exchange, which had been closed for more than 10 years as the most conspicuous symbol of capitalism, has been revived with great fanfare as the regime's unique achievement, and used as a major vehicle for privatizing state enterprises. Furthermore, to top it all, Articles 43 and 44 of Iran's Constitution, which placed all the 'commanding heights' of the economy in state hands, were rescinded by the Expediency Council in October 2004, enabling all major industries and basic economic activities (except for oil and gas) to be owned and operated by the private sector under certain conditions.

The third evaluation approach—a comparison with the past—would also turn in the Islamic regime's disfavour. During the 1960–76 period, Iran enjoyed one of the fastest growth rates in the world at an average annual rate of 9.8%, and an increase in per head income of 7%—resulting in a five-fold expansion of GDP. By contrast, in 2003 per head GDP was still nearly 14% below that of 1976. The unemployment rate that measured a mere 2.9% in 1976 has been in double digits for much of the post-revolution period.

According to official reports, while the consumer price index averaged 5.7% per year in 1960–76, it registered double-digit figures in all but two of the last 35 years, ranging from 10.4% to 49.7%, and averaging 20.8%, with the highest figures being recorded during the Rafsanjani and Ahmadinejad administrations. Private estimates of the consumer price index have always been much higher.

Altogether, despite official efforts to magnify positive achievements, and equally strenuous attempts to downplay obvious setbacks, the consensus among non-partisan observers is that Iran's economy is now in many ways worse than it was before the revolution. Based on the Government's own statistics, almost all common indicators of economic progress lag behind pre-revolution figures. State dominance over the economy is more obtrusive. Dependence on oil exports is greater, economic growth is lower and inflation is higher. Unemployment and underemployment are more widespread and the income gap between households is wider. The Government is in vastly deeper debt to the Central Bank. According to the 2014 annual report of the Heritage Foundation: 'Iran had one of the Middle East's most advanced economies before the 1979 Islamic revolution. Today, the economy is in shambles thanks to a policy agenda characterized by large subsidies to favored sectors, a bloated public sector and high inflation.'

The current deputy speaker of the Majlis, one of the stalwarts of the regime, provided a particularly succinct evaluation of the Islamic Republic's economic performance. Addressing the assembly in April 2014, he said: 'With 3.3% average annual GDP growth between 1979 and 2012, some 20% average annual inflation, and 12.2% protracted unemployment the Islamic Republic has not been able to present a successful economic model to itself and to the world despite the abundance of capabilities such as a favourable geographic position, and enormous deposits of oil and gas.'

Underlying causes

During the last quarter century the Islamic Republic has shown an extraordinary resilience against all odds, a canny instinct for survival, and an astounding resistance against all adversities. Despite the early loss of many of its top leaders at the hands of domestic opposition groups, a long, bloody and disastrous war with Iraq, ethnic separatist insurrections, crippling international sanctions, burgeoning population, and frequent natural disasters, the clerical establishment has managed to stay in power. Why, then, has it earned such an unenviable economic record? Why does the economy still remain a bleak spot in its 35-year history and a potential threat to its long-term survival?

On careful scrutiny, the precarious state of Iran's current economy, and the root causes of its formidable shortfalls, may be found in its basic structure that is built upon hazardous fault lines. The Iranian economy may best be described as being state-dominated, excessively regulated, inward-oriented, insufficiently competitive, under-taxed, overly subsidized, environmentally negligent, and excessively dependent on oil exports. Each one of these characteristics is individually and jointly responsible for the country's economic malaise.

First, state dominance over the economy is the main culprit. The Government owns and operates all major industries (led by oil, gas and petrochemicals), public utilities, banks, insurance companies, transport and communications, agribusinesses, and many trades and services. Some 25% of the total labour force is employed in the public sector. The state itself employs 3m. people, up from 550,000 prior to the revolution. Despite the Islamic Republic leadership's repeated emphasis on the need for privatization, and a favourable interpretation of the Islamic Republic's left-leaning Constitution, the central Government and state-affiliated entities continue to own, manage, or control hundreds of economic enterprises. Interestingly enough, even after the adoption of privatization as an official policy in the early 1990s, the situation has hardly changed. According to the Rouhani administration's Minister of the Economy, of the total sale of state enterprises in the last few years, valued at IR 1,500,000,000m., only 12.5% has been obtained by the legitimate private sector, while the rest has either been purchased by the state banks' subsidiary holding companies and semi-public agencies, ceded to other quasi-public organizations in lieu of government debt, or purchased by some influential insiders. Even when a genuine denationalization has occurred, as in the case of banking, private entities have not been able to match their state rivals. By one estimate, for example, in 2014 the country's 17 private banks had some 2,780 branches around the country but these were fewer in number than those of just one state bank. According to some official estimates, in 2014 nearly 70% of the economy was controlled by the state, while the state enterprises' budget still amounted to 53% of GDP. However, if the vast ownership of the *bonyads* and their affiliated conglomerates, the extensive business holdings of the IRGC, and Khamenei's multi-billion-dollar controlled business empire (called *Setad-e Ejrai-ye Farman-e Hazrat-e Emam*) were added to those of the public sector proper, total public control might exceed 80%. The Heritage Foundation's 2014 Index of Economic Freedom placed Iran in the 'closed country' category, ranking 173rd among 178 countries.

The gargantuan size of the public sector and the total number of people on the public payroll are other indicators of the state's dominance. While Iran's population almost doubled between 1979 and 2014, government employment has increased almost six-fold. According to the latest estimates, in 2014 some 4.7m. individuals—active employees and retired public servants in both the civil service and the military—were on the government payroll. The substandard qualifications of many public employees is another distressing factor. According to a high-ranking official at the Management and Human Capital Development Bureau, although public servants are supposed by law to possess a college degree, in practice only 39% have been educated to that level, while 2% are simply illiterate.

In addition to extensive business ownership and employment, excessive government rules and regulations (for example, in just one year a single agency distributed 180 circulars) are the second debilitating feature of the Iranian economy. From the registration and licensing of business enterprises to wage/price decisions, labour relations, banking operations, trade practices and capital flows, Big Brother's hand is conspicuous. The report by the Heritage Foundation, measuring 10 factors affecting the extent of government interference in the economy (e.g. wage/price controls, foreign exchange regulations, trade barriers and overall government interventions) classifies the Islamic Republic as a highly regulated economy. The Global Competitive Report ranks Iran in 69th place among 139 countries in terms of the climate for trade and business.

A direct consequence of such excessive regulation is widespread corruption—a fact that ironically is recognized and regretted by the Supreme Leader himself as well as by all former presidents, all seven candidates in the 2014 presidential election, and most recently by President Rouhani. According to an influential Majlis deputy, corruption has now become institutionalized and endemic in all public offices, including the judiciary. As mentioned before in Transparency International's Corruption Perceptions Index 2013 Iran is named as one of the world's most corrupt nations. The World Justice Project's Rule of Law Index 2014 indicates Iran's ranking at 82nd among 99 countries with regard to the impartiality of the judiciary. Another nefarious consequence of over-regulation is the worsening trade and business environment, which is stifling foreign investment. According to the 2014 World Bank Ease of Doing Business report, Iran ranks 152nd among 189 counties world-wide, and 13th among 15 nations in the Middle East and North Africa in terms of ease of conducting trade and business. With respect to the bankruptcy rate Iran ranked 129th among 189 nations, three places lower than in 2013. A Bloomberg Global Poll conducted in January 2014 showed that 57% of respondents did not think Iran would be a good place for investment in the next five years, against 27% who did.

Inward orientation and a skewed public investment policy is the third outstanding feature of Iran's economy. This isolationist posture goes back to a misconceived revolutionary emphasis on economic self-sufficiency as a symbol of political independence. Thus, while Iran has about 1% of the world population and 7% of world resources, its average annual registered exports amount to only about four-tenths of 1% of the world trade. Despite some recent trade liberalizations, Iran's average tariff rate has been one of the highest of countries surveyed by the IMF. Closely associated with this policy is the concentration of state attention on certain specific projects to the exclusion of others. In an uncanny resemblance to the old Soviet economic model, the Government's main focus, interest, investments and activities have been mainly concentrated on certain strategic projects, e.g. nuclear energy, space exploration, defence equipment (satellites, missiles, drones, speed boats, submarines), medical research and nano-technology—at any price, and at the expense of the people's welfare at all costs.

Fourth, the Iranian economy is insufficiently competitive in the global markets due to low capital productivity, a relatively small active labour force, and low total factor efficiency. Among the reasons cited for poor capital productivity are a high capital-labour ratio, a long gestation period for projects, the obsolescence of equipment, unused enterprise capacity and faulty investments. Of Iran's current population of 77m., some 63m. are of working age, but only 23m. (or 36%) form the active labour force—one of the world's lowest. Some 2.5m. of this labour force are officially reported as unemployed. In addition, there has been low and declining factor productivity. According to a report by the National Productivity Organization, published in May 2014 after years of inactivity, the projection for a 2.5-point annual productivity growth during the Fourth Development Plan (2005–10) never materialized, and the index, which was expected to reach 120.9 at the end of the period, ended up at 106.1. Factors cited for low labour productivity include a shortage of human capital, a rigid labour market, a poor correlation between wages and product value, a lack of personal interest and enthusiasm for one's job, acceptance of positions to earn an income rather than to be useful or creative, the lack of sufficient job security and the absence of proper job supervision. According to a report published in March 2014 by the *Jomhouri Eslami* newspaper, the average daily *productive* work of Iran's public workers has decreased to 22 minutes, and that of employees in the private sector to about 126 minutes. According to another estimate, with 25 days of official holiday per year, plus weekends and the 30-day annual vacation, the average productive work of Iranian workers can be put at 80 hours, or 10 days, per year. A recent book by Hossein Ghadiri on the economy entitled *Petroleum Misperceptions and Relaxed Economy* gauges the useful service of a government employee during 30 years of service to add up to the equivalent of only 65 weeks! Suspected culprits for negative figures in the case of capital and total factor productivity may be found in the mismatching of formal education and national economic needs, inadequate training, use of antiquated technology, poor selection of projects, and diversion of research into non-civilian activities. Iran has not been able yet to eradicate illiteracy. According to a recent estimate, about 10m. of the country's 67m. inhabitants over the age of six can neither read nor write. UNESCO ranks Iran in 86th place among 164 countries.

Low productivity is particularly pronounced in the public service. Several thousand public corporations with privileged access to low-cost bank credit, government subsidies and import protection are over-staffed, poorly managed and closed to public scrutiny. According to some unofficial estimates, one-half of all public servants and one-third of workers in public corporations are redundant. Furthermore, domestic markets are controlled by numerous private and public monopolies. The business playing field in Iran is neither level nor open. The priority given to Islamic and revolutionary commitments in the selection of managerial cadres and lucrative projects has deprived the country of the requisite professional expertise and competence. As a result, according to a report published in 2012 by *Jomhouri Eslami*, the cost of certain basic products in Iran is three times the global average.

The fifth unfavourable characteristic of the Iranian economy is its relatively low level of taxation. The Islamic Republic is one of the few countries in the world with the lowest ratio of taxes to total government revenue. Taxes generate only about 45% of the state's annual budget, and less than 7% of GDP. Tax exemptions are extensive as some 40 different entities engaged in trade and business operate legally or effectively tax-free. A considerable proportion of government employees' wages and salaries is also tax-free. Altogether, according to the Government's top tax administrator, some 50% of Iran's GDP currently is exempt from all taxes. Furthermore, some 26% of the taxable sector avoids paying taxes. While major producers' guilds (*asnaf*) produce some 30% of GDP, their taxes amount to only 6% of total collected taxes. Adding to the harmful effects of low taxation is the large percentage of cash and non-cash subsidies responsible for recent fiscal deficits and inflation.

Sixth, Iran's natural resources (oil and gas, water, forests) are mercilessly overused. According to a May 2014 report by the National Productivity Organization, per head energy consumption in the household sector is twice the global average; in agriculture, three times; and in industry and transportation 1.2 times. Iran's energy intensity is 70 units higher than the global mean. High per head water consumption (70% higher than the world average), prolonged periods of drought and poor water management have brought the country to the verge of a water crisis. According to Massoumeh Ebtekar, Vice-President and Head of the Organization for the Protection of the Environment, in terms of environmental protection Iran's ranking among 132 countries has dropped 61 places in the last 10 years; the country is now the seventh biggest producer of greenhouse gases; and it has warmed by 3% during the period. Shirin Abolghassemi, the director of the Forests Protection Project, has reported that in the three years to 2014 two-thirds of the Zagros forests have been totally wiped out. Another recent report shows that 1m. hectares (ha) of land in Iran now face subsidence and soil erosion. The Government's General Inspectorate reported in 2014 that 1m. b/d of oil is burned up and wasted during production. Water shortage is predicted to occur within a decade.

Finally, petroleum has been Iran's economic lifeblood, and the state-supported economy is heavily dependent on oil exports earnings.[13] While the oil sector's share of GDP has remained less than 20% in recent years (before the imposition of universal sanctions), crude oil exports have continued to be the mainstay of Iran's economy. Revenues from petroleum sales provide about four-fifths of the country's total annual foreign exchange receipts. Significantly, the well-being of the economy is closely linked to world oil prices. The six distinct economic cycles of stagnation-recession and renewal-recovery in the last 35 years have been invariably linked to oil bust and boom. The recessions of 1979–81, 1986–89, 1993–99, and 2011–14 can be traced to periods of global oil price slumps. By contrast, the economically vibrant years of 1982–85, 1990–92 and 2000–05 correspond with periods of high world oil prices. Nor is this correlation hard to detect. Oil booms increase the Treasury's receipts, reduce budget deficits, expand public investment, finance the industry's need for raw materials and semi-processed imports, enable the Government to import large volumes of consumer goods to curb inflation, and help the state banks to pay back their external debt. An oil bust operates in a reverse manner by depressing all those factors.[14]

Favourable prospects

Despite these many fault lines and handicaps, Iran can still become a thriving and prosperous country under an improved economic structure, competent leadership, prudent dealings with the world community, and luck. Currently, the country's annual GDP measures US $485,000m., and is dominated by the services sector, at 55%. Industry provides 20% of the total, with agriculture claiming 14%, and oil and gas merely 9%. An improvement in industrial and agricultural activity with curtailment of the duplication of services is badly needed. Supreme Leader Khamenei has frequently referred to Iran's woes as 'poverty, discrimination and corruption'. These three ills require proper care and attention for their cure.

Although Iran has only 1% of the world's population, the country ranks seventh globally in mineral wealth—it possesses 10% of proven global petroleum reserves, and 16% of global natural gas deposits. New mineral wealth continues to be discovered each year, and a large part of the country still remains unexplored. Iran is now called the region's most 'wired' nation, with more than one-third of its 77m. inhabitants having access to the internet. Two-thirds of the population are under the age of 30, and are educated young men and women who are willing to participate in building a thriving and prosperous Iran. Given the implementation of the appropriate policies, the country's diverse climate and favourable topography would allow a rich agricultural sector to flourish. With its strategic location, surrounded by 15 land and sea neighbours, Iran could serve as a lucrative trade and transit route in both north–south and east–west directions. Its abundant natural and human resources would also be magnets for foreign direct investment were a hospitable business climate with sufficient incentives to prevail. Finally, given proper maintenance, the basic infrastructure (roads, railroads, air and sea ports, up-to-date communications) is already in place to promote and sustain growth and development. All that is needed for progress and prosperity is strong leadership and rational policies.[15]

Notes

1 "The Iranian Economy before and after the Revolution", *Middle East Journal*, Summer 1992.
2 "Islamic Fundamentalism in Action", *Middle East Policy*, Spring 1995.
3 "Iran's Unemployment Crisis", *Middle East Economic Survey*, October 11, 2004.
4 "Islamic Social Justice: Iranian Style", *Middle East Policy*, Fall 2007.
5 "Iran's 20-year Economic Perspective", *Middle East Policy*, Fall 2009.
6 "Iran's Oil Stabilization Fund: A Misnomer", *Middle East Economic Survey*, November 21, 2005.
7 "Khatami's Legacy: Dashed Hopes", *Middle East Journal*, Winter 2006.
8 "Sanctioning the Islamic Republic: A New Global Wave", *Middle East Economic Survey*, November 1, 2010.
9 "Iran: The Rial Saga", *Middle East Economic Survey*, August 6, 2012.
10 "Iran: The Subsidy Dilemma", *Middle East Economic Survey*, December 10, 2013.
11 "Ahmadinejad's Legacy", *Middle East Policy*, Winter 2013.
12 "Nuclear Iran: Perils and Prospects", *Middle East Policy*, Summer 2006.
13 "Iran's Oil as a Blessing and a Curse", *The Brown Journal of World Affairs*, Fall–Winter 2008.
14 "The Islamic Republic of Iran: Facts and Fiction", *Middle East Policy*, Spring 2012.
15 "Iran's Economy Facing a Challenging Year", *Middle East Economic Survey*, April 5, 2013.

Articles

1 The Iranian economy before and after the revolution*

The victory of Algeria's Islamic Salvation Front (FIS) in the December 1991 general elections—not long after the solidification of an Islamic government under General Umar Hassan al-Bashir in Sudan—has renewed fears of the rise to power of Islamists in North Africa and elsewhere. The FIS triumph has likewise emboldened religious militants, and raised their hopes of government takeovers through democratic means. Some Islamists in Asia, the Middle East, and Africa now confidently talk of a day when Islamic rule—some modeled after Iran's—will be established in their homelands and with it an era of spiritual liberation, economic prosperity, and social justice.

Curiously enough, of those who long for a theocratic government of the Iranian variety, few among the hundreds of thousands of demonstrators and political activists in Algeria, Egypt, Indonesia, Jordan, Morocco, Tunisia, and elsewhere seem to know much about Iran's past or present. The publicized picture of Iran before the 1979 revolution is often of an economy mired by stagnation, suffering from an intolerable chasm between the rich and the poor, with agriculture neglected for the sake of rapid industrialization, and oil revenues largely squandered on useless weaponry. In contrast, the publicized image of the new Iran is that of a balanced, prosperous economy, with reduced inequalities of wealth and income, relying on its own resources, defending Islam against a hostile world, standing up for the rights of the poor, and challenging the "forces of imperialism and Zionism."

Because such misconceptions can lead to a hasty rejection of the status quo, or the mistaken pursuit of an uncertain future, a realistic assessment of the Iranian experience should be of interest to those who now favor such a regime as well as those who dread its emergence. This article discusses the economic elements of the Iranian experience.

The Pahlavi years and post-revolution developments

The story of Iran's economic development under the Pahlavis, with all its successes and setbacks, is well documented. Between 1946 and 1979, Iran was gradually transformed from a largely farm-based economy to a modern society by way of major changes in the traditional socioeconomic order.

Through public planning, urbanization, industrialization, diversification, and infrastructural investment, the state guided the economy and achieved sustained growth. Through control of imports, management assistance, and low-cost credit, the government helped the private sector, and maintained an essentially free-market system. In those years, and particularly the decade and a half ending in 1978, the government was successful in achieving most of its economic, social, and military objectives.

Data published by the World Bank show that, compared with other Third World countries during 1960–77, Iran's annual real growth rate of nearly 9.6 percent was about double the average of countries in its category, and higher than the average for any other group of countries in the world.[1] Impressive rates of growth were also achieved in other areas: investment, savings, consumption, employment, and per capita income. All sectors of the economy showed significant expansion, albeit at different rates. Inflation was kept at a low rate until 1974, when the oil boom pushed price indices to double-digit heights. The overall external payments balance for much of the 1970s was positive. The exchange and trading system was liberal even by Western standards. The Iranian rial became effectively a convertible currency toward the end of this period. Government finances, while in deficit, were in good order, and internal debt was easily manageable as was external borrowing. Thanks to considerable outlays allocated to education and health, great strides were made in improving social welfare. Infant mortality, malnutrition, endemic diseases, and illiteracy were significantly reduced. Caloric intake, life expectancy, and school enrollment were all markedly increased. While rural-urban income gaps (and income inequalities within each sector) did not narrow, indicators showed that absolute poverty was measurably reduced.

The shah's quest for military superiority in the region, combined with his drive to see Iran join the ranks of the world's major industrial powers within a generation, and his desire to create a West European-style welfare state—all simultaneously with the aid of oil money—proved to be too ambitious a target to reach and too heavy a burden. The country's significant socioeconomic achievements, and considerable military preparedness, thus failed to establish a solid base of support for the leadership. Despite an elaborate military-industrial superstructure, the regime's sociopolitical foundations were not strong enough to withstand the onslaught of growing public dissatisfaction, or to ward off the challenge of a would-be savior. The country's sizeable investments in infrastructures, human resources, and defense under the shah, however, would enable the Islamic regime that came to power in 1979 to cope with many formidable problems much better than expected or imagined. The subsequent ability of the Islamic Republic to defend Iran's territorial integrity against the Iraqi invasion, to sustain its fast-growing population (albeit at a reduced level), and to reduce its external debt was due to a very large extent to the enormous investments and capital accumulation during the shah's reign.

In short, while the shah's basic development strategy, and his principal socioeconomic policies, were a matter of controversy throughout the period—and the debates continue to this day—today's Islamic militants' image of pre-1979 Iran is skewed. Most specifically, Iran's pre-revolution economy was far from stagnant: it was registering positive growth every year between 1963 and 1977, and unemployment was relatively small and localized. Domestic income distribution, while not ideal, was no worse than most developing, and some developed, countries'. Agricultural growth was higher than in all but a handful of nations. Industrialization was pushed through not at the expense of agriculture, but thanks to oil revenues. Although oil income was used to purchase a sizeable volume of sophisticated arms, it also served as the mainstay of foreign exchange needs for infrastructural expansion and for investments.[2]

The religious elements that coalesced behind Ayatollah Ruhollah Khomeini and ultimately triumphed over the other revolutionary groups opposed to the shah had no clear economic agenda beyond repudiating Pahlavi strategies and policies. The shah's regime was castigated for having adopted a Western development model that made the country's economic survival and prosperity dependent on foreign raw materials, managerial know-how, technology, and trade. The regime was further faulted for the too-rapid exploitation of oil reserves, insufficient investment in agriculture, an industrialization drive geared to assembly-plant operation, undue reliance on oil export revenues to finance domestic public expenditure, scant attention to non-oil exports, a widening gap between individuals, classes, and regions, and the promotion of a "consumerist" economy.[3]

An Islamic and appropriate model had thus to be found to right these wrongs, develop a healthy economy, and reduce the country's economic dependence on the outside world. This model—frequently idealized by the religious leadership, but never clearly delineated—was ultimately defined from different ideological tendencies within the clerical hierarchy. The 1979 constitution served as the initial step toward the Islamization of the Iranian economy. The crucial difference between the new constitution and those of other contemporary nations—including Iran's own 1906 constitution—is in its emphasis on life's purpose. The economy, the 1979 constitution declares, is not an "end in itself" but only a "means" of moving toward God. To this end, it has to be planned in a proper and just manner to abolish all forms of unmet needs with respect to life's basic necessities and to attain national self-sufficiency in output, science, and technology. The chapters dealing exclusively with economic matters and the people's rights provide a mixture of "Big Brother" controls, comprehensive welfarism, cooperative associations, and private enterprise. The document as a whole prescribes an idealistic model wherein a benevolent theocratic government controls the commanding heights of the economy—basic industry, banking, insurance, foreign trade, and public utilities; cooperatives engage in vital production and distribution functions; and the private sector plays an important but residual role.

In line with these constitutional provisions, a series of measures were taken to expand the role of the state in the economy beyond what had been the case under the shah. All major industries were taken over from private owner-managers and placed in state hands. Banking and insurance were totally nationalized. Thousands of business firms in farming, industry, and trade that belonged to supporters of the previous regime were confiscated and turned over to a number of new revolutionary "foundations." In two principal areas, however—land reform and foreign trade—the conservative clergy rebuffed all moves toward radicalization; the matter is still in legal limbo. The most specific action taken in the direction of economic Islamization was the enactment of interest-free banking legislation in 1982. Islamic transaction modes replaced regular bank lending practices, and bank depositors, instead of being creditors, subsequently became partners in profit-sharing. The nationalized banks also became owners of a large number of money-losing public industrial enterprises, previously confiscated from, or abandoned by, their former private owners. The end of the war with Iraq in August 1988, the death of Ayatollah Khomeini in June 1989, the need for reconstruction, and problems from delayed development ushered in a new era. The ideological compass shifted in the direction of pragmatic considerations and fiscal realism. The election of Ali Akbar Hashemi Rafsanjani to the presidency, following an amendment to the constitution, and the inauguration of the Five-Year Development Plan (1989/90–1993/94) provided the impetus for a shift in development strategy, and changes in economic policy. Although deplored and denounced by the radical press and an articulate faction within the ruling clergy, the regime's new socioeconomic orientation and agenda began to overshadow revolutionary slogans and religious dogma. As a result, since 1989 the government's declarations and actions have differed from the ideas and ideals expressed at the outset of the revolution. Except in inspirational terms, or in nomenclature, major economic policies now make scant reference to things specifically Islamic.

Talk in government circles as well as in the bazaar is no longer about rejection of materialism, the imposition of a frugal consumption model, the establishment of a classless society (*ommat-e vahed*), or a return to Islamic social justice, piety, and brotherhood according to the Prophet's prescriptions. The principal concerns are inflation, employment opportunities for college graduates, sales of state factories to the private sector, joint ventures with foreign firms for increased automobile production, expansion of electric power production, promotion of foreign investment in oil and petrochemicals, abolition of rationing and subsidies, deregulation of industry, establishment of free-trade zones, and promotion of non-oil exports.[4] The expansion of oil output, renewed emphasis on industrialization (including the assembly-plant variety), defense build-up, and the pre-1979 goal of "grow first, redistribute later" are again in vogue. Export promotion strategy seems to have replaced the import-substitution dogma.

The statistics

In the 13 years since the revolution, the Iranian economy has experienced four cycles: a deep recession immediately after the establishment of the

Islamic Republic in 1979; a strong revival between 1981 and 1986; a mild recession between 1987 and 1989; and a respectable recovery since the cease-fire with Iraq. Despite the regime's early intention of reducing dependence on the petroleum sector, during this entire 13-year period the economy has been closely tied to oil revenues. Several internal and external factors also affected the country's economic course. Internal factors included political turmoil, the mass exodus of talent and capital, economic uncertainties regarding private property, ideological strictures relating to wealth and income, legal ambiguities concerning land tenure, and the preference for Islamic commitment over professional expertise in the choice of managers. Significant external considerations included the long and costly war with Iraq, major fluctuations in world oil prices, the freezing of Iranian foreign exchange assets abroad following the seizure of the US embassy and hostages, Western credit and trade sanctions, diplomatic isolation, and the influx of an estimated 3–4 million refugees from Afghanistan and Iraq. Post-revolution economic developments reflect the impact of these adverse factors. Their influence, however, has been mitigated by an extensive infrastructure, a large industrial capacity, foreign exchange reserves, and trained bureaucratic cadres inherited from the previous regime. Nevertheless, as extensively reported in both the local and the foreign press, and widely acknowledged by the political leadership and high government officials, the economy's performance has been anything but laudatory.

According to the government's own figures,[5] Iran's gross domestic product (GDP) at constant prices declined by some 1.5 percent a year on average between 1977/78 and 1988/89, with the result that the total GDP in the latter year was approximately equal to that 15 years earlier, i.e., 1973/74. In the postwar period of reform and reconstruction, GDP registered 7.2 percent annual growth on average in 1989/90–1990/91. Real output at the end of the decade, however, was still below that of 1977/78. Due to an estimated average 3.5 percent annual rise in population during the post-revolutionary period—largely in response to an initial government policy of encouraging early marriages and high birth rates—per capita GDP at constant prices in 1988/89 was not much more than the level 21 years earlier. Private per capita consumption in real terms—as the best indicator of material well-being—dropped from 153,000 rials in 1977/78 to 125,000 rials in 1990/91. Added to this already reduced per capita consumption are such problems as periodic shortages of necessities, power blackouts, rationing, long waiting lines, polluted air, and other daily aggravations prevalent during the 1980s compared to the 1970s and 1960s.

Other major economic indices show similar unfavorable trends. The share of aggregate consumption in GDP rose from about 62 percent in 1977/78 to more than 77 percent in 1990/91 while that of total investment fell from 33 percent to about 12 percent during the same period, with public investment outlays down to 7 percent from more than 18 percent of GDP. Figures on employment are sketchy, but also discouraging. The 1986/87 official population survey showed a total population of 49.4 million, an active labor force of 13 million, and an employed portion of 11 million—indicating an official jobless rate of 14 percent. Private estimates put total unemployment at twice that figure. Nearly one-third of the jobs were in the public sector. According to unofficial estimates, between 1979 and 1991, employment in the agriculture sector increased by about 10 percent, while service sector employment nearly doubled. The largest number of workers in the private services was engaged in small retail and itinerant petty trade, with relatively low labor productivity.

Individual economic sectors showed vastly different rates of growth, and their share in GDP changed accordingly. Because of the attention and official priority attached to agriculture, and the adoption of policies designed to increase farm productivity, the agriculture sector performed better than the rest of the economy. Total farm output is shown by the authorities to have grown on average by 4 percent a year between 1978/79 and 1990/91 due to an increase in yield per acre and area under food grain production. The share of farming in GDP thus rose from 12.4 percent in 1977/78 to more than 18 percent by the decade's end. Nevertheless, some 17 percent of the country's total annual imports on average consisted of foodstuffs. While this sector performed better than other sectors, its annual growth, according to World Bank data, was no more than the rates achieved in the 1970s and 1960s. Not only was self-sufficiency in agricultural staples not achieved by the end of the decade as promised, but national dependence on imported food items actually increased. Imports of cereals and grains—wheat, barley, rice, and corn—which amounted to less than 2.7 million tons in 1977/78 reached more than 8.2 million tons in 1989/90. Foreign purchases of sugar, red meat, and edible oil were also much larger than before.

Performance and growth in the oil and gas sector were severely affected by the war with Iraq and its damage to oil installations and facilities. Crude production fell to a low of 1.46 million barrels a day (b/d) in 1980/81 and 1981/82, compared to 5.6 million b/d in 1976, but subsequently ranged between 2.2–2.9 million b/d for the rest of the decade—less than Iran's Organization of the Petroleum Exporting Countries quota in some years, and exceeding it in others. After the cease-fire with Iraq, production increased to some 3.2–3.4 million b/d but was still less than the peak volume in the 1970s. As a result, the share of the oil sector in GDP declined sharply from 30–40 percent in the mid-1970s to only 9–17 percent in the 1980s. Several diverse factors were responsible for the decline in petroleum production, exports, and oil revenues: the initial decision to save oil reserves by cutting output; damage suffered from the war; gyrations in world prices of crude petroleum; and poor maintenance of oil wells because of capital and other shortages. Oil income continued to account for about 90 percent of total foreign exchange receipts each year, and according to some estimates, no more than $50 billion of the $200 billion oil income received thus far since the revolution has been spent on fixed capital formation.[6]

The industrial sector experienced equally unfavorable developments after 1979. The political climate of the early years and revolutionary excesses led to a massive exodus of industrial entrepreneurs, managers, and skilled workers, as well as large-scale capital flight. The freezing of Iranian assets abroad, Western economic sanctions, and negative government policies toward multinational corporations resulted in the departure of foreign specialists and the cessation of foreign investment. Inexperienced new managers, labor disputes, and disruptive meddling by members of revolutionary *komitehs* (Islamic watchdog committees), established in each factory, further reduced output. The situation was aggravated by the Iran–Iraq War, which damaged or destroyed production facilities. Reductions in oil revenues sharply cut into the import of industrial parts, raw materials, and processed goods. Added to the industrial sector's problems were the wholesale nationalization of hundreds of privately owned enterprises, regulations impeding growth, and lack of coordination among government ministries and agencies in charge of industrial development. Uncertainty regarding the state's treatment of private property rights, lack of incentives, and the limited profitability of short-term commercial transactions discouraged new long-term investment by the private sector. In six of the 13 years in the post-revolutionary period, this sector experienced negative growth. Capacity utilization near the end of the decade was below 40 percent in many industries before it picked up after the cease-fire, thanks to a number of incentives and the availability of foreign exchange.

The service sector had a mixed record. While it was somewhat positively affected in terms of both output and employment shares in GDP, this sector also registered negative growth in five of the 13 years. The output share rose from 36 percent to 46 percent of GDP between 1979 and 1990. In terms of employment, the services' share went up from 33 percent to 46 percent of total employment. The sector was particularly noteworthy in absorbing the lion's share of new entrants into the job market. Positive growth was achieved in the trading subsector, but the picture was flat in banking, public services, and tourism.

The economy was also beset by a number of other adverse developments. All major indicators were negatively affected by unfavorable domestic and foreign events. Under the pressure of war, slow economic growth, and rising public expenditures, the central government has experienced a budget deficit every year since the revolution. The gap ranged from a huge 15 percent of GDP in 1980/81 to about 3 percent of GDP in 1991/92, with an average of about 7 percent. In some years, the deficit was larger than the government's total regular revenues. Since the budget shortfalls were almost totally financed by credit from the Central Bank, the money supply rose nearly 10 times during the period. This liquidity explosion pushed retail and wholesale prices upward year after year. With many items in the consumer's basket subject to price ceilings, rationing, or subsidies, the true rate of inflation is not easy to determine. According to government statistics, the consumer price index rose by 637.5 percent between 1979 and 1991, or at an average annual rate of about 18 percent (compounded).[7] Unofficial estimates point to much larger figures. Official statistics show a steady decline in real wages and compensations in large-scale industrial establishments after 1980. There are other indications of similar reductions in the real incomes of middle- and lower-class workers.[8] The rising prices of goods and services, perennial shortages, and demands of war combined to cause an increase in the balance of payments deficit. The official external balance figures on the current account show a deficit for 10 out of the 13 years.

Finally, despite the regime's declared policy of improving the lot of the poor (*mostazafan*), for whom the revolution itself was ostensibly launched, the evidence suggests little or no measurable success. Data on wages and salaries are not adequate or reliable. Figures on family disposable incomes and rural-urban disparities are also frequently murky and unilluminating.[9] Based on all indications, however, nominal wages and salaries have persistently lagged behind inflation. According to a Majlis deputy, government employees' salaries and bonuses went up by only 142 percent between the revolution and 1991, while the cost of living soared more than six times, leaving "more than 90 percent of public servants below the poverty line."[10] In the absence of relevant and detailed information on wages and salaries, such claims cannot be easily verified or denied.

Regarding changes in the internal distribution of income, the official line is that the poor are now better off than before the revolution. This is undoubtedly true for certain groups of people who have been especially well positioned within the regime, such as most members of the Revolutionary Guards, many families of the war dead, some among the subsidized urban proletariat, a number of *basij* (paramilitary) volunteers, and others coming from extremely low-income households. Whether or not this is true of the entire population is still an open question. In a study shortly after the revolution, it was found that in 1972 some 44 percent of the population were living "under the subsistence poverty line."[11] According to a former head of the government's Plan and Budget Organization, absolute poverty increased by 43 percent during the 1979–85 period, and the trend was continuing.[12] Other reports indicate "absolute poverty" spreading among as many as 65–75 percent of the population in 1988.[13]

Performance in proper perspective

The foregoing data on Iran's post-revolution developments point to many undeniable economic shortfalls and setbacks.[14] An objective evaluation of this rather dark picture, however, must be made against the backdrop of the regime's numerous handicaps and disadvantages. The economy, in particular, must be given credit for its resilience in the face of enormous odds. As indicated earlier, immediately after its establishment, the Islamic Republic faced the massive exodus of experienced businessmen and managers, thousands of leaderless enterprises bogged down for lack of working capital, a shaky banking system, flight of funds out of the country, management–labor disputes, and total chaos in intersectoral relations. Shortly after that, the regime was confronted with a freeze on its badly needed foreign assets, a trade embargo, and harsh financial sanctions.

Before the disputes with the United States could be settled, the country was invaded by Iraqi forces in September 1980 with subsequent heavy damage to factories, power stations, oil installations, and other parts of its infrastructure—recently reported by a UN team, on the basis of official claims, to equal $97 billion (while the government puts the total at $1 trillion).[15] Meanwhile, the regime partially lost the core of its political leadership through internal uprising and terror tactics of the opposition. Finally, the oil industry, the mainstay of the economy, underwent disruptive fluctuations in output and price because of factors largely outside the regime's control.

Notwithstanding these handicaps and hardships, the economy—thanks to a continuous stream of oil export revenues—managed to avoid life-threatening shortages, runaway inflation, and mounting foreign debt. Even at the height of the Iran–Iraq War, food and other basic necessities were available for a modest level of living. There never was famine. Even "non-necessities" were adequate for those who could afford them at free-market prices. Inflation, even by outsiders' estimates, was never close to the level experienced in some developing economies in recent times. Despite the heavy cost of war, the regime avoided recourse to foreign borrowing on a large scale, and even paid off some of its long-term debt—albeit partly from reserves inherited from the shah's regime. Public expenditures on defense were kept from rising steeply by mobilizing private financial contributions for the war effort. The budget deficit was held on average below 8 percent of GDP by cutting down on non-priority outlays, albeit at the expense of public services and investment. Adverse effects of inflation on low- and fixed-income groups were reduced through price subsidies, rationing, and direct distribution of certain essential goods, although at a reported cost of increased inefficiency and corruption.[16]

At the same time, it should be noted that while some of the adverse elements were beyond the government's control, other factors responsible for keeping both output and income down were of the regime's own making. Specifically, two policy decisions stand out. First, the regime's self-appointed mission as exporter of Islamic revolution throughout the Muslim world (and beyond) was clearly an overly ambitious and unrealistic objective for which the country was politically, financially, and technically ill-prepared. Not only was most of the world against such adventurism but, as the nearly universal support for the Baghdad government after its imminent collapse in 1982 made apparent, Tehran's own Muslim allies in Damascus, Tripoli, and Algiers were not ready to embrace Ayatollah Khomeini's brand of Islam and thus risk the destabilization of their own regimes. Preoccupation with this unrealistic mission sapped a great deal of the country's energy and increased the government's diplomatic isolation.

The second policy decision that hampered economic growth was the choice of an old (and already discredited) Marxist economic model, long practiced in India and also in parts of Latin America with disastrous results. Largely under pressure from its radical faction, and partly due to war requirements and exigencies, the Islamic Republic during 1982–88 resorted to public ownership, price control, industrial regulation, import substitution, and overall economic regimentation designed to produce an elusive self-sufficiency. Using wartime conditions as an excuse to harness the economy, the government tried everything to expand government ownership and operations. By 1987, an estimated 60–70 percent of the entire domestic economy and 90 percent of foreign trade were directly or indirectly in state hands. Although public expenditures by the central government as a percentage of GDP (at current market prices) fell from 42 percent in 1977/78 to 22 percent in 1990/91, the share of the general government (including public enterprises and parastatal "foundations") increased progressively.[17]

The regime's foreign exchange system was, up to 1989, highly restrictive, complex, and arbitrary. There were a multitude of exchange rates for different transactions. The direction of trade was shifted deliberately from the United States and the West in favor of neighboring countries, the Eastern bloc, the Third World, and smaller partners. The result has been a mushrooming bureaucracy, which now employs twice as many people as there were in the shah's time, sheer inefficiency, lower per capita output, and related problems.

The road ahead

The period of "postwar reconstruction" began in earnest after the cease-fire with Iraq, the revision of the constitution, and the election of Rafsanjani to the presidency. A five-year plan has been underway since 1989. It targets 8 percent annual real growth for GDP, with promises of increased employment, and higher per capita income. Planned outlays are to be financed mainly from domestic resources and owned foreign income (i.e., earnings from oil and gas). Total gross fixed capital investment from central government sources is estimated at about 27 percent of total government expenditures.[18] While slightly larger than the last 10 years' average, this share is measurably smaller than similar ratios in the pre-revolution plans.

In a major policy shift from the past, the government and its top spokesmen now clearly admit that regulation and regimentation have been harmful to the economy.[19] Through a series of Majlis laws and cabinet decisions, the private sector is now asked to participate in non-strategic manufacturing, social services, transportation, tourism, and trade. One-fourth of state-owned enterprises have become candidates for privatization. Free trade zones have been established on Qeshm and Kish islands. The new strategy of "economic adjustment and reforms" aims at the establishment of a market mechanism for determining the prices of goods, foreign exchange, and money; privatization of non-strategic industries now under government control; deregulation of cumbersome bureaucratic rules; and reorganization of state machinery in the service of marketization. The policies designed to achieve some of these objectives relate to tax laws, import-export regulations, accounting procedures, exchange system, and monetary and banking guidelines. The ultimate goal is to enhance people's participation in economic activities and decision making, and reduce state controls. Prospects for these new policies remain somewhat uncertain due to strong resistance from powerful vested interests already entrenched at the various levels of the bureaucracy and the economy as a whole. Apart from hurdles involved in the resolution of conflicting philosophies and approaches among various clerical factions to many essential policy issues, some of the targets of the 1989–93 plan relating to inflation, balance-of-payments, budget deficit, housing, non-oil exports, job creation, and private investment seem rather ambitious. The government's reported determination to rebuild its shattered military, expand its regional assistance, and support Islamic groups in Afghanistan, Algeria, Lebanon, and Sudan may make the domestic task even more difficult.[20] The plan's performance in its first two-and-a-half years of operation is far from reassuring. Scattered information filtering through government offices and agencies indicates shortfalls from target goals in many areas.[21] The plan's overall success will require, in addition to the peaceful resolution of internal and external conflict, a series of sustained structural adjustment measures including the gradual unification of exchange rates; stringent fiscal reforms aimed at eliminating perennial budget deficits; speedy removal of price controls, rationing and subsidies; a serious demand management strategy to harness inflation; the dismantling of the regulatory mechanisms on credit, trade, and private enterprise; restoration of the accountability of the parastatal organizations; streamlining of public administration; and the adoption of clear long-term policies on energy, agriculture, industry, and foreign trade. Without such a substantial restructuring of the economy, the country is likely to face further inflation, larger fiscal deficits, reduced efficiency, a decline in output growth, a deterioration in the external account, and a possible recession. Even reasonable headway toward these objectives requires further rethinking of a number of political, ideological, and even constitutional preferences, priorities, and prescriptions. Preparations are now being made for the second five-year economic plan (1994/95–1998/99) to be submitted to the Majlis later this year or in early 1993. Thus far, significant deviations from current plan targets have raised questions at home and abroad regarding the usefulness and relevance of the Iranian planning mechanism in helping to shape the country's economic development. These questions have become even more pertinent now that the private sector is officially mandated to serve as a main force for growth in the next plan. The results of the April–May 1992 nationwide elections for the fourth Majlis have been widely interpreted as a confirmation of President Rafsanjani's pragmatic economic policies and a good omen for the country's sustained growth and political calm. Some Western observers have seen the hardliners' defeat as a mandate to proceed with industrial privatization, government deregulation, and the economy's integration into the global market. While this prognosis seems plausible, its optimistic undertones remain to be tested. Iran's current economic problems need much more than a friendly Majlis; they call for an improved international political image of the Tehran regime, greater private sector confidence, increased foreign exchange, newer technologies, higher labor productivity, a cleaner bureaucracy, and less income disparity. An accommodating Majlis can at best be a catalyst for change, but it cannot be an ultimate solution. The new "moderate" Majlis may support the government in further opening the country to the West—even to the United States—streamlining the bureaucracy, shedding some money-losing enterprises and costly regulations, and seeking foreign assistance. These reforms, however, are not without cost. If the experience of Eastern Europe and the former Soviet Union serves as a guide, Rafsanjani's perestroika—raising taxes, rationalizing interest rates, cutting off subsidies, unifying the exchange rate, liberalizing trade, and linking wage hikes to productivity—will have similar widely unpopular repercussions. These restructuring measures, although ultimately rewarding, are bound in the short term to produce further inflation, unemployment, bankruptcies, and deprivations unwelcome not only to opposition politicians but to an overwhelming majority of the rank and file Iranians who, after 13 years of patient waiting, would like to see the regime's promises of prosperity and plenty fulfilled. In the fluid political climate of today's Iran, it is too soon to count the new Majlis's blessings.

Notes

* First published in the *Middle East Journal*, Summer 1992, The Middle East Institute. Reproduced with permission.

1 *World Development Report* (Washington, DC: World Bank, August 1979), pp. 128–29.

2 For a discussion of economic strategies and policies under the Pahlavis and their criticisms see Jahangir Amuzegar, *The Dynamic of the Iranian Revolution* (Albany, NY: Suny Press, 1991), Chapter 4 and Part 2.

3 For a typical exposition of these criticisms, see "Bar-rasi-e tahavvolat-e eqtesadi-e keshvar baad az enqelab" (A Review of Economic Developments after the Revolution) (Tehran: Bank Markazi [Central Bank], [1984]); see also Hooshang Amirahmadi, *Revolution and Economic Transition: The Iranian Experience* (Albany, NY: SUNY Press, 1990), pp. 1–16.

4 See, for example, *Middle East Economic Digest* (MEED), November 15, 1991, p. 4.

5 Facts and figures cited in the following paragraphs are all compiled, calculated, and analyzed by the author from the following sources. (1) Bank Markazi: Hesabhaye melli-i Iran, 1353–66 (Iran's national accounts) (Tehran, 1992); Gozaresh-e eqtesadi va taraznameh (Annual economic report and balance sheet), for each year from 1977/78 to 1989/90; Annual Review, 1369 (1990/91). (2) Plan and Budget Organization, Gozaresh-e eqtesadi (Annual economic report), for each year from 1984/85 to 1990/91. (3) Iranian Statistical Center, Salnameh-e amari (Statistical yearbook), various years 1977/78–1990/91. (4) Iran's Customs Administration, Foreign Trade Statistics, annual. (5) Organization of Petroleum Exporting Countries, Annual Statistical Bulletins; International Monetary Fund, International Financial Statistics, monthly; IMF Survey, July 30, 1990, and other data; World Bank, World Development Report, annual, and other data.

6 See Majlis debates on the 1992/93 national budget, *Kayhan Havai*, January 22, 1992, p. 24.
7 *Kayhan Havai*, January 15, 1992, p. 24.
8 For price and wage indices see Bank Markazi's annual reports each year from 1978/79 to 1989/90.
9 Bank Markazi publishes average annual budgets of rural and urban households based on regular surveys, but the information is inadequate for a meaningful determination of disparities.
10 *Kayhan Havai*, January 15, 1992, p. 24.
11 Hossein Azimi, "Aspects of Poverty and Income Distribution in Iran, 1960–72" (Ph.D diss., Oxford University, 1980), p. 145.
12 *Kayhan* (Tehran), March 19, 1986, p. 18.
13 See Amirahmadi, *Revolution and Economic Transition*, pp. 194–202 and 292; and *Iran Times* (Washington), 7 Aban 1367 [1987], p. 5.
14 For a candid reference to some of these failings see President Rafsanjani's Friday prayer sermon, *Kayhan Havai*, August 14, 1991, p. 9 ff.
15 See UN Security Council, S/23322, December 24, 1991.
16 See Dilip Hiro, "War Unsettles Iran's Economy," *Washington Post*, January 9, 1986; see also, "A Teheran Spring," *New Yorker*, June 22, 1992.
17 In the fiscal year 1992/93, the public enterprise budget was one and one-half times the national budget. The budget of the parastatal "foundations" was also an additional 50 percent. See *Kayhan Havai*, February 19, 1992, pp. 24–26.
18 See A Summarized Version of the First Five-Year Economic, Social, and Cultural Development Plan of the Islamic Republic of Iran, 1989–93 (Tehran: Plan and Budget Organization, 1990).
19 See *New York Times*, May 28, 1991, and July 2, 1991; *Iran Focus*, May 1990; and MEED, November 15, 1991, p. 4.
20 David Hoffman, "Iran's Rebuilding Seen as Challenge to West," *Washington Post*, February 2, 1992.
21 Arzyabi amalkard barnameh aval dar salhaye, 1368 va 1369 (Performance Evaluation of the First Development Plan for 1989/90–1990/91) (Tehran: Plan and Budget Organization [1991?]).

2 Islamic fundamentalism in action

The case of Iran*

During the Cold War, Muslim intellectuals in the Middle East and North Africa did their best to portray Islam as a "third way" between Karl Marx's proletarian utopia and Adam Smith's capitalist bliss. The overall reaction, even among countries allied with neither camp, was one of indifference, if not disbelief. Since the 1979 Iranian revolution, however, Islamic fundamentalism has been depicted as a serious challenge not only to the established Western-oriented order in many secular Muslim countries, but to the West itself. Concern over this threat has sparked a global debate on the nature and implications of Islam as a new political force for change.[1]

Stripped of its emotive and prejudicial ramifications, the debate revolves around five main issues: Is Islam compatible with Western democracy? Will Islamic fundamentalists once in power tolerate or reject native cultures? Can a modern economy be managed by an Islamic theocracy? Does Islamic militancy pose a threat to non-Islamic societies? And, finally, is Islamic fundamentalism a solid trend or a passing phenomenon?

Those troubled by the militancy of radical Islamic groups find political Islam antidemocratic, absolutist, narrowly focused and anti-Western (particularly anti-American).[2] The Islamic Sharia, or code of conduct, while avowedly subject to wide interpretation, is seen as clearly opposed to the Universal Declaration of Human Rights, democratic governance, religious tolerance, ethnic diversity and political pluralism.[3] Minorities under Islamic rule are said to enjoy protection at best, not equal status. Since Islam is a polity ruled by God, disobedience toward God's surrogate rulers is seen as not only a sin against the Almighty but a crime against the state, leaving no room for criticism, disagreement or dissent—features that are essential to liberal democracy.[4] Sophisticated analysts acknowledge Islam's theological heterogeneity, compatibility with modern science and technology, and lack of a conspiratorial nucleus. But they still find Islamic fundamentalism a threat to Western security, legitimacy and way of life. Islamic movements are believed to be bent on a holy war against democracy, modernization, secularization and humanism. More ardent foes regard radical Islam as essentially violent, coercive, intolerant and terror-linked. Moderate political Islam is in turn viewed by some as oxymoronic. They believe that Islam is bent on changing fundamental aspects of national culture and long-standing ethnic traditions. The West is, accordingly, urged to confront the Islamic menace firmly and, if necessary, by force.[5]

Defenders in and out of Muslim countries claim Islam to be a vital source of inspiration, with deep spiritual content. The tolerant, moderate, progressive Islamic majority is said to oppose terroristic militancy and favor the establishment of peaceful and farsighted Islamic entities. Unlike international communism, Islam is denoted not as a menacing global ideology threatening the West or an esoteric belief competing with Western democracy, but as a rich and effective means of mobilizing people toward a compelling moral and religious society.[6]

As part of a worldwide religious revival, the Islamic resurgence is described as a movement away from what Zbigniew Brzezinski terms the West's "permissive cornucopia" or a system of unbridled materialistic self-indulgence.[7] In this view, militant fundamentalists are considered anti-Muslim rebels against whom true Islam is currently on the defensive.[8] Islamic parties that may come to power through democratic elections, it is believed, cannot *a priori* be expected to impose an intolerant, undemocratic order on society. Furthermore, any Islamic takeover of existing governments in the Middle East and North Africa is depicted as a "transitional phase" in the process of transformation from an old and decadent order to new democracy, a phase that is inherently short-lived. As Islamic rulers prove unable to "deliver the goods," it is argued, the unbearable burden of coping with mundane socioeconomic problems will inevitably lead them to seek coalitions with other groups, thus paving the way for the emergence of secular opposition governments.[9] The West's long-term real interests, therefore, are seen to require maintaining friendly relations with the new Islamic governments; encouraging democratic and liberal elements in Muslim countries; expanding trade and investment relations with them; and, instead of pressuring them into isolation, helping them integrate with the world community.[10]

These contradictory interpretations and recommendations, baffling as they are to an uninitiated observer, prove most frustrating to Western policy strategists who must devise appropriate plans for different eventualities. Uncertainty as to what Islamic fundamentalists might do once they gain power could lead either to a costly confrontation with the Muslim world resembling a new Cold War, or a false sense of security verging on equally costly indecision.

To be sure, nobody knows whether Islamic winners would abide by democratic norms of behavior. No one, including the Islamic agitators themselves, can predict what might happen in Algeria, Egypt, Jordan, Pakistan and elsewhere if Muslim extremists come to power whether through bullets or ballots. Would they respect minority rights, and give up power if later defeated at the polls? Or would they revert to a new dark age of obscurantist and fanatical rule, imposing their will and values on others? Would they remain law-abiding members of the international community or defy the West and Western allies by their overt or covert transgressions?

Is Iran's present the wave of the future?

In the search for answers to some of these questions, Iran's post-revolution experiment with Islamic governance may provide a fairly good clue as to what an Islamic state may or may not be able to do once in power. Iran's Islamic Republic is the modern world's first and most celebrated example of conversion to theocracy. Critics and supporters of Islam both cite Iran as an example of an Islamic government in action. The country is called by some a moderate force for stability in the region, and by others an "international outlaw" and a "dangerous state."

The five basic questions mentioned above may be posed in the Iranian case as follows: Does Iranian rule give any indication of the compatibility of Islam with Western democracy, as supporters claim? Has the regime been able to radically Islamize Iranian society or impose fundamental Islamic values on the Persian culture, as the critics expect? Has the theocracy been able to solve the country's immense politico-economic problems, as originally promised? Is Islamic Iran a direct or indirect threat to its neighbors' sovereignty or interests, as is often argued? Finally, can the regime withstand the threats to its survival?

Democracy's litmus test

Iran's current Islamic government gained power in 1979 after successfully eliminating all of the secular coalition partners who took part in a nationwide revolution against the Pahlavi monarchy. Overriding the demands of the radical left and the liberal center, the framers of the 1979 constitution, under Ayatollah Ruhollah Khomeini's strict orders, opted for an Islamic republic and a theocratic state. The ayatollah himself enjoined the jurists from using the term "democratic," which he denounced as a Western concept. The Islamic regime and its supporters in the West now often cite periodic elections for members of the Majlis (national consultative assembly), for the president of the republic and for members of other political bodies as proof of democratic rule in Iran. This claim is also frequently buttressed by reference to occasional criticism of the government in the Majlis and the press. The regime's political nomenclature, too, includes such democratic concepts as the constitution, people's rights, separation of powers, political parties, government accountability to the elected representatives, etc. Yet, upon reflection, it would not be difficult to conclude that while some of the *necessary* conditions of democracy (e.g., the ballot box) may exist in the Islamic Republic, the *sufficient* requirements (e.g., a civil society, individual liberties, a free press, an independent judiciary, and the separation of mosque and state) are clearly absent.

In Iran's [Shia] Islamic theocracy, absolute sovereignty over the world and man belongs to God (Article 56 of the 1979 constitution) and through Him to Prophet Muhammad, his descendant *imams*, and the Islamic jurist (*vali-e-faqih*). In the absence of the Hidden Imam, as God's last designated surrogate and Lord of the Age, the governance and leadership of the nation devolves upon the just and pious *faqih*, who rules over and supervises the legislative, executive and judicial powers (Articles 5 and 57). These powers, while separate and independent of each other, all emanate from the *faqih* himself, and are subject to confirmation by him as the Supreme Leader. The Majlis, as a legislative assembly, consists of the "selected" representatives of the people, but it may not always represent the people's will. While presumably symbolizing popular expression and reflecting popular needs, Majlis laws derive their legitimacy only in the observance of divinely inspired edicts. The majority vote is subordinate to God's will: It is legitimate and valid only when it conforms to the official religion. All legislation is subject to a veto by the Council of Guardians if not in conformity with Islam (Article 72). While there is a provision for amending the constitution, there is no possibility of changing the Islamic character of the regime, its republican mode of government, the supreme power of the *faqih*, or Shiism as Iran's official religion—features that are deemed irrevocable and unalterable "forever."

In the Iranian Islamic jurisprudence, human rights are not universal, absolute, inalienable or free from the Shia belief system. Individual freedoms exist only within the context of duties before God (Article 20). Respect for individual dignity and liberty is not inherent, but a function of Shia ideology and dogma. Thus, Muslim and non-Muslim citizens do not enjoy the same political or civil rights; nor do women. In the 1979 constitution's chapter on the Rights of the People, equality before the law is guaranteed only in conformity with Islamic criteria. Rights to life, property, dwelling and employment are theoretically valid, but they may be denied by law (Article 22). Freedom of the press, speech and publication are recognized except when detrimental to the fundamental principles of Islam (Article 24). Political parties and associations are permitted as long as they do not violate Islamic edicts or the Shia basis of the Islamic Republic (Article 26). Habeas corpus and protection against censorship, torture and arbitrary arrest are guaranteed only to the extent permitted by law.

In practice, freedom of speech, assembly and political association (including the much-publicized "free" debates in the Majlis) are allowed only as long as the inviolability of the Islamic tenets, the irreversibility of the revolution, and the absolute sovereignty of the *faqih* are not questioned. Private property is sanctioned under certain stringent conditions, but free enterprise (as the so-called economic counterpart of democracy) is considered a Western concept and alien to Iran's independent Islamic venue.

The International Covenant on Civil and Political Rights (to which the shah's government was a signatory) is branded a cultural imperialistic ploy of the West; its observance must therefore be subject to Islamic laws. Embracing Islam and practicing Shiism by non-Muslims are welcomed and encouraged. But renouncing the Islamic faith or engaging in derogatory behavior against Islam by Muslims entails harsh penalties, even death. Religious minorities, i.e., Zoroastrians, Christians and Jews, are allowed religious freedom, and given their own separate, token representation in the Majlis, but they are deprived of high governmental, and all judicial, positions. The Bahais, as followers of a renegade Islamic sect, are considered apostates and frequently persecuted on charges of disloyalty. Observance of religious holidays, the Islamic dress code, prohibition against alcohol consumption, dietary rules and other ordinances are mandatory.

The judiciary, as the principal protector of individual rights, executor of law and order, and the ultimate guarantor of democracy itself is constitutionally independent of the other two branches but still subordinate to the Supreme Leader, who alone has the power to appoint and dismiss the Chief Judge. It is also a male bastion, as women are not allowed to serve as judges and are not treated equally before the law as witnesses or as plaintiffs in marital disputes. Judges are not removable or transferable without their consent except when it is in "the interest of society" at the pleasure of the Chief Judge. There is no appeal procedure from many judicial verdicts.

A curious feature of Iran's present regime can be seen in its convoluted political configuration. Iran's Islamic Republic is a religious *oligarchy* of intricate, overlapping relationships among the leading clerics, who function in an exclusive, close-knit process of mutual loyalty and support. At the apex of the political pyramid is the Supreme Leader (*rahbar*) who is the spiritual guide of the nation, the official head of state, the commander-in-chief of the armed forces and, as *vali-e-faqih*, the protector of the faith. He is constitutionally elected for life by the Assembly of Experts, who are elected by the people. But all candidates for the Assembly of Experts must first be approved by the 12-member Council of Guardians composed of six clerics (*faqihs*) and six lay jurists. The Council is the highest constitutional court of the realm; it has veto power over all legislation and supervisory responsibility over all elections. But half of the Council members are directly appointed by the Supreme Leader, and the other half—the lay lawyers—are elected by the Majlis from among individuals nominated by the Chief Judge. The Chief Judge, however, is himself appointed by the Supreme Leader. And, Majlis deputies, who are to elect the six lay jurists, are men and women who, before standing for popular elections, must be pre-screened and approved for their religious and revolutionary qualifications by the Council of Guardians. In this merry-go-round all major players thus owe their positions to each other in one way or another: the Supreme Leader to the Assembly of Experts; the Assembly of Experts to the Council of Guardians; the Council of Guardians to the Supreme Leader and the Majlis; and Majlis deputies to the Council of Guardians. The president of the republic, too, must first be anointed by the Council of Guardians, and, after popular elections, confirmed by the *rahbar*, who is elected by the Assembly of the Experts where the current president sits as vice-chairman.

The *formal* checks and balances that are stipulated in the constitution between the three so-called "independent" branches of government are just that—formal and abstract. The heavy hand of clerical absolutism actually moves the ship of state; the *rahbar* or *vali-e-faqih* is constitutionally at the helm. All other facets of Iranian politics take their cue from the top in a pseudo-democratic manner. For instance, a deadlock between the Majlis and the Council of Guardians—when deputies vote for successive versions of a particular bill and councilmen veto them—is resolved by the Council on the Expediency of the (Islamic) Order (CEO), a group representing all three branches of the government. But it is the Supreme Leader who ultimately determines the Council's membership and agenda and the president of the republic who conducts its affairs as chairman. Any revision of the constitution must also be initiated by the *rahbar* after consultation with CEO members whose majority he himself designates. Any amendment to the constitution must first be approved by a special council whose majority membership is appointed by the Supreme Leader directly or indirectly.

In this incestuous political process, the *rahbar*'s theocratic power does not end there. The heads of various national *bonyads*—the semi-public religious and charitable organizations that produce and control a sizable (although never disclosed) portion of Iran's national income—are appointed by the Supreme Leader and are solely responsible to him. So is the head of the country's entire propaganda machine, the radio and television networks. In short, whatever "democracy" is practiced in Islamic Iran, it is by no stretch of the imagination of a participatory and pluralistic variety.

Islamization of the social order

Has the Islamic Republic rewoven the fabric of Iranian society? On the surface and in official descriptions, the metamorphosis of Iranian society is highly visible. But from the evidence at hand it would be difficult to conclude that a genuine and pervasive change favoring greater Islamic fervor has taken place. Endowed with an ancient culture and rich traditions, a great sense of national pride, and an extraordinary penchant for modernization and progress, the Iranian majority have, in fact, surprised both themselves and the new regime by their resistance to Islamic change.

Despite Iran's long and tumultuous history of alternation between authoritarianism and anarchy, with only a few brief periods of experimentation with Western-type democracy in this century, an awakened popular desire for personal freedom and social justice has proven hard to suppress. While much is made of the traditional devotion to Islam and Shiism, a unique popular ambivalence about religion is often noticeable. For the vast majority in Iran, there is a palpably ingrained faith in God, an adulation for Prophet Muhammad and his descendants, an enthusiasm for some evocative Shia rites and a concurrence with some Islamic symbols and idioms. Yet there is also a frequently subtle and covert resistance to ecclesiastic coercion, a lack of fealty to any one *marjá* (source of emulation), a resentment toward religion's undue infringements on private life and a strong enmity to Islamic thought control.

This ambivalence is clearly borne out by recent post-revolutionary history. While extensive superficial transformations have been introduced by the regime, the Persian national psyche has remained true to its rich and compelling traditional origins. Institutionally, a number of revolutionary organs have been created to implement clerical domination of the state and promote the Islamic agenda. The educational system, from kindergarten to postgraduate studies, has been radically revamped in the direction of Islamic doctrines, theological dogma and Iran's post-Islamic history. Preference has been given, in both university enrollment and academic faculty recruitment, to the commitment to Islam rather than intellectual prowess or professional expertise. Western values have been denounced in classrooms, Friday sermons, Majlis debates and press commentaries as decadent, hedonistic, oppressive, exploitative and imperialistic. Western and modern Persian music has been banned from radio and television. The press law has made illegal any publication of materials offensive to Islam, religious divines or the revolution. Broadcasts by state radio and television networks as well as domestic movies and publications are strictly censored to preserve ideological Islamic correctness. Satellite dishes are banned.

Yet despite these Islamization efforts and cultural engineering, Iranian society has continued to function in much the same fashion as before, not even remotely close to Ayatollah Khomeini's ideas and ideals. While state-sponsored demonstrations still display pro-Islamic and anti-American signs and slogans, the revolutionary fervor has been replaced by concern over inflation, unemployment, pollution, traffic congestion and daily discomfort. And except for some superficial and cosmetic changes in political symbols and economic idioms, basic social relationships show a great measure of continuity from the shah's time.

The most visible and by far the boldest success of the regime lies in the public enforcement of an Islamic dress code (veiled, ghost-like women, and tieless, unshaven men), the closing of bars and casinos, and separation of the sexes in public gatherings (including classrooms). Yet popular sentiment regarding symbols of modernity has hardly been altered. In private and away from the vengeful eyes of the vigilantes charged with "enforcing good and enjoining evil," individual conduct has been different."[11] Private parties featuring the latest dance craze, high-stakes gambling, drinking, fashionable dress and other forbidden behavior are not only high society's open secrets; they are widely practiced by the nouveau riche and palpably envied by the majority of the population. According to foreign correspondents' personal observations, despite the expulsion of the so-called "Westoxicated" elements from the universities, government agencies and semi-public institutions, the popularity of all things Western has scarcely diminished.[12] The demand for smuggled Western pictures, video cassettes, music CDs and bleached jeans seems virtually insatiable, and their underground market flourishes. Broadcasts by the BBC, the Voice of America and CNN are far more eagerly awaited by the public at large than the sermons on chastity or the joy of martyrdom.

Even bazaar merchants and small shopkeepers, who are said to have spearheaded Ayatollah Khomeini's "anti-modernization" drive, openly complain about the lack of entertainment programs on domestic radio and television.

Other signs of resistance to forced Islamization are also apparent. The ideological and financial difficulties of enrolling in domestic colleges and universities and the declining quality of education have driven up the demand for studies abroad. At the same time, the number of clergy in the Majlis has dropped from 45 percent in the 1980–84 assembly to a low of 18 percent in the 1992–96 session despite a thorough Islamic scrutiny of candidates and tight "management" of the elections. Attendance at Friday prayer meetings has been on a steady decline, maintained at a minimum level by various material incentives. Audience and viewership of state radio and television have notably dwindled. Despite years of incessant admonition against material wealth, luxurious living and consumerism, no dent has been made in society's yearning for "the good life." Tehran shops are stacked with imported goods of every variety. City billboards are covered with ads for everything from Dole bananas to Sony Walkmans, replacing revolutionary exhortations and anti-American graffiti. A frugal "consumption model," repeatedly demanded by Islamic radicals, has yet to be forged. High clerical leaders themselves are often criticized in the press for throwing extra-lavish wedding parties for their offspring.

In short, despite more than 16 years of Islamic proselytizing and promotion of Islam as the sole basis of political legitimacy, the Iranian society has successfully defied the regime's efforts to remake it in an Islamic image, except for certain deceptive facades. Iranian nationalism, the indomitable Persian spirit and the nurturing force of Persian culture have vied with Shiism as equal partners in forming the "moral basis" of government. Eighty years of secularization, modernization and Westernization since the constitutional reforms of 1906–11 seem to have immunized Iranian society against wholesale reindoctrination and fanaticism.

The economic performance test

How has the theocracy coped with the country's economic problems? Have the mullahs been able to deliver the goods?

Islamic revolutionaries blamed the shah's government for undue reliance on oil exports for financing domestic needs; for unwise dependence on foreign capital, technology and markets at the neglect of national self-sufficiency; for the mistaken priority given to assembly-line industrialization at the expense of agriculture; for excessive exploitation of precious national resources (oil) to purchase useless military equipment and pursue nuclear technology; and, finally, for relentless encouragement of materialism, conspicuous consumption, and greed.

By promising to reverse this "deviate" course, the people were assured of the dawn of an equitable and moral society imbued with growing economic independence, declining poverty, enjoyment of adequate basic needs and a clean environment. In an effort to reach these goals, the regime undertook to follow a new strategy aimed at making agriculture totally self-sufficient in one decade and turning it to a developmental "pivot"; reducing oil production and exports to a minimum level needed for the country's own requirements; increasing non-oil exports and revenues to finance domestic development and the defense budget; taxing the rich and redistributing income to deprived regions and dispossessed people; cutting military expenditures; guaranteeing employment for all; and designing a frugal and healthy consumption model to fight against waste, prodigality and luxury living.

Against this list of promises, the regime's performance, as candidly acknowledged by the leadership itself, has fallen far short of expectations. Thanks to a steady stream of oil-export revenues, the regime has been able to finance needed imports and subsidize both domestic production and consumption. Some development projects in transportation, irrigation, energy, petrochemicals and metals—all designed, initiated, or under construction during the shah's reign—have finally been completed. But, based on the regime's own published data, none of the common, universal indicators of economic development (e.g., sustained growth, full employment, price stability, external balance, or fiscal piety) has behaved satisfactorily. National output in real terms has barely risen above the 1979 level; per capita income is probably one-third less due in part to a much larger population. Unemployment is officially put at 11 percent but privately estimated to be at least twice that. Inflation, by government calculations, has run about 20–30 percent a year in recent years but is privately put at 40–60 percent. The Iranian rial has lost more than 90 percent of its value since the revolution. Balance of overall payments has been in deficit most of the time, and the budget has been perennially in the red.[13]

The revolution's goal of "economic independence" is a long way off as Iran is now relatively more dependent on foreign markets, technology and investment than before the revolution. The lot of the poor has, if anything, further deteriorated as more families have fallen below the official poverty line. And environmental decay (air pollution, soil erosion, deforestation and water siltation) has worsened. Nor is Iranian society healthier, more cohesive, safer or less hedonistic than before. Drug addiction reportedly has afflicted more than 2 million people despite wholesale executions of drug dealers. Administrative inefficiency, pervasive corruption and fraudulent activities of different varieties at high echelons of the government have accompanied growing poverty and social discord. Conflicts and clashes have surged not only between the regime and its opponents but also among the clerical establishmentarians.

On specific promises, too, the regime admits its glaring shortfalls and wholesale policy reversals. Agricultural self-sufficiency has missed the 1990 target, and it is highly doubtful it will be reached soon. Domestic energy policy has shed its early emphasis on minimum oil exploitation and the cancellation of the nuclear-power program. Instead, the government is now desperately trying to raise domestic oil-production capacity toward the pre-1979 levels and has provoked Washington's wrath by attempting to rebuild a nuclear-energy complex that it disdainfully abandoned in 1979. Reliance on oil revenues for defense and development needs is now greater than ever before. Military expenditures are again on the rise. Capital-intensive investments in metals, petrochemicals and power projects have kept the goal of full employment a distant dream. And no "consumption model" has ever been devised.

A threat to the non-Islamic world?

The perception in the West, reinforced by partly self-serving claims from certain countries and quarters, is that Iran is the civilized world's number-one enemy. Tehran is accused of fomenting a global conspiracy aimed at assisting Islamic extremists politically, logistically and financially against secular or Western-oriented Muslim governments. Although many informed analysts regard these claims as highly exaggerated and Tehran steadfastly denies any territorial ambition or involvement in terrorist activities abroad, the allegations and concerns continue.

No one disputes that Iranian and Western (particularly American) interests in the region do not always coincide. The Islamic regime sees the US military presence in the region as a threat to its own survival. Radical Iranian clerics are opposed to US support for Israel and to the Middle East peace process, regarding the Jewish state as illegitimate and vowing to destroy it. The Islamic Republic envies Israel, its perceived nemesis, for the latter's conventional and nuclear military strength. Being the largest, most populous and potentially a strong military/industrial power in the Middle East, Iran legitimately aspires to be a major, if not dominant, regional player.

The United States, however, holds strong reservations about virtually every one of these positions. Washington sees Iran as an "unfriendly tyrant," an extremist and rejectionist state with aggressive, expansionist and hegemonic intentions toward its neighbors. Iran's military buildup is considered beyond its legitimate defense needs. The Islamic state's alleged efforts to acquire chemical, biological and nuclear capabilities are seen as a means of facilitating the export of Islamic revolution by violent means. In a word, Iran is thought ultimately capable of challenging US interests in the Gulf.

Despite these clear and avowed conflicts of interest, the possibility that Iran could mount a real or sustained military or foreign-policy challenge to the West, now or in the immediate future, remains doubtful. Iran still feels exhausted from a costly, devastating war with Iraq; its modernizing and replacing of lost weapons is hampered by an insufficient supply of hard currencies. Its decimated armed forces are not organizationally modern. The economy suffers from severe internal and external imbalances. There is virtually no indigenous research matching the West's. The military budget, although reportedly on the rise in recent months, is one of the lowest in the region by almost any criterion. Under no conceivable scenario can Iran alone pose a serious military threat to Western interests in the region.

The possibility of a collective Islamic challenge—i.e., some 40 countries with a Muslim majority banding together under Iran's leadership to challenge the non-Muslim world—is even more absurd. Shiism, Iran's brand of Islam, is adhered to by less than 15 percent of the world's Muslims. Tehran is in recurrent rows with other Muslim countries (Iraq, Saudi Arabia, the United Arab Emirates, Egypt, Jordan, Algeria, and Yasser Arafat's Palestinian group). Ayatollah Khomeini's dream of a global, borderless *Dar-al Islam* has now reverted to a fiercely nationalist concept of a majestic Iran whose every inch of territory must be defended against all outsiders and, conspicuously, its Muslim neighbors to the south. No Muslim country in the world has been willing to accept Iran's leadership on any diplomatic position, much less a holy war against the West. Even Syria, Libya and Sudan, whom Tehran can still call its friends, do not see eye to eye with the Islamic Republic on all issues.

A more imminent real threat, however, may come in the form of covert political subversion or assistance to native uprisings in susceptible Muslim countries. Tehran has, in fact, been frequently accused of fomenting anti-government insurgencies in the Middle East and North Africa. While the regime admits only to offering "moral" support to Islamic "freedom fighters" in oppressive systems, and denies any involvement in subversive actions anywhere, neither the mischief some of its rogue elements may have engaged in, nor the possible copy-cat effects of its early revolutionary actions against the shah, can be ruled out. Nor should the incalculable damage caused by virtually "costless" acts of sabotage (e.g., blowing up an airplane or bombing a large office tower) by its sympathizers be ignored. Yet, in all such cases where the Iranian clergy's hand may be clearly identified, a large part of the responsibility should be placed on festering local inequities, injustices and indifference, not on foreign instigators. The most Tehran can do in such foreign adventures, if anything, is to ignite the fuse on the powder keg; it can neither plant the seeds of internal discontent nor initiate the causes of local grievance.

The survival test

The final hypothesis to be tested is the issue of endurance. Can Iran's Islamic Republic cope with internal and external challenges to its survival?

The Islamic leadership in Iran, and its supporters abroad, are doing their utmost, with words and deeds, to present the regime as a strong, fiercely independent and leading member of the Islamic world, confident of its own future and the days when Islam will peacefully conquer the hearts and minds of people everywhere. Yet, a continuing struggle for power within the clerical oligarchy since Khomeini's death—as evidenced by open or veiled friction between the Supreme Leader, the president, Majlis deputies, the judiciary, and the independent ayatollahs not affiliated with the government—gives a strong indication that the regime itself has not been able to establish, once and for all, its quintessential principle of the *velayat-e faqih* (a polity led by the supreme Islamic jurist) as the moral basis of Islamic government. A series of clearly anti-clerical acts by the people at large, mostly in private but occasionally in the open, also attests to the still shallow imprint of Khomeinism on Iranian politics. Civil disobedience, bureaucratic shenanigans, flagrant evasion of taxes, the ingenious thwarting of unpopular rules and even occasional defiance of authority through riots and demonstrations all point to the regime's increasingly fragile popular base. The religious content of the 1979 revolution, too, is being increasingly eroded by burgeoning sociopolitical movements toward the creation of a civil society where Iranian nationalism is expected to supersede Islamic unity and solidarity.

The leadership, discreetly worried about growing popular dissatisfaction, has launched an aggressive campaign of damage control. The regime's obvious and admitted failures are routinely blamed on such extraordinary (and presumably uncontrollable) factors as the lingering effects of the shah's "decadent" policies, the "imposed" war with Iraq, Washington's acts of "aggression" against Iran, Western sanctions, oil-market weakness and natural disasters. The clerical spin doctors have also adopted two further lines of defense. First, in sympathy with the Shia glorification of martyrdom, Iran is depicted as a valiant nation beleaguered by Western trade and credit restrictions, victimized by the biased Western press and vilified by enemies of Islam ("Zionists and imperialists"). Second, foreign criticism of the regime is rebutted by giving an Orwellian twist to all objective reality.[14] Thus, while foreign observers describe the current economy as a shambles, the president claims that economic progress in the past five years has been unprecedented in Iran's last 2,500 years of history since the Medes. While the Supreme Leader has banned "ideologically corrupt" candidates from the Majlis, Iran is still called a "well-rooted" democracy by President Rafsanjani. While various watchdog groups routinely report flagrant human-rights violations in Iran, the supreme leadership claims the people's current freedom in Iran to be "unprecedented in history." While a hapless journalist is given a long prison sentence for publishing a caricature of Ayatollah Khomeini, the head of the judiciary claims that no one in Iran is prosecuted for exercising freedom of speech or expression. While punishment for the so-called Islamic offenses has been brutally stiffened in recent years, Iran's civil and criminal codes are declared the "most progressive" in the world. While women are deprived of their many common universal rights, the head of state speaks of the Islamic woman as a "world model" of dignity, morality and pride. And a female deputy in the Majlis glorifies *hijab* (the veil) as the most outstanding symbol of feminist liberation.[15]

This line of propaganda, never widely effective among the majority of informed citizenry, is now being further undermined by mounting economic hardships and growing social inconveniences. As the regime is forced to make more and more mid-course corrections, the latter are bound to become the catalyst for further decentralization of authority, heightened popular participation in decision making and greater freedom of expression, not only in economics but in politics as well. For an oil-based country such as Iran, economic survival in an eventual oil-less economy is contingent upon preparation for keener international competitiveness and greater integration into the global economy. But any such successful integration is bound to intensify popular demand for political freedom and social deregulation. The rising strength of the middle class, the eye-opening effects of new information technologies on the technocratic elite, and the homogenizing impact of foreign contacts on the national lifestyle (the universalization of music, films, food and fashion) are, in turn, bound to bring the Islamic conception of the state into question. As the people's innate distaste for self-delusion grows, pressures for change will become irresistible.

Pointers for the future

Looking into the future of Islamic fundamentalism through the prism of Iran may not provide satisfactory answers to all the questions raised before. Nor can it offer omnibus guidelines for a Western policy position. Country conditions are different; so are Islamic militant groups. The outcome in a given country may be less—or more—explosive than Iran's. Fundamentalists may win peacefully or by other means in some highly vulnerable countries, and the resulting restrictions, brutality, and chaos may exceed or lag behind Iran's. But the Iranian experience still provides some relevant pointers. First, an Islamic regime may use certain democratic institutions (periodic elections, limited official tenure, separation of powers, etc.), but a Western participatory democracy is not compatible with radical Islam. Second, the extent of Islamization and cultural engineering will depend on the strength of ethnic traditions, with younger and less entrenched societies probably being easier to influence than well-established cultures. Third, success in managing the economy is contingent upon the stage of domestic development and the extent of integration into the world economy: an export-led and import-dependent economy is, as a rule, more difficult to manage under strictly Islamic scriptures than a fairly self-sufficient rural entity. Fourth, an inherent threat to the West from an Islamic regime would be exceptional. The Islamic Republic, since its inception, has enjoyed close and profitable trade and exchange relations with almost the whole world. Sabotage, terrorist assaults and acts of violence against Israeli and American interests may continue by certain militant Islamic factions, but a serious military or security challenge would seem rather far-fetched. Finally, an Islamic fundamentalist state would be easy to establish but so too would be its eventual transmutation. The people's free spirit and their instinctive preference for progress and prosperity over retrogression and deprivation are bound to pave the way for the emergence of a more moderate, secular government. History shows systems that ignore human proclivities will not work, and systems that are unworkable tend to implode. Islamic fundamentalist regimes are no exception.

Notes

* First published in *Middle East Policy*, Summer 1995. Reproduced with permission.

1 See, for example, S.P. Huntington, "The Coming Clash of Civilizations," *New York Times*, June 6, 1993; and Bernard Lewis, *Islam and the West* (New York: Oxford University Press, 1993).

2 For an eloquent presentation of some of these views see Judith Miller, "The Islamic Wave," *New York Times Magazine*, May 31, 1992, and "The Challenge of Radical Islam," *Foreign Affairs* (Spring 1993).

3 See, for example, Martin Kramer, "Islam vs. Democracy," *Commentary*, January 1993.

4 See Bernard Lewis, "Islam and Liberal Democracy," *Atlantic Monthly*, February 1993.

5 See B.R. McCuinn and Gad Yaacobi, "Letters to the Editor," *New York Times*, March 22–23, 1993.

6 For example, Robin Wright, "Islam, Democracy and the West," *Foreign Affairs* (Summer 1992); L.T. Hadar, "What Green Peril?" *Foreign Affairs* (Spring 1993); and N.R. Keddie, "Arguments for Islam," *New York Times*, April 29, 1993.

7 Zbigniew Brzezinski, *Out of Control* (New York: Scribners, 1993).

8 Mohammed Arkoun, *Rethinking Islam* (Boulder, CO: Westview Press, 1994).

9 For support of these views see John EsDosito, *The Islamic Threat: Myth or Reality?* (New York: Oxford University Press, 1992); and E.W. Said, "The Phony Islamic Threat," *New York Times Magazine*, November 21, 1993.

10 Sally Ann Baynard, "Fundamentalist Error," *Washington Post*, August 29, 1994. For a policy of benign neglect toward Islamic fundamentalism, see E.G. Shirley, "Is Iran's Present Algeria's Future?" *Foreign Affairs*, May–June 1995.

11 See Chris Hedges "With Mullahs' Sleuths Eluded, Hijinks in the Hills," *New York Times*, August 8, 1994.

12 See Geraldine Brooks, "Teen-Age Infidels Hanging Out," *New York Times Magazine*, April 30, 1995.

13 For the sources of these statistics, see Jahangir Amuzegar, *Iran's Economy under the Islamic Republic* (London: I.B. Tauris, 1993).

14 All quotations are translated from various issues of the Persian weekly, *Kayhan Havai*, for the years 1993, 1994 and 1995.

15 Words such as democracy, human rights, freedom, progress, dignity and liberation in the Islamic Republic's political vocabulary remind one of Lewis Carroll's Humpty-Dumpty telling Alice in *Through the Looking-glass* that "when I use a word … it means just what I choose it to mean—neither more nor less."

3 Iran's unemployment crisis*

Stubborn, double-digit unemployment is currently the Islamic Republic's most acute single economic concern. Providing gainful, even if not equally productive, jobs for millions of job seekers now tops the list of the theocratic oligarchy's unrelenting headaches. The challenge is formidable not only because of unemployment's debilitating impact on the economy, but also due to its dire political, social, and even cultural consequences for the regime's stability and staying power. While shortages of job opportunities have been a structural phenomenon in Iran for some time, the acceleration in the growth of the labor force since the late 1990s has now reached a critical mass—defying all attempted solutions.

Despite the enormity of the challenge, statistics on Iran's employment and unemployment are the flimsiest, least reliable, and most contested of all basic indicators. The principal sources of data are either out of reach, limited, or largely conjectural. Iran's total population itself—and thus the size of its labor force—is based on conflicting *estimates.* And estimated figures for any given year vary between those of the UN Secretariat, Iran's Statistics Center, other local authorities, and foreign organizations—often with a 10% margin of difference. The size of the labor force is subject to even greater variety of guesswork. And the official estimate is highly misleading because it suffers from technical, conceptual, and methodological flaws.

Iran's current working age population, i.e., persons between the ages of 15 and 64, is broadly estimated to be about 37mn of which some 21mn (or less than 32% of the total population) constitute the active labor force. This figure compares poorly with the 50–60% labor participation in other countries, partly because it leaves out some 5mn or so deprived job seekers, i.e., women (not including housewives). The total also excludes children below 15 and older men above 64 who are still in the job market due to poverty or inadequate social security benefits. The estimated employed number is equally questionable because it includes seasonal workers, everyone who works at least two days a week, and all those who have a job at the time of census-taking regardless of their status shortly before or after.

Data collection and dissemination methods used by several competing organizations are defective because they lack a unified scientific basis. Labor market statistics are offered by at least five separate agencies: Iran's Statistics Center; the Management and Plan Organization; the Ministry of Labor; the Central Bank of Iran; and the House of Labor—with notable differences among them. And since there is no requirement for authentication, and no penalty for unfounded statements, government officials, individual Majlis deputies, newspaper reporters and private analysts also often cite employment figures of their own on various occasions. For instance, the vice-president, the minister of economy and finance, and the head of the labor ministry each give a different rate of unemployment for the first quarter of the current Iranian year (2004–05)—ranging from 10.4% to 11.8%. On top of all this, the reliability of each agency's aggregate data are subject to doubt since the politically sensitive nature of the subject invites sleight-of-hand manipulations on the part of interested parties.

The jobless paradox

Disregarding differences between public and private unemployment estimates, and relying on the figures published by Iran's Statistics Center (as the sole organization responsible by law for the collection and dissemination of national data) the jobless numbers remain confusing and questionable because of their inconsistencies. For example, while Iran's economy has admittedly failed to absorb all the new entrants into the job market during the last four years, the Center's data show a decline in annual unemployment.

According to the projections of the Third Economic Development Plan for 2000–05, in order to bring the unemployment rate from 15% in 2000 down to 11.5% in 2005 (and thus keep the total jobless number from rising further), a total of 3.8mn jobs (or 760,000 a year on average) had to be created. Now, the figures released by the High Employment Council chaired by the President show the number of jobs created each year during 2000–04 to have been 431,000, 493,000, 690,000, and 700,000, respectively. Citing these figures in his annual state-of-the economy reports to the Majlis, President Khatami acknowledged more than once that the 2.3mn jobs created during the first four years of the Plan have fallen considerably short of the Plan's target. By his count nearly one fourth of the new job seekers have failed to find gainful employment. Nevertheless, Iran's Statistic Center shows the unemployment rate for the same four years as 14.3%, 14.2%, 12.8%, and 11.6%, respectively—without any explanation. According to these numbers, the jobless rate—instead of increasing by at least 3.5% in the last four years—has actually declined by 2.6%!

Theoretically, the only way this could have happened would have been with a situation where some disappointed job seekers gave up hope for finding work, and dropped out of the active work force. But Iran's statistical apparatus is neither equipped, nor has ever tried, to measure this particular aberration.

Nonetheless, in his August 2004 report to the Supreme Leader, detailing his administration's latest "achievements," President Khatami offers a novel clue to the unemployment enigma. In his words "the usual lack of accuracy in statistics" has this time worked in his government's favor as merely 590,000–600,000 people have entered the job market each year. Consequently, he concluded, the average jobless rate in the last four-year period has been 13%—or 2% less than in 2000. These numbers, however, have been refuted by the Supreme Center of the Islamic Association of Labor, which gave the unemployed rate in August 2004 at more than 16%, and dismissed smaller figures as politically tainted. The *Iran Daily* newspaper reports the rate to be 16–20%. Information based on the Central Bank's data also shows a much larger figure than those of the Statistics Center.

Due to these ambiguities and discrepancies, the true number of current unemployed workers in Iran is subject to wide speculation. By the Statistics Center's account the total is no more than 2.5mn, while other sources put the figure at more than 3mn, and private estimates by Iranian and foreign analysts run as high as 4–4.5mn depending on the size of disguised employment or virtual underemployment. Larger numbers are routinely cited by the opposition at home and abroad.

Unemployment characteristics

While the lowest double-digit official figure for the early 2004 unemployment may not be unduly alarming on a comparative global scale, the number is still discomforting for its five specific undesirable features. First, unemployment is especially high at 34% among the 15–24-year-olds who officially constitute 25% of the labor force; it is 22% for men and 41% for women.

A report commissioned by the Management and Plan Organization and released in early September 2004 puts the total national unemployment rate at 13.2%, and predicts that if this level holds up, then the jobless rate among the 15–29 age group will reach 52% within two years. Among these idle job seekers, more than 10% are classified as college graduates, and 30% high school diploma holders. Second, the duration of unemployment is not short for most of the people out of work. Some 70% of current jobless workers have been idle for more than two years; others have been looking for jobs much longer. Third, unemployment is highest among women of all ages. While women's participation in the labor force is only slightly more than 13%, their unemployment rate is more than 40%. By some private estimates, only 15% of female university graduates are able to find suitable work. Fourth, more than 43% of the employed group is listed as illiterate or barely literate—with significant unfavorable implications for potential economic growth. Fifth, and by far the most worrisome aspect of the picture is that some 76% of the unemployed are technically classified as "unskilled" including thousands of high school and college graduates.

Principal causes of disequilibria

Iran's protracted and intractable unemployment crisis may be traced to several separate factors. The first culprit is what a seasoned foreign reporter has called Iran's "demographic juggernaut," i.e., the 3.9% annual population growth during 1979–88 encouraged by the Islamic Republic's desire to create a "20mn army" of Islamic revolutionaries. A left-leaning and anti-Western administration, which implemented this ultimately disastrous pro-natalist policy, unabashedly prided itself in the mid-1980s of having produced 10mn new "soldiers of Islam." The 1980s baby-boom generation has now come of age facing a bleak job market and bedeviling the hapless Khatami government. The fateful irony is that a majority of these would-be Islamic soldiers have now turned out to be not only ardent secularists but also eager draft-dodgers by legal or extra-legal means (i.e., buying out their service obligation for cash, or emigrating abroad). The increased unemployment caused by the 1980s population bulge has, in turn, been exacerbated by an enormous labor surplus in rural areas, as well as the unprecedented influx of more than 2.5mn refugees and workers from Afghanistan, Iraq, Pakistan and other neighboring countries. These poor, desperate, and often unregistered workers have effectively chased native unskilled laborers out of the strained job market by demanding lower wages, and being willing to work in less pleasant or more hazardous occupations.

The second factor for the double-digit unemployment has to do with the inadequate pace of economic growth. By a consensus of Iranian and foreign economists, Iran's gross domestic product (GDP) must grow at a rate of at least 8% a year in real terms in order to absorb all the new job seekers, and by 9.5% to reduce unemployment below 10%. The Iranian economy's 5.4% average yearly growth in the last four years, however, has not been vibrant enough to generate needed outlets for all the new entrants with the result that the demand for new labor has lagged behind its supply by some 30%.

Aggravating inadequate output growth has been the third factor: absence of labor-intensive investment schemes. With the bulk of the national economy in the state's hands, and with the bulk of public sector investments earmarked for large capital-intensive projects in such heavy industries as oil, petrochemicals, iron and steel, base metals, and military hardware, even a respectable 5.4% annual GDP growth has failed to accommodate new job seekers. Directly resulting from this investment bias has been the low labor intensity of growth. According to an IMF report, while Iran's annual output growth has been comparable to the performance of "peer" countries in Asia, Africa, and Latin America, its employment elasticity (i.e., change in employment as a percentage of the labor force with respect to change in real non-oil GDP) has been relatively low at 0.5. This figure compares unfavorably with 0.7 in Pakistan, 0.9 in Jordan, and 1.4 in Algeria. Still other factors such as substantial state subsidies on energy and other productive factors, negative or low interest rates offered by state banks to favored clients, and certain other rent-based amenities have induced the private sector to substitute capital for labor.

The fourth factor for the mushrooming of young job applicants has been the mismatching of Iran's education system with the country's occupational needs. The large number of unemployed college graduates classified as "unskilled" suggests that their formal training is not suitable for the market place's requirements. Government officials often boast about the number of university students having increased five-fold in the last 10 years. But for one thing, they neglect to realize that a real impetus for the increased enrollment has been the absence of gainful employment outlets—making the opportunity cost of attending a tuition-free public university next to zero. College attendance has thus been simply a means of postponing the day of reckoning. For another, they tend to overlook the students' choice of academic studies and their relevance to the economy's requirements. Statistics cited in an IMF report show that Iran's university graduates in humanities and Islamic studies outpace those in social sciences, commerce, and business administration by a factor of 4 to 1. This glaring imbalance between the kind of skills needed for sustained growth and the purely abstract knowledge acquired through a poorly designed academic curriculum lies at the roots of Iran's "educated" jobless.

Thus while most government departments complain about their need for technical and professional staff, thousands of college graduates in medicine, health care, law, engineering, agriculture, and social sciences reportedly drive taxis, or engage in low-paying clerical or sales jobs. The key to the dilemma is that many degree holders across the land are just that—holders of college certificates—but in reality are certified unemployables. Of these job seekers 80% are reportedly the products of Iran's Islamic Free University—a multi-branched, private, tuition-based, diploma mill without a qualified faculty, and with no standard laboratory, library, or research facilities.

Fifth, the early job havens, i.e., government agencies and state-owned economic enterprises, have now run out of steam. These vast outlets that in the first post-revolution decade absorbed the bulk of job seekers as employers of first resort, are now hugely overstaffed and deeply in debt. By accommodating almost indiscriminately most of the newcomers to the job market, government employees have grown four times from 550,000 in 1979 to more than 3.2mn in 2003 while the total population has merely doubled. Generous hiring policies of state enterprises and their mushrooming subsidiaries have resulted in some of their manufacturing units employing seven times as many workers as a similar factory in the West. Public sector employees increased from 19% of the employed population in 1976 to 32% in 1986. Now, the government perennial budget deficits no longer allow bureaucratic agencies to expand their politically accommodating work force. Nor can state enterprises, operating largely in the red and kept on life support by fiscal subsidies or bank loans, easily add to their job roster.

Sporadic and largely unsuccessful privatization efforts in the last few years have also aggravated the jobless situation as the new private owners have fired redundant workers. Alarming bankruptcies of an estimated 1,400 inefficient private firms in the textiles and similarly vulnerable industries during the last four years have had their share of the increased unemployment—with resulting frequent "illegal" labor strikes in major cities.

Sixth, and by some accounts, the strongest deterrent to high employment has been labor-market rigidities caused in part by the country's anti-business labor code, passed by a previous left-leaning Majlis. The law, which is now fiercely defended by workers and their friends in high places, imposes onerous burdens on small and mid-size firms that serve as the largest job providers. The code requires employers to pay no less than a minimum wage; observe limited number of hours of work; provide compensation for overtime; give regular annual bonuses regardless of their financial position; pay 30% of workers' social security, health and unemployment insurance costs; and provide free training, housing and transportation expenses for their employees. Workers are also entitled to annual holidays and sick leave with pay, and receive a hefty severance pay if fired, even for cause—thus reducing annual employee turnovers to a minimum. By one private estimate, non-wage expenses often amount to 1.5–2 times the wage bill for an average employer. For these reasons, in the last few years, entrepreneurs have remained reluctant to hire full-time workers on a "permanent" basis, and chosen to fill their vacancies with fixed-term contract employees, in order to escape most of those obligations.

Finally, responsible for inadequate job creation have been such other structural market deficiencies as insufficient wage flexibility, absence of independent labor unions, low labor mobility, lack of collective bargaining, and imperfect information needed to match labor's supply and demand.

Collateral implications

Economic costs of unemployment as a drag on the economy are highly transparent and calculable. Labor is the most perishable of all productive factors, and a non-retrievable asset when lost. But socio-political and other non-material consequences of idleness—while equally deplorable human tragedies—are usually hidden and often not easily measurable. In Iran, as elsewhere, widespread joblessness as a straight road to poverty has been a destabilizing social force. According to the latest claim by a high welfare organization official, some 12% of Iran's total population, or about 9mn persons, live below the poverty line, and as many as another 17%, or 11mn are considered "needy." Private estimates show as high as 40% of the population under absolute or relative poverty lines—with unemployment often cited as a major contributing factor. Jobless-related poverty, in turn, has been frequently found to be the main cause of countless "social ills" including suicides, dysfunctional families, high divorce rates, drug addiction, illegal underground activities, violent crimes, prostitution, graft and corruption. Some 60% of nationwide suicides in Iran are directly traced to the absence of paying jobs.

Unemployment has also had its significant cultural backlash. Lack of suitable work for more than 300,000 college graduates each year has been a crucial factor in the "intellectual hollowing out" of the country. Estimates of Iran's technical and professional cadres leaving the motherland each year have ranged from 100,000 to 225,000 young men and women. Poor prospects for finding satisfying work have led thousands of Iranians studying abroad—including some 4,000 recipients of government scholarship—to choose not to return home even at the cost of forfeiting their "return pledge" bonds.

A shortage of adequate jobs is also an alarming threat to political stability. No matter which metaphor one wishes to accept or reject regarding the Islamic Republic's current unemployment malaise—the Achilles' heels of the regime, a time-bomb ticking to go off, or the last straw on the clerics' back—there could be no denying that the government's inability to meet this challenge is the most acute single issue. State officials—from the president on down to local police chiefs—regularly express their concerns regarding the eerie potential of a protracted unemployment slump. Apart from clear prospects of street demonstrations, sit-ins, clandestine sabotage, and open riots, the unemployed youth are prone to fall prey to the pernicious appeal of fanatical elements, anti-social cults, and outright terror groups. Potential for political mischief is embedded in stressful idleness.

A challenging decade ahead

Concerted government measures to put people to work—vocational training, establishment of an information data base, tax holidays, subsidized credits, and direct budgetary support to high unemployment sectors and depressed areas—have so far produced scant results. Efforts to send idle workers to Europe, Southeast Asia and other countries in the region have hardly made a dent—a total of a few thousand from a pool of millions. Iranian unskilled workers have been unable to compete with lowest wage laborers from India and Bangladesh, and the "skilled" contingent have not been professionally up to par with those from Eastern Europe and other developed countries. A much-heralded supplemental emergency fund of IR9 trillion (around $1bn), ear-marked in 2002 for lending to small private firms at a minimal interest rate in order to create 300,000 new jobs, has failed to reach its goal, and has been fraught with a number of unintended consequences. A memorandum of understanding signed with the UN in August 2004 to resolve the problem of youth unemployment remains to be tested.

Official desperation has reached such a low level that incumbent officials as well as aspiring politicians now actually welcome the brain drain. President Khatami has called it a natural phenomenon. The speaker of the new Majlis believes that Iran needs only half of its highly educated elite. And a presidential contender argues that if some 250,000 young university graduates leave the country voluntarily each year, this decade's unemployment problem will be solved!

Harmful and self-defeating as this culturally humiliating and economically damaging remedy may be, the diagnosed duration of the problem is not off the mark. Thanks largely to the successful national family planning followed by the government since 1989—in a 180-degree reversal of an earlier stand—the fertility rate among women of childbearing age has dropped from seven to three. As a result, annual population growth has fallen from 3.9% in the 1980s to an estimated 1.4% now. Under these circumstances, the baby-boomers' pressure on the job supply is expected to end by the end of this decade, and the natural rate of employment restored. In fact, if economic growth during 2010–20 should match the pre-revolution peaks, Iran might again become a labor importer, as was the case in the 1970s.

The critical period is thus here and now. Generating nearly 1mn jobs a year up to 2010 is a Herculean task, which requires a series of resolute and painful measures ranging from some short-term emergency measures of the American Works Progress Administration variety to the long-term restructuring of the economy. Such a fundamental overhaul needed to replace the oil-based growth of the last three years by a labor-based development model in the next seven, would need due diligence on the part of the current 7th Majlis, and next year's winner of the presidential race.

Note

* First published in the *Middle East Economic Survey*, October 11, 2004. Reproduced with permission.

4 Islamic social justice

Iranian style*

The ideal of social justice was a prime goal of Iran's 1979 revolution. The monarchy was mercilessly chastised by Ayatollah Ruhollah Khomeini for having neglected the plight of the poor and the disenfranchised, the *mostazafan*. A new constitution adopted under his supervision after the revolution is replete with references to justice and equity as two of the main Quranic principles of governance. Eradication of poverty and deprivation thus became one of the Islamic Republic's principal duties and its leaders' principal aims. And the dominance of public sector over the national economy, specified in the constitution, was expected to guarantee the achievement of that objective.

The fact that, after nearly three decades of "Islamic" rule, millions of Iranians are still living below the poverty line and the gap between rich and poor has actually widened is not surprising, in view of gross economic mismanagement. The real surprise lies in the recent ideological turnaround by the regime and the candid rejection of the state as an anti-poverty agent. This review intends to (a) discuss the Islamic Republic's several privatization programs in the last 18 years to reduce state economic dominance and the way in which the 1979 Constitution has been amended to reach that goal; (b) examine President Ahmadinejad's cherished scheme to distribute a portion of public assets among the poor as "justice shares" (*saham-e edalat*); and (c) appraise the new measures' prospects for achieving the goal of social justice.

The economy's new cornerstones

To Ayatollah Khomeini, the ascetic spiritual founder of the Islamic Republic, economics was a dismal and distasteful subject. He is frequently quoted as having referred to economics in highly derogatory terms. In the preamble of the 1979 Constitution, adopted under the ayatollah's direction, economics is described as a *means* and not an *end*. The economy's main task is defined as the satisfaction of man's basic "material needs" in the course of his "journey toward God." This unique and somewhat bizarre concept (which was hardly understood and seldom practiced by the majority who voted for the Basic Law) was presented as a distinct feature of Islamic government "in contrast" to non-Islamic economic systems, in which the goal is "the concentration and accumulation of wealth."[1] Taking his cue from the founding father, current Supreme Leader Seyyed Ali Khamenei, for the first 15 years into the revolution, also praised "spiritual virtues" (*taqva*) as life's main goals and asked the faithful to shun material possessions (*zakharef*). On other occasions, he openly cursed "those who made Iran dependent on oil" and wished the country could afford to shut down all its oil wells.[2]

The body of the Basic Law that was drafted by the first Assembly of Experts functioning as a constitutional convention, however, makes no further reference to this puritanical Islamic concept and, in fact, requires the government to provide for the people's basic needs in the fullest possible manner from cradle to grave. The assembly, composed of delegates from various ideologically diverse factions that had joined Khomeini's "rainbow coalition" against the monarchy, initially had a hard time agreeing on an "Islamic" economic regime. In the final give-and-take among the factions, the *Tudeh* (communist) and other leftist members of the assembly were given the task of drafting the economic segment of the document as long as Khomeini diehards were equally allowed to provide the political segment. In the ultimate compromise that was finally reached, the "Islamic Marxists" accepted the principle of the *velayet-e faqih* (rule by an Islamic jurist) as the new regime's political foundation in exchange for inserting their own favored economic version. The new constitution's Chapter IV on the economy (Articles 43 to 55) thus became a communist-style economic manifesto in which the "commanding heights" of the economy were to be in the government's hands. The rest was to be divided between the "cooperative" and the "private" sector with the priority belonging to the former. Thus, ironically, an essential segment of an "Islamic" constitution that was supposed to help people "move toward God" was drafted by a cabal of godless ideologues who subscribed to a totally different agenda. According to Article 44, the public sector includes "all large-scale and key industries; foreign trade; major mineral resources; banking, insurance; energy; dams and larger-scale irrigation networks; radio and television; post, telegraph and telephone; aviation; shipping; roads, railroads and the like." To placate other Islamic clerics in the assembly who defended Islam's respect for private property, Article 44 also adds: "Public ownership described in this article is sanctioned as long as it does not work against the interests of society."

By virtue of this provision, hundreds of prosperous and well-managed private enterprises in industry, agriculture and trade that had already been confiscated by the revolutionary government and nationalized without due compensation became the legal wards of the state. They were placed at the disposal of several *bonyads* (charitable foundations) and two government agencies: the National Iranian Industries Organization and the Industrial Development and Renovation Organization. Following the beginning of war with Iraq in 1980, the scope of government operations and involvement quickly expanded. As a result, by the end of the war in 1988, state enterprises and *bonyads* became the dominant players in the economy. Large-scale economic activities in the energy, industry and other strategic sectors remained in state hands. The private sector was limited to small-scale agriculture, domestic trade and services, and minor mining and manufacturing.

Meanwhile, dire wartime economic conditions were further aggravated by the misguided policies of Mir Hossein Mussavi, a leftist prime minister, and carried out by a Soviet-type bureaucracy run largely by dogmatic, incompetent or corrupt managers. Bent on financing the ruinous war with meager domestic resources, the Mussavi administration played havoc with the economy. Inflation was artificially kept low through strict rationing, comprehensive wage and price controls and massive subsidies. The exchange rate between the Iranian rial and the US dollar was allowed to become increasingly overvalued by means of strict annual foreign-currency appropriations, exchange rationing and a multiple-exchange-rates regime. The result was a steady decline in gross national product and growing overall poverty. According to the Central Bank's latest revised calculation, Iran's national income by the end of the war in 1988 fell to 64 percent of its 1978 level in real terms. And, due to the government's disastrous pro-natalist policy, designed to produce more soldiers for Islam, per capita income plummeted to 37 percent of its pre-revolution high. Growing cost/price distortions, accompanied by an increasingly overvalued rial, produced shortages of basic goods and services, widespread public dissatisfaction and a near revolt by consumers. The result was the election of a new centrist and pro-business government under President Ali Akbar Hashemi Rafsanjani that promised to make up for wartime hardships by reversing course.

Initial attempts at privatization

The early effort toward reducing state economic dominance was made in the context of the first Five-Year Economic Development Plan (1989–94) under Rafsanjani's so-called "structural adjustment" (*taadeel*) program.[3] The declared goals, under the banner of privatization (*khosousi sazi*), were (a) to cut back the number of state-owned enterprises (SOEs) that had mushroomed since the 1979 revolution to over a thousand; (b) to get the government out of its "non-essential" functions; and (c) to increase total national-factor productivity. An enabling decree by the Council of Ministers in spring 1991 ordered the privatization of public enterprises through three methods: the Tehran Stock Exchange, open auctions and negotiations with potential buyers.

The first period of privatization, 1990–94, was carried out by virtue of the First Development Plan's authorization, albeit in an unplanned, haphazard and chaotic manner, with total sales of public assets worth 1.7 trillion rials. The procedure that was followed in the first 20 months, however, had to be stopped in the winter of 1992 due to widespread reports of flagrant corruption, cronyism and no-bid sales of moneymaking enterprises to selected groups at below-market prices. A new ministerial decree with added safeguards against abuses proved to be equally flawed. The Majlis in mid-summer 1994 put a temporary end to all privatization efforts until previous infractions were rectified. The second phase, 1995–97, was carried out under the Second Plan's mandate according to a special Majlis law limiting the transfer of public assets—totaling 1.8 trillion rials—only to workers and war veterans on specially favored terms. In the third period, 1998–99, some 3.1 trillion rials changed hands under annual budget laws as well as the Second Plan's statutory authorization.

As total sales figures annually fell considerably below budgeted sums in the first ten years of privatization, and the whole program failed to achieve the objectives of downsizing the bureaucracy, the Third Plan (2000–05) devoted a special section to the process. Accordingly, three new organs—the Privatization Organization of Iran (POI), the High Council on Shares Distribution and a series of Conglomerates called "mother" corporations—were established. The POI was given the exclusive mandate to dispose of enterprises belonging to all government ministries and agencies. The High Council, composed of cabinet ministers, was to decide which industries or enterprises were to be privatized. Conglomerates or holding companies were to take over individual enterprises in a specific field and put them together in a basket destined for privatization. The fourth period, 2000–05, thus followed the Third Plan's authorization and managed total sales of 2.9 trillion rials in the first two years, following a tighter and more focused program.

Reliable data regarding total privatized assets during the 1990–2006 period are not available. As in most official statistics in the Islamic Republic, published figures are replete with contradictions, ambiguities and misinformation. A report based on the POI data and covering the first 12-year period of operation values total privatized assets at 10.1 trillion rials (about $1.6 billion).[4] According to another report, by the Majlis' Research Center for the 16-year period, the POI has transferred total shares worth 23 trillion rials (about $2.4 billion).[5] The head of the Privatization Organization, and the minister of economy and finance both put the total at $3 billion.[6] President Ahmadinejad has on different occasions talked about $3.2 billion[7] and $3.5 billion.[8]

The percentage of total privatized assets as a portion of the total government holdings is hard to assess. Data regarding the number of enterprises belonging to the government and other public and semi-public organizations, their balance sheets and net worth are scarce, unreliable or unavailable. By one official's estimate, the number of public corporations and their second-, third-, fourth- and fifth-generation subsidiaries has reached 2,500.[9] A government report to the Majlis in early 2003 showed the total capital of the 460 largest entities, one-fourth of which were listed as money losing, to be $62.5 billion.[10] Another report by the National Accounting Organization refers to 1,038 entities with total assets of about $92 billion and liabilities of $55 billion.[11] A knowledgeable Majlis deputy values all SOEs at $150 billion.[12]

Regardless of the exact worth of privatized assets and the total worth of government holdings, however, the maximum transferred shares has been a minute portion of total public wealth. Two other related factors must also be kept in mind in assessing the magnitude of privatization. First, some major buyers of "privatized" shares were financial subsidiaries of state banks, state insurance companies, and other semi-public enterprises that were not part of the private sector. A major portion of total "privatized" assets also consisted of transfers to the Social Security Fund and the Government Employees' Pension Fund as part of the treasury's past-due contributions; they were not truly "private sector" participants. Second, and more startling, is the fact that during the privatization exercise the government, instead of shrinking as mandated by law, had actually become ever bigger. According to a high government official, while a maximum of $3 billion of SOE shares were reportedly transferred during 1990–2006, state banks and other SOEs had an annual return on their capital of about $12 billion, of which 45 percent, or about $5 billion, was left at their disposal for reinvestment. By this calculation, the public sector grew by nearly $5 billion each year[13] through these reinvestments alone. Altogether, during the period an estimated $132 billion in totally new public investments—or 40 times total privatized assets—were made in the oil, gas, petrochemical, steel, aluminum, copper and other ongoing or new public projects.[14]

Privatization's early setbacks

A number of factors are frequently cited for the slow pace and insignificant scale of privatization. Some of these factors were similar to the experiences of other countries; others are more country specific. In general, privatization in any state-dominated economy is an issue with a diffuse, unorganized and silent constituency, i.e., consumers who may eventually enjoy better products at lower prices. These beneficiaries, however, while in the numerical majority, are normally outflanked by a minority of vested interests that will go to any lengths to preserve its prerogatives in public ownership. For example, government agencies in charge of state enterprises resist privatization because they lose part of their political power by giving up their economic clout. Politically appointed boards of public corporations, along with incompetent or corrupt managers and tenured employees who might lose their jobs and perks are other privatization opponents. Privileged suppliers and customers of public enterprises who would be deprived of their usual sweetheart deals would similarly engage in a tooth-and-nail fight to keep those businesses in public hands.

In the case of the Islamic Republic, several other factors acted as additional handicaps. First, there was an absence of national consensus about the very benefits of privatization. There were lingering suspicions, if not actual hostility, among the left-leaning bureaucrats held over from the Mussavi government toward capital, capitalists, private investments and the profit motive. Privatization also faced a skeptical public that saw the process as a squandering of national wealth and an enrichment of government cronies.[15] Second, since each state enterprise often embodied the economic power of a political or clerical faction in the country, a source of employment and income to faction supporters, and a vehicle for transferring rent to its satellite private businesses, there was a great deal of reluctance by managers, who feared losing these prerogatives. Third, there was a lack of enthusiasm on the part of potential investors because enterprises that were destined for privatization were not, as a rule, highly profitable. They had two to three times as many workers as normally needed; they were operating mostly under old technologies; they were in some cases heavily in debt to state banks; and many owed unpaid taxes.[16] Fourth, even a few profitable entities offered for sale had annual returns of between 10 and 15 percent at best. High as these rates may seem in a global context, they were actually rather meager in a country with an average annual inflation rate of the same magnitude.[17] Furthermore, the 10–15 percent taxable rates of return did not compete favorably with the 17 percent risk less and tax free annual "profit" (interest) rates paid on government "participation papers" (bonds), or higher long-term deposit rates in state banks—not to speak of the 30–45 percent returns in the "informal" economy of the bazaar. Fifth, extensive deficiencies in the operation of the Tehran Stock Exchange, where privatized shares were to be traded (including the absence of market-makers and lack of both liquidity and transparency) played against their attraction. Sixth, with the country's formal capital market nearly monopolized by inefficient and struggling state banks and insurance companies, the public's access to funds for financing purchases of privatized shares was highly limited. Seventh, there was strong opposition by the politically active labor lobby. Although Western-type labor unions do not exist in Iran, an Islamic House of Labor, with a Majlis deputy as its secretary general, is there to champion the cause of workers. The House of Labor has opposed privatization from its early inception, calling it an exercise in dismissing workers, downsizing the labor force, lowering wages and creating more poverty. It has further argued that privatization in a majority of developing countries has caused nothing but chaos, ruin and the shredding of the social fabric.[18] Eighth, there were significant ambiguities in the Third Plan law regarding priorities in the sale of public enterprises (e.g., banks vs. industrial units). Ninth, Iran's small and orphaned private sector had neither the technical nor managerial capabilities for absorbing the bulk of privatized businesses. Finally, but by no means least significant, the pervasive and exclusive definition of the "public sector" in Article 44 of the Constitution kept many risk-averse private investors from purchasing shares of key industries that were still clearly categorized as belonging to the state.

Transition to a market economy

The Islamic Republic's experience with privatization under the first two economic development plans, 1990–2000, was, as already discussed, by no means a success. The budgeted revenues from sales of SOEs perennially fell short of targets, in some years by as much as 65 percent.[19] With no proper safeguard in a number of well-publicized cases, the new owners decided to shut down the plant, fire workers, sell the company's most valuable asset—the land—to private builders, and liquidate the enterprise.[20] Due to pressure from the dismissed workers, the government was forced to take back privatized firms in a few cases.[21]

As early as the middle of the Second Plan, it was thus becoming increasingly clear that the costs of keeping the overstaffed, mismanaged and money-losing state enterprises on life support through budget subsidies could neither be justified nor continued for long. A detectable national consensus seemed to indicate that the constitutional language and implications of Chapter IV, and specifically Article 44, was the main stumbling block to wholesale privatization. Amending the Constitution, however, was neither easy nor politically prudent. The procedures for amendment were time-consuming and highly complicated. But, more significant, any attempt at amending Chapter IV could have opened a Pandora's box. There were no guarantees that other parts of the Constitution, particularly the crucial principle of *velayat-e faqih*, would not be raised for "discussion."

Two convenient escape routes thus suggested themselves: simply ignoring the mandate of Article 44 and proceeding with the transfer of public-sector assets, or searching for an enabling "interpretation." Unthinkable as the violation option might appear in a Western legal context, the decision was not precedent setting in the Islamic Republic. In previous years, various administrations had routinely sidestepped, bypassed, ignored or even boldly violated various principles of the country's 1979 Constitution and its 1989 amendment. Constitutional guarantees had frequently been ignored by over-zealous security agents, corrupt prosecutors or politicized judges. Glaring violations occurred in many areas: the rights of ethnic and religious minorities (Articles 12 and 19); the sanctity of one's life, home and property (Article 22); freedom of thought and expression (Article 23); an uncensored press (Article 24); political-party formation and activities (Article 26); peaceful demonstrations (Article 27); habeas corpus rights (Article 32); the prohibition against torture and forced testimony (Article 38); Majlis oversight authority in all national affairs (Article 76); the immunity of Majlis deputies in the discharge of their duties (Article 86); and jury trials for political and press offenses (Article 168). In foreign affairs, Article 11, calling for unity and solidarity with the Muslim world, and Article 152, regarding non-alignment with any superior power and defending the rights of Muslims everywhere under the slogan of "neither East nor West," had also been virtually ignored and forgotten. Close and extensive political and economic ties with Russia and China, both major powers mistreating their Muslim citizens, had dominated the Islamic Republic's foreign policy. A watchdog commission set up during the Khatami administration to record and report constitutional infringements by government employees and agencies was later terminated when its workload became unbearable.

Yet, in no case up to 1992, had any of the original mandates regarding the structure and direction of the economy and the Islamic Republic's basic economic ideology been formally countermanded. Furthermore, the option of ignoring the Constitution could not be easily extended to Article 44 without palpable costs. Other provisions of the Constitution had been disregarded only at the (unquantifiable) expense of the regime's legal and political "reputation." Ignoring Article 44 would have affected the pocketbook, driving away both domestic and foreign investors.

A plausible alternative thus favored the "interpretation" route. Interpreting the Constitution, however, was the prerogative and responsibility of the Council of Guardians (Article 98). But this organ could neither be expected to come up with a favorable verdict, nor was it technically equipped to offer detailed operational provisions. As in other difficult cases, the Expediency Council, as the final arbiter of all legislation in Iran, came to the rescue. Invoking its duty under Article 110 of the Constitution—"advising the Supreme Leader in the establishment of the regime's principal national policies"—the Council began a long and arduous process of finding a solution. And, after five years, in late 1997, it reached a consensus that the ambiguities embodied in Article 44 were indeed partly responsible for the slow progress of privatization. Citing the last sentence of the article, it concluded that continued extensive public ownership during peacetime was indeed against the national interest and, therefore, should be relaxed. In March 1998, the Supreme Leader agreed with the Council's findings and ordered it to proceed with necessary clarifications. Protracted studies and deliberations within the Council and further instructions from the Supreme Leader took another six years. The final document was resubmitted to him in late 2004 in five parts.[22] Four parts of the new "Guidelines" were approved immediately and ordered to be implemented in May 2005; the more crucial one, dealing with Article 44, was finalized in July 2006,[23] authorizing a major divestiture by the state of some of its major possessions.

Parts A and C of the Guidelines set up the essential course for government actions. Part A deals with basic policies aimed at expanding the role of the non-public sectors (private and cooperative) and preventing further expansion of the bureaucracy. First, it essentially puts an end to government monopoly in the commanding heights of the economy. It gives the green light, with clearly defined exceptions, for the private and cooperative sectors to invest, own and manage most areas and activities already in the domain of Article 44: basic industries and mining, foreign trade, banking, insurance, electric-power generation, dams and irrigation, post and telecommunications, railways, airlines, shipping, and downstream oil and gas. Of equal significance, it also enjoins the government from entering into any new economic activities outside the parameters of the existing Article 44.[24] Furthermore, it calls on the government to transfer to the non-public sector any involvement in the domain outside Article 44 by 20 percent a year. In the so-called "liberated" areas, the non-public sector can enter and compete with the public sector.

Part C, which the Supreme Leader took much longer to approve, complements Part A by calling for the overhaul of the state-dominated economy through divestiture of existing activities and assets in a wholesale manner. Accordingly, the government role is to change from direct ownership and management of the economy to that of policy making, guidance and supervision. The private sector is to be strengthened and assisted in its international competitiveness. To these ends, 80 percent of the government's shares in the areas falling under Article 44 (with some major exceptions, notably up-stream oil and gas industries) are earmarked to be transferred to the private and cooperative sectors.[25] Part C also provides other enabling requirements for wholesale divestiture in terms of share pricing, sales conditions, publicity and other related matters.[26] It is expected that, with full implementation of the program, the government would eventually own no more than 20 percent of the economy, consisting only of "mother" or strategic industries.

The new mandates reflect a near-total change from both the letter and the spirit of the original Constitution: they involve an overhaul of Iran's economic structure and a historic revision of private-public relationships, defining the proper roles of the state and the market. Most astonishingly, they reflect a dramatic ideological shift in the Supreme Leader's own creeds. An avowedly austere cleric who had persistently enjoined the devout from seeking worldly goods seems to have lately changed his mind and gone on record stating that "the accumulation of national wealth and the establishment of social justice" are indeed "the two main pillars of Islamic economics."[27] The official in charge of privatization has recently gone even further by claiming that the Supreme Leader, anxious to ensure national economic security, believes that "the creation of wealth is not only a necessity, but actually precedes its distribution."[28]

Social-justice shares: Ahmadinejad's initiative

The Ahmadinejad government that came to power in summer 2005, calling itself the "justice-driven administration" under the banner of *mehrvarzi* (compassion) represents in fact populism of the right rivaling Mussavi's compassionate socialism of the left. The scheme, dedicated to the cause of the poor and deprived regions of the country, proposed a different direction to accomplish the privatization task. The president himself was widely quoted as having denounced the past actions as corrupt, ineffective, contrary to workers' interest and tantamount to giving away the ranch. He openly accused the previous two administrations of selling public assets on favorable terms without proper safeguards to friends, relatives and cronies at one-fifth to one-eighth of their true worth—and all on credit.[29] He even vowed to take back properties that were unjustly ceded to a few privileged individuals, calling the transfers null and void.[30] To reverse past injustices, the new president promised to change course and follow the privatization drive through the distribution of what he termed "justice shares" (*saham-e edalat*).

The scheme, however, was neither original nor highly valued in informed circles. It was rooted in Ayatollah Khomeini's repeated references to "Islamic justice."[31] Proposals to transfer shares of SOEs to the people in different forms and under different terms had also been offered by other sources as early as 1996.[32] A published study, entitled *Popular Privatization*, had already proposed a detailed plan for giving every citizen "stock coupons," redeemable in cash or exchangeable with shares of SOEs, in order to raise national productivity and spread social justice at the same time.[33] Rafsanjani's campaign for the presidency in 2005 also promised a nationwide distribution of "stock coupons." A Tehran Stock Exchange manager had suggested a similar proposal. Based on these varied schemes, the Ahmadinejad plan to distribute ownership was presented to the Majlis in October 2005, with the initial objective of granting stock rights to the lowest-income families.[34] The program encompassed the distribution of shares of all government enterprises and semi-public entities under government jurisdiction. Interestingly, the scheme was presented not as a replacement, but as an adjunct to privatization with a set of other complementary objectives: equitable distribution of wealth combined with steady income for the poor; propagation of the culture of stock ownership; increasing enterprise productivity; changing the public's negative view of private enterprise; and enhancement of the share of the cooperative sector in the national economy. The Ministry of Welfare and Social Security was given the task of identifying prospective families among the lowest-income recipients in the country. The Ministry of Economy and Finance was to serve as a conduit for the transfer of shares.

As finally put together, the multi-layered and complex program now involves (1) an initial sale on credit of SOE shares by designated enterprises to the Privatization Organization in 20-year installments; (2) subsequent sales by the POI to an intermediary agency called the Corporation for Transfer of Justice Shares (CTJS) within the Ministry of Economy and Finance on the same conditions; (3) separate agreements by CTJS with each of the country's 30 *Ostan* (region) Justice Shares Cooperatives; (4) sale by the Ostan JSC to 337 *Shahrestan* (province) JSCs; and (5) issuance by the latter of coupons to eligible recipients.[35] In this complicated vertical lineup, individual coupon recipients are shareholders of their Shahrestan cooperative; Shahrestan cooperatives are shareholders of the Ostan holding companies; Ostan holding companies are shareholders of the Transfer Corporation; and the latter holds shares of privatized SOEs on behalf of the government.

Based on various official declarations, the Ahmadinejad administration intends to transfer to the public 80 percent of the shares of all designated state enterprises, estimated at $115–$120 billion within three years. Previously, an eight-year time horizon had been announced for the entire process.[36] Forty percent of the assets are to be distributed under the justice-shares program, 35 percent offered to public investors through the Tehran Stock Exchange or sold through auction, and 5 percent earmarked for the workers and managers of the privatizing entities. The state will retain 20 percent of shares.[37] The POI has announced an ambitious program of offering shares of 240 state enterprises up to March 2008. By the end of the period, the public sector's share of the national economy is to be reduced to 20 percent from the current 65 percent, the private sector's share will rise from 30 to 55 percent, and the share of the cooperative sector will go up to 25 percent from the present 5 percent.[38]

In the current perspective, share distribution is to reach some 21 million of the poorest 30 percent of the population, who will receive a total of 420 trillion rials (about $46 billion) in public-enterprise shares in three phases. In Phase I, the lowest-income 10 percent—an estimated 5.6 million individuals with an income of less than 300,000 rials a month ($32) and currently supported by various welfare schemes, would receive about 27 trillion rials.[39] In Phase II, another estimated 7.4 million rural residents and migrating tribes will be included, receiving 6.5 trillion rials. In Phase III, the program will be extended to an estimated 8 million government employees, workers, retired army and security personnel, and civilian retirees—comprising the six lowest deciles of income receivers—who would receive about 10.5 trillion rials. Each member of a designated family of five (maximum) would initially receive 5 million rials worth of justice shares, and eventually 20 million rials. The beneficiaries are to pay for the coupons in 10 to 20 years out of the annual dividends on their shares. According to a special decree by the Supreme Leader, the lowest 20 percent of income earners are entitled to a 50 percent discount in the purchase price of their shares. Discounts or other benefits are also provided for workers and managers of privatizing firms. There are detailed provisions regarding further transactions in distributed coupons.

The program has, from the start, faced five major challenges to its basic design. As the judiciary chief in a rare public statement has noted, there have been "strong differences of opinion" among the Islamic Republic's various power centers regarding policies and actions in the implementation of Article 44 and the basic direction by the Supreme Leader and the Expediency Council[40]—implying some resistance by the enterprises in voluntarily relinquishing their shares. The second hurdle has been the difficulty of identifying a reasonably accurate number of the "poor" in all three phases. Due to a near total absence of income-distribution data in Iran, figures regarding the size and status of the "poor" are both controversial and unreliable, with estimates ranging from zero to 30 percent of the total population. According to the current minister of welfare, "no one" in Iran was under the absolute poverty line.[41] He later admitted that some 9.2 million of Iran's total urban and rural population of 70 million are under the absolute or relative poverty line.[42] A Management and Plan Organization official and a Majlis deputy, however, give estimates of 10–12 percent. Two other members of the Majlis welfare committee put the figure at 13 and 20 percent, respectively, while a radical private economist raises the figure to 30 percent.[43]

The third challenge has been the selection of enterprises whose shares are to be transferred. If these entities were in the red and kept alive on public subsidies, transferring their shares would be tantamount to distributing poverty, not plenty. And if they were profitable businesses, the government could lose even more budgeted revenues from their operation and face larger deficits with more dire consequences. Fourth, obtaining an accurate, cost-based pricing of enterprise shares has been a thorny problem, given the companies' opaque accounting system, the unpublished amounts of annual state subsidies, loans received from state banks on favorable terms, unpaid taxes and other market data. In view of difficulties encountered in pricing the total worth of even a small public enterprise in the earlier privatization exercises—sometimes stretching to several months—share pricing of the current mammoth government entities is likely to entail interminable disagreements among company accountants and POI appraisers. Fifth, the elaborate, complex and ill-defined administrative and bureaucratic processes involved in carrying out various phases of the scheme constitute a new daunting task for the already overwhelmed bureaucracy. Finally, there have been no specific sources of financing officially designated for the elaborate administrative costs of the various agencies involved.

Matching these multiple challenges faced by the program's supporters is an apparent lack of enthusiastic demands on the part of the public as well as share recipients.[44] This attitude reflects partly the insignificant immediate impact of the program on their daily lives, and it manifests the national financial culture that exhibits a clear preference for tangible wealth such as land, property, gold, jewelry, antiques and even mobile telephones compared to financial assets.[45] The poorer the income group, the less interest is shown in owning financial papers. Emblematic of this phenomenon is the fact that less than 10 percent of the Iranian population's total possessions is in financial assets, compared to more than 60 percent in advanced countries.

Published information about the justice-shares program so far is sketchy, contradictory and full of ambiguities. Actual share distribution reportedly began in February 2006 among the poorest group in four relatively "deprived" Ostans each of which received 5 million rials ($540). Within a year, a total of 5.6 million individuals reportedly received a total of about 27 trillion rials worth of shares.[46] In defending his privatization record against widespread criticism, President Ahmadinejad has boasted that, in the previous 15 years, only 35 trillion rials of government shares had been privatized, while his government had thus far distributed more than 26 trillion, and intends to transfer another 60 trillion in the current and coming years.[47]

Assuming that the program succeeds in reaching its primary objective, there is no evidence, or even a reasonable assurance as yet, that other objectives of the program—increasing income, expediting privatization, downsizing the bureaucracy, promoting stock ownership habits, and enhancing enterprise efficiency—might be tackled or even approached. A palpable redistribution of income, the program's prime objective, can hardly be accomplished with the promised 11–15 percent annual dividend[48] on the initial $50 or even the ultimate $200 distributed shares to a poor family member, half of which has to be paid back annually. Furthermore, there is no guarantee that privatized

SOEs will have a double-digit return year after year and pay regular dividends so that the recipients can pay for their shares.[49] Second, expediting the privatization process as the next major goal of the program is also difficult to imagine.[50] In fact, it has been all too clear from the start that the objective of privatization (downsizing the public sector), and the goal of social justice (wealth redistribution), could not be optimized or even accomplished by one stroke, as the minister of economy and finance claimed.[51] Privatization could not be achieved through a justice-shares program that leaves 20 percent ownership (and thus effective management control) in state hands. The program could at best be called partial *denationalization* rather than privatization. Third, downsizing the government through reduced ownership is equally dubious, given the nightmarish multi-stage structure of the share-distribution program. The Central Headquarters, led by the president and composed of nine ministers, the mammoth Holding Company possessing large shares of 500 SOEs, the 30 *Ostan* and 337 *Shahrestan* cooperatives—each with its board of directors, managers, accountants, auditors, inspectors, etc.—would add to the government's size instead of reducing it. Fourth, enhancing total-factor productivity as another crucial goal of the scheme is also questionable.[52] There are already grave doubts about the technical, managerial and fiduciary ability of the Privatization Organization, the main Holding Corporation, and that of the regional and provincial cooperative societies to perform their fiduciary duties.[53] The only objective of the program that is perhaps within reach, and has been partly achieved, is expanding the share of the cooperatives sector—so far the orphan segment of the national economy. For this reason, the justice-shares program has been dubbed cooperativization rather than privatization.[54]

Furthermore, despite continued statements and repeated assurances, there is great doubt that the program will be able to distribute even the first 5-million-rial tranche of the 20 million rials promised to its 21 million eligible recipients by February 2008.[55] Fully aware of the difficulties involved in altering the recipients' preference for tangible assets and alerted by the sad experiences of privatization in the former Soviet Union and Eastern Europe, the framers of the justice-shares program have placed a two-year total ban on the sale of distributed coupons. They also strongly advise the recipients to hang onto their papers for steady returns and claim that the shares' value has already gone up in the Tehran Stock Exchange. Nevertheless, there are scattered reports that, in certain *Shahrestans*, the coupons are already being sold in the "informal" market at half their face value.[56] And, notwithstanding the various legal restrictions imposed on the sale of distributed coupons, private analysts believe that a majority of the recipients are likely to bypass those restrictions and create a black market in shares in Iran's underground economy. Or, they may take advantage of several loopholes in the program by selling their shares back to their local cooperatives, making the latter a new, semi-public, large institutional shareholder. In either case, the effect would not only negate the program's original intent but may entail new hazards for the economy. Many private economists warn about further fueling the already alarming double-digit inflation.[57] Others argue that even those who may hang on to their coupons are likely to increase their consumption, stimulated by the wealth effect. The Iranians' legendary low propensity to save and the bitter memories of the Tehran Stock Exchange crash in 2004 underscore these pessimistic forecasts.

Altogether a cursory examination of the justice-shares program so far is sufficient to indicate that the scheme is an ad hoc populist program—poorly conceived, inadequately prepared and highly complex—with insufficient prior cost-benefit analyses or calculations of its socioeconomic consequences.[58] For these reasons, even during the first phase of implementation, it has undergone repeated changes in its major provisions and continues to do so.[59] A great deal more data are needed to predict the ultimate success of the scheme.

Iran's privatization paradox

By a consensus of both domestic and foreign observers, the Islamic Republic's 18-year privatization attempt has not been a success. The new scheme under the Guidelines also faces a multitude of challenges. As already mentioned, during the nearly two decades of privatization efforts, the public sector, if anything, has continued to expand several times faster than the privatized segment. The share of the national budget in GDP has nearly doubled; private savings and investments in relation to GDP have remained the same; and national-factor productivity has actually declined.[60] The number of major SOEs listed in the comprehensive annual budgets (excluding their subsidiaries) has reached more than 500 from fewer than 270 in 1989, and their share of total public expenditure has risen to 73 percent from about 53 percent.[61] More significantly still, after nearly two years since the Guidelines proclamation, which the Supreme Leader termed "an economic revolution,"[62] not much interest has been shown by the private sector in the newly opened fields. While the constitutional "interpretation" of Article 44 was at the time hailed as the key to large-scale privatization, subsequent developments significantly tempered the initial euphoria. In the nearly two years since the first proclamation, no more than 10 percent of projected privatization revenues in the 2005 and 2006 national budgets actually materialized. This setback was so keenly felt that the Supreme Leader, in an unusual gesture, publicly chastised the government for the slow pace of privatization.[63] As it turned out, however, the process had encountered another major obstacle. An ad hoc Majlis committee, established to watch and expedite the privatization process, ultimately came to the conclusion that the main reason for the shortfall was the fact that the implementation of the Guidelines still required special enabling legislation from the Majlis. Without a specific parliamentary authorization, the privatizing agencies could not be found negligent in their transfer delays, and courts were not able to sanction the legality of transferred assets.[64] According to a Privatization Organization official, despite repeated advertisements in newspapers, no offer has been received from the private sector for some of the public enterprises put up for sale.[65]

Although the Islamic Republic's current domestic and international political climate, the real or imaginary winds of war with the United States or Israel, a shortage of domestic private capital and the paucity of foreign direct investments are often cited as the main causes of the economic malaise, the underlying cause may, in fact, lie in a more fundamental paradox. To be sure, under the Ahmadinejad government, which is accused of having "a clear anti-bourgeoisie policy aimed at paralyzing big investments by the private sector"[66] and giving conflicting signals regarding government policy,[67] the climate for liberalization, marketization and privatization has palpably deteriorated. Ahmadinejad's own quasi-dictatorial interventions in various domestic economic arenas—goods, capital, labor and trade—have also actually intensified. Such various factors as his objection to streamlining energy prices, mandatory increases in workers' paychecks, the mandated lowering of interest rates, compulsory earmarking of bank credits for the government's favored but questionable projects,[68] forced changes in private banks' management, the arbitrary raising and lowering of tariffs on scores of items, threatening to take back the questionably transferred enterprises, the granting of lucrative contracts to certain special entities on a no-bid basis,[69] the haphazard allocation of oil money to hundreds of small and questionable projects demanded by welcoming crowds during the president's travels around the country, and allegations of government interference in the election of the Iran Chamber of Commerce president[70] have all been pointed out as inimical to long-term domestic private investment.[71] A longer and more specific list of challenges to the implementation of the Guidelines is presented by private-sector leaders and high government officials.[72]

A belligerent stance by the president on the nuclear-proliferation issue and a clumsy and needlessly hostile position toward Washington and Tel Aviv have also resulted in a reluctance by foreign oil companies to invest in Iran; and de facto sanctions by European and other foreign financial and credit institutions under pressure from Washington have virtually shut off badly needed foreign direct investment.[73] After President Ahmadinejad's repeated statements that the UN and American sanctions have had no adverse effects on the economy or his nuclear policies and that Iran was unfazed by the prospect of further sanctions, the oil minister recently admitted that sanctions are hurting the oil industry.[74] The Tehran Stock Exchange's lackluster performance during the current administration and its recent erratic receptions to the initial public offering of four giant state steel, aluminum and copper enterprises, coupled with widespread reports about Iranian capital flight to Dubai, seem to confirm the political uncertainty hanging over the economy.[75] To help the private sector finance its purchases of privatized shares, the government has decided to turn one of its state banks into a cooperatives bank with an additional 3,500 billion rials in capital, and has ordered other state banks to set aside 15 trillion rials in credit for large buyers of state enterprises in return for a 30 percent down payment in cash.[76] It remains to be seen how these marginal measures may deal with the problem.

Even in the absence of the current obstacles, however, an effective and measurable privatization drive remains an elusive goal due to the influence of a seemingly insoluble systemic paradox. On the one hand, there is no doubt that Iran's current economic woes—high unemployment, virulent inflation, low factor productivity, slow growth, low levels of domestic savings and foreign direct investment, and relatively high but unprofitable public outlays—cannot be remedied without the creation and promotion of a strong private sector.[77] Privatization is not an option but a necessity. On the other hand, there are certain indisputable indications that neither the institutional nor the ideological underpinning of the Islamic regime would allow such a transformation.[78]

Institutionally, privatization is a daunting, if not impossible, task in an oil exporting country like Iran, where (a) the mainstay of the economy—oil reserves and revenues—is a government monopoly; (b) petroleum-export incomes are too large and far beyond government needs to finance and maintain the basic infrastructure and provide public goods; (c) oil revenues are not directly distributed among citizens as in Alaska; and (d) oil windfalls are not placed in a "lock box," to be invested abroad and drawn upon only during oil shortfalls and other emergencies as in Kuwait or Norway.[79] In the absence of these four conditions, extra oil income received by the government would invariably be invested in new public enterprises and would always exceed the simultaneous privatization of existing ones. In Iran's case, additional factors are also at play. Even in the most successful implementation of the current privatization program, 20 percent of the ownership of privatized enterprises is to be retained by the government, another 40–45 percent of shares will also remain in state hands because the managers of privatized enterprises and the leadership of cooperatives will still be appointed by the ministries of finance, industry, commerce, cooperatives, and others. As a result, meaningful privatization would probably never be achieved since the Islamic Republic's sub-par performance lies not in public ownership but in poor management.[80]

Ideologically, too, privatization is anathema to the Islamic Republic's political fabric and essence. True privatization requires, first, a clear legal recognition of private ownership rights with solemn guarantees regarding the impossibility of expropriation without due compensation. Second, it calls for the sanctity and security of contracts, business transparency, a modernized and private banking system, removal of inhibiting regulations, wage/price decontrol, trade liberalization and a market-friendly labor code. Third, it requires a modern business and commercial law with proper safeguards against monopoly, unfair trade practices, and deceitful advertising strengthened by special provisions against stock fraud, price manipulation and insider information deals. Finally, the need is for an independent, honest, accessible non-political and business-savvy judiciary.

None of these conditions exists in the highly regulated, rent-oriented, corruption-gripped, and non-transparent Islamic Republic. In fact, a recent report details the prevalence of preferential import licenses, access to interest-free or cheap credit for well-connected groups, guaranteed market shares for favored religious centers, and other such discriminatory practices.[81] Furthermore, there is no doubt that such a firmly institutionalized and powerful private sector would inevitably cause the growth of competing political-power centers: private manufacturing associations, business roundtables, labor unions, an independent press, civic groups and political parties. All such developments would be an existential threat to the supremacy of the *velayat-e faqih*, the Supreme Leadership. The resolve to get the government out of economic ownership and management is thus as fragile as the regime's confidence in its own survival.

For these reasons, privatization has remained a process based on mutual reluctance. That is, in addition to the economic, political, financial and managerial opposition on the part of government agencies to offer their enterprises for sale, there has been a significant lack of interest by the public. The lack of enthusiasm on the demand side may be traced to the yet unchanged structure of the Iranian economy—the prevailing anti-business environment, continued price controls, trade restrictions and protection, unfair and misplaced public subsidies, a crippling labor law, absence of incentives for foreign investments, inadequate money and capital markets, a significant lowering of Iran's ranking by Transparency International, and the earlier botched privatization efforts.[82] In the candid opinion of a government official, other factors such as dependence of state entities on subsidies (particularly on energy), lack of transparency in investment opportunities, voluminous and ever-changing government regulations, and other inhospitable conditions constitute further barriers to private-sector demand.[83] As a prospective private investor told a recent industrial conference in Tehran, private businesses will obviously be reluctant to invest in the country or even to bid for government shares under present conditions, where they still have to observe government price ceilings while their wage bill and other costs are increasing, the commerce ministry raises and lowers tariffs at will and permits or restricts exports without notice, and the Central Bank keeps the exchange rate unchanged despite continued high inflation.[84]

End of an era?

Privatization is now the ruling elite's declared priority. From the Supreme Leader to government ministers, agency heads, religious luminaries and security officials, all sing the praises of a large private-sector role. The Privatization Organization persistently announces imminent offers of new enterprises going on the block, covering oil and gas, petrochemicals, telecommunication, steel, aluminum, copper, cement, electrical power, state banks, insurance companies and other state entities.[85] Yet, there are legions of skeptics in and out of the country who still believe that the whole program is nothing but a clever ploy by the government to raise revenue to cover part of annual budget deficits. In any case, achieving the goal of social justice through a genuine privatization program, including social-justice shares, requires substantial prior changes in the Islamic Republic's institutional and ideological underpinnings. It is becoming increasingly clear that, if the current schemes are to succeed, economic liberalization, de-monopolization and political democratization must precede them. However, in the frank opinion of the minister of finance, Iran is not yet ready for liberalization, and this ideal would take several more years to materialize.[86] A comprehensive piece of legislation currently submitted for debate to the outgoing Seventh Majlis—designed to allow the legal divestiture of Article 44 enterprises by the government and to provide a more hospitable and secure climate for private-sector expansion—may turn out to be of some help.[87] But the essential privatization paradox still remains to be dealt with.

Notes

* First published in *Middle East Policy* vol. XIV, no. 3, Fall 2007. Reproduced with permission.

1 For all quotations see *The Constitution of the Islamic Republic of Iran* (Berkeley, CA: Mizan Press, 1980).

2 See, for example, *Kayhan Havai* (Tehran) 20, *mordad* 12 *Aban*, and 4 *Esfand* 1372 (June to February 1993).

3 For a brief description of early attempts, see Jahangir Amuzegar, "Iran's Privatization Saga," *Middle East Economic Survey*, June 17, 2002.

4 For a breakdown of sales figures by various government agencies as well as methods of sales (negotiation, auction, and the use of the stock market) during the first 12-year period, see "Trends of Privatization in Iran," available at www.hamshahri.net, November 10 and 13, 2002, and January 16, 2003. See also statement by the privatization director, available at www.radioazadi.org, May 9, 2002.

5 www.jomhourieslami.com, October 10, 2006.

6 www.donya-e-eqtesad.com, July 4, 2006.

7 www.donya-e-eqtesad.com, October 28, 2006.

8 www.donya-e-eqtesad.com, March 7, 2007.

9 www.hamshahri.net/news, June 15, 2007.

10 www.hamshahri.net, February 1, 2003.

11 www.hamshahri.net, May 20, 2003.

12 *Iran Economics*, November 2006.

13 www.donya-e-eqtesad.com, June 20, 2006, and www.jomhourieslami.com, December 30, 2005.

14 Statement by the head of the Privatization Organization, available at www.donya-e-eqtesad.com, July 4, 2006.

15 According to a poll taken by the Ministry of Culture and Islamic Guidance, between 66 and 82 percent of the ordinary citizens opposed the privatization of banks, insurance companies, universities, hospitals, public utilities, air transportation, telecommunications and, most strongly, oil and gas. See www.hamshahri.net, August 18, 2004.

16 For example, of the 64 operating airports destined for privatization, only one, according to the head of National Aviation Organization, was profitable. See www.hamshahri.net, August 30, 2005.

17 See "Money and Inflation in the Islamic Republic of Iran," IMF Working Paper WP/07/119, May 2007.
18 See statement by Ali Reza Mahjoob, available at www.jomhourieslami.com, November 17, 2004.
19 For a sample of numerous shortfall reports, see www.radiofarda.com, April 29, 2002, and www.hamshahri.net, November 2, 2002.
20 www.radioazadi.org/Iran, November 8, 2002.
21 Five such cases were returned to their original state agencies. See www.hamshahri.net, June 27, 2002.
22 See "Private ownership in large economic spheres is legalized," available at www.hamshahri.net, October 2, 2004.
23 For the background and details of the process, see *Iran Economics*, November 2006.
24 According to a knowledgeable Majlis deputy, the government owned more than 2,000 enterprises of which 1,500 were outside the mandate of Article 44. See www.hamshahri.net, August 17, 2004.
25 Up to that date, only 49 percent of SOEs could be transferred.
26 For a comprehensive description of the five parts and a full discussion of related matters, see "Methods and Requirements of Article 44 Implementation," *Iran Economics*, November 2006.
27 Statement reported in www.radiofarda.com/Article, February 19, 2007.
28 Statement by the head of the POI, available at www.jomhourieslami.com, June 5, 2007.
29 www.radiofarda.com, March 7, 2007; and www.donya-e-eqtesad.com, March 7, 2007.
30 For a typical criticism, see his speeches in Arak and Saveh, available at www.emrooz.info, May 18, 2006.
31 See "Imam's economic viewpoints," available at www.hamshahri.net, June 2, 2005.
32 For references, see "A Critique of Justice Shares," available at http://emruz.info, February 4, 2007.
33 See "Details of Shares Participation Through Coupons," at www.donya-e-eqtead.com, October 16, 2005.
34 For details of the initial proposal, see www.donya-e-eqtesad.com, October 28, 2005.
35 www.hamshahri.net, October 22, 2006.
36 Statement by the head of the POI, available at www.hamshahri.net/news, November 26, 2006.
37 Statement by the finance minister, available at www.jomhourieslami.com, May 1, 2007.
38 Statement by deputy finance minister, available at www.donya-e-eqtesad.com, January 8, 2007.
39 www.donya-e-eqtesad.com, July 3, 2006; and www.hamshahri.net, May 8, 2007.
40 See www.donya-e-eqtesad.com, April 18, 2007.
41 See "The Minister's Claim," available at http://emruz.info, March 13, 2007.
42 See www.iran-emrooz.net, August 12, 2007.
43 For sources of respective figures, see www.iranmania.com/news, May 15, 2007; http://emruz.info, April 29, 2007; www.jomhourieslami.com, May 2, 2007; and the *Guardian*, April 30, 2007; *Kayhan* (London), June 27, 2007.
44 See the dialogue between the minister of finance and the members of the Tehran Chamber of Commerce, available at www.donya-e-eqtesad, July 22, 2007.
45 This attitude resembles the situation during the shah's time, when peasants showed significant resistance to cede the titles to their newly acquired small pieces of land under the land reform program to an agricultural cooperative in exchange for the cooperatives' shares.

46 www.donya-e-eqtesad.com, April 22, 2007.
47 www. donya-e-eqtesad.com, May 19, 2007.
48 See statement by the head of POI, available at www.hamshahri.net/news, May 12, 2007.
49 No dividend has so far been declared or distributed to coupon recipients, and no payment made for their receipts.
50 For a fuller discussion of the subject, see *Islamic Republic of Iran: Managing the Transition to a Market Economy* (Washington, DC: International Monetary Fund, 2007).
51 www.donya-e-eqtesad.com, March 13, 2006.
52 For doubts in this regard expressed by the government's Management and Plan Organization publication, see www.donya-e-eqtesad.com, January 23, 2007.
53 For an official airing of these ambiguities and doubts, see "Three Unknowns about Justice Shares," available at www.donya-e-eqtesad, January 23, 2007; and a statement by an influential Majlis deputy, available at www.jomhourieslami.com, June 20, 2007.
54 http://emruz.info, February 4, 2007.
55 Statement by deputy minister of finance, available at in www.hamshahri.net/news, May 8, 2007.
56 www.donya-e-eqtesad.com, April 17, 2007.
57 The World Bank and the Economist Intelligence Unit in their latest reports both predict higher inflation and slower GDP growth of the Iranian economy in the next three years. See www.radiofarda.com, June 2, 2007.
58 See statement by a member of the Tehran Chamber of Commerce, available at www.donya-e-eqtesad.com, July 24, 2007.
59 For a detailed critique of the program, see http://emruz.info, February 4, 2007, and May 21, 2007.
60 For details, see *Iran Economics*, June 2007.
61 For an evaluation of the privatization program, see *Iran Economics*, June 2007.
62 www hamshahri.net, January 22, 2007.
63 See www.radiofarda.com, February 19, 2007.
64 See statement by Elias Naderan, www.donya-e-eqtesad.com, April 6, 2007.
65 www.jomhourieslami.com, June 20, 2007.
66 See statement by a former president of the Tehran Chamber of Commerce, *Financial Times*, May 28, 2007.
67 www.jomhourieslami.com, June 22, 2007.
68 For the misuse of bank loans in the "quick return" projects see www.donya-e-eqtesad.com, June 18, 2007.
69 For details see the *Wall Street Journal*, October 14–15, 2006; and the *Financial Times*, March 16, 2007.
70 www.radiofarda.com, June 13, 2007.
71 See BBC Persian.com, June 12, 2007; www.radiofarda.com, June 13, 2007; and specifically the letter written to President Ahmadinejad by 57 economics professors at various Iranian universities, available at www.iran-emrooz.net, June 11, 2007.
72 See www.jomhourieslami.com, July 8, 2007; and www.donya-e-eqtesad.com, July 1, 2007.
73 www.payvand.com/news, May 12, 2007; and Associated Press, May 24, 2007.
74 Agence France-Presse, July 4, 2007.
75 For the warm reception of four attractively priced and dividend-paying state metal companies see www. donya-e-eqtesad.com, August 11, 2007. For promises of starting the second and third phases of justice share distribution soon, and the first dividends to be paid on already distributed shares see www.jomhourieslami.com, August 14, 2007.
76 www.hamshahri.net, June 8, 2007; and www. donya-e-eqtesad.com, June 8, 2007.

77 In the candid opinion of the current minister of commerce, "without creating a genuinely competitive climate in the country, privatization would be meaningless." See www.donya-e-eqtesad.com, June 18, 2007.
78 For more detailed references to some of these factors see "The Third Letter of Economists to Ahmadinejad," available at www.iran-emrooz.net, July 15, 2007.
79 See Jahangir Amuzegar, "Iran's Oil Stabilization Fund: A Misnomer," *Middle East Economic Survey*, November 25, 2005.
80 For the significance of this factor see "Should State-owned Financial Institutions Be Privatized or Reformed?" *IMF Survey*, May 31, 2004.
81 See "New Era for Iran's Private Sector," available at ISN Security Watch, www.isn.ethz.ch/news, June 26, 2007.
82 See statement by a Management and Plan Organization official, available at www.donya-e-eqtesad.com, December 9, 2006.
83 Statement by the head of the POI, available at www.hamshashri.net/news, May 1, 2007.
84 www.donya-e-eqtesad.com, June 22, 2007.
85 For various lists of state enterprises put up for sale this year, see www.jomhourieslami.com, June 23 and 27, 2007, and July, 22, 29, and 31, 2007; and www.hamshahri.net, July 16, 2007.
86 www.hamshahri.net, July 22, 2007.
87 For details see www.donya-e-eqtesad.com, August 11, 2007.

5 Iran's 20-year economic perspective

Promises and pitfalls*

With the start of its fourth five-year economic development plan in March 2005, the Iranian government issued a document called *Iran's 20-Year Economic Perspective*, outlining a road map for the country's economic, political, social and cultural development during the next two decades. The Perspective's preamble promised that by 2025, i.e., after the completion of four five-year development plans, Iran would be a fully advanced country, rising to the number-one rank in economic, scientific and technological progress among 28 nations in the Middle East and Southeast Asia. By that time, Iran was to be a nation with an Islamic and revolutionary identity, offering a guiding light for the Islamic world while engaged in effective and constructive interaction with the rest of the global community.[1]

The widely publicized document called for (a) achievement of fast-paced and sustainable economic growth; (b) creation of durable employment opportunities; (c) enhancement of factor productivity; (d) active presence in regional and international markets; (e) development of a diverse, knowledge-based economy free of inflation and blessed by food security; and (f) establishment of a market environment conducive to domestic and international business entrepreneurship.

With the first of the four five-year plans nearing its end without reaching any of its major targets (e.g., rapid growth, price stability, high employment, increased investment and reduced reliance on oil-export receipts), a fresh appraisal seems appropriate.[2] And, since the Islamic Republic currently lags far behind other countries in the region in most of those measures, there is no doubt that unless the causes of such poor performance are clearly recognized and effectively dealt with, the next three plans will have no better outcome than the first one. A careful new look at the Perspective's prospects, challenges and requirements is thus in order.[3]

Favorable prospects

The Perspective's 20-year objectives actually contain some reasonably favorable potential. With only 1 percent of the world's population, Iran ranks seventh in mineral wealth, possessing 10 percent of proven global petroleum reserves and 16 percent of the earth's natural-gas deposits. New mineral wealth is being discovered each year, and a large part of the country is still unexplored. Iran is now called the region's most "wired" nation, with more than one-third of its 72 million people having access to the Internet. The two-thirds under 30 are also educated young men and women ready to participate in building a thriving and prosperous Iran. Variegated climate and favorable topography allow for a rich agriculture under conducive policies. With a strategic location, surrounded by 15 land and sea neighbors, Iran can serve as a lucrative trade and transit route in both north-south and east-west directions. Its abundant natural and human resources would be magnets for foreign direct investment if a hospitable business climate and sufficient incentives should prevail. Finally, the minimal infrastructure needed for growth and development (roads, railroads, air and sea ports, modern communications) is already in place to promote and sustain growth under proper maintenance.

There is no doubt that such an overly ambitious scheme not only requires sufficient material and human resources, but also a hospitable environment free from ideological, political, economic, managerial, technological, socio-cultural or external challenges that may impede the achievement of its lofty goals. The following brief references to each of these existential obstacles may show the enormity of the task ahead and the need for urgent rescue efforts.

Ideological shackles

The foremost obstacle to the realization of the Perspective's goals is the Islamic Republic's theocratic oligarchy, based upon an anachronistic, retrogressive and somewhat xenophobic constitution that is inimical to economic growth and wealth creation. This fundamental law, adopted in 1979 and amended in 1989, is based on a hotly disputed theological doctrine called *velayat-e faqih* (guardianship of a jurist), formulated by Ayatollah Khomeini before the 1979 Iranian revolution. This theology, challenged from the start by Shiite divines both in Iran and across the Middle East, bestows dictatorial power on a *vali* (*rahbar*, or supreme leader), who is presumably infallible. A unique constitutional process in the Islamic Republic virtually allows this *vali* to appoint himself for life and be answerable to no one.[4] He sets the country's major domestic and foreign policies, commands the armed forces, oversees the state radio and television monopoly, appoints the six clerical members of the veto-wielding Council of Guardians, and selects the members of the Expediency Council as the final arbiter of all national legislation. The basic law also contains a distinct ideological bias in favor of the poor (*mostazafan*) under a banner of "Islamic social justice" that is never clearly defined. In this bias, akin to equating poverty with virtue, the primacy of money and wealth is called into question, as is the pursuit of pleasure. There is also an ill-concealed hostility toward capitalism, free enterprise and the Western way of life, presumably because they are based on "secular, humanistic and liberalist" principles instead of theistic foundations.[5] Real economic development, it is held, may not be attained by adopting foreign economic models, but only through a genuine "national, home-grown and Islamic" paradigm compatible with Iran's own history, geography, politics and culture.[6]

Searching for this elusive economic model for nearly 30 years, the government has been operating under a series of five-year development plans that have never been strictly adhered to, never attained their targets and never taught a useful lesson. Yet, this exercise in futility still continues in the preparation of the Fifth Plan (2010–15). Meanwhile, in search of a culture-specific model, the regime has shifted from one awkward strategy to another.[7] The irony is that such a specific, domestic-oriented model, even if it could be fashioned, would not only lack scientific or rational underpinning, it would also actually go against Iran's own basic national interest. For a small, isolated, rural and self-sufficient island nation, an inward-looking paradigm might perhaps have been tolerable. But for a large and populous country, dependent for as much as 40 percent of its gross domestic product on foreign trade, it would be patently absurd. Furthermore, the adoption of such a xenophobic model would be against the Perspective's promise of "collaboration" with the global community.

Political handicaps

Politics and governance in Iran is based on the regime's self-described Islamic democracy, an oxymoron that identifies neither a true Islamic state nor a modern pluralistic, representative government. The regime's virtually apartheid character discriminates between *khodi* (ours) and *gheyr khodi* (others); but *khodis* themselves are treated differently on the basis of gender, revolutionary credentials, blood relations and inclusion in the *nomenklatura.* Even women who are *khodis,* for example, are treated as second-class citizens in matters such as marriage, divorce, inheritance, child custody and court testimony. Denied access to many occupations, they constitute a small segment of the labor force and deprive the economy of their productive contribution. Members of the *pasdaran* (Islamic Revolutionary Guard Corps), the *basij* (volunteer militia) and the martyrs' families are given special educational, professional and financial privileges. Clergymen enjoy special advantages, occupy supervisory positions in all government organizations, head most of the charitable foundations and have their own court of justice. Grandees—offspring and siblings of eminent ayatollahs—are shown favoritism in government projects and no-bid contracts and treated with kid gloves in judicial proceedings.

There is also no equality before the law for all, regardless of religion, gender or political beliefs, as real democracy requires. Sunnis, Christians, Jews, Zoroastrians and Bahais do not enjoy the same rights and privileges as Shiites. The Islamic Republic continues to be on the list of countries accused of religious discrimination by the United Nations and the United States. Those labeled liberals, secularists, monarchists and pro-Westerners are denied many of their civil rights. Political parties, labor unions, business associations and nongovernmental organizations are not free to organize and function, despite constitutional guarantees. There are more than 100 political "parties" officially registered and recognized, but none has a national base, sizeable membership, party discipline or meaningful platform beyond some attention-getting slogans. In the 2009 presidential election, for example, the general secretary of a major party backed the candidate of another party! Even the periodic elections that the regime routinely claims as proof of its democracy are by no means free or fair.[8]

Governance in Iran may be characterized essentially as rule by men and not by law, even God's law. There is a unique jurisdictional power-sharing arrangement, or political satrapy, among various clerical, military and technocratic power brokers. The national constitution remains largely a law on paper only; more than a dozen of its essential clauses are routinely disregarded with impunity. A commission established during the Khatami administration to monitor and report such violations was abolished in 2000 after only a year, during which it found hundreds of them. Laws are frequently passed by the Majlis (legislature) but ignored or selectively enforced by the executive branch or the supposedly "independent" judiciary. The supreme leader issues lofty proclamations (against corruption and profligate consumption, in favor of the sale of public entities) with no follow-up. Disregard for the budget and fiscal discipline manifests itself in the hundreds of projects approved on the spot by cabinet members touring the country, with no visible means of fiscal support.[9] The Expediency Council orders various state councils unlawfully abolished by the executive branch to be reinstated to their legal status, but the order is not obeyed. The Council of Guardians orders the incumbent president to halt his provincial tours paid by the state funds during presidential campaigns, and he defies the order with no consequences. The judiciary chief gives strict instructions on judicial procedures and sentencing practices, but they are openly ignored by lower-court judges. Court orders on individual or business-rights cases are issued but not enforced by responsible state agencies. Prosecutors use cruel and unusual means to exact confessions from political prisoners on trumped-up charges, despite strict constitutional prohibition. And, while no official raises his voice, whistleblowers themselves end up in jail. Security agencies run their own prisons. The sitting president, in a televised campaign debate, openly accuses the three former heads of government of corruption and misfeasance, and everyone listens with utter indifference. State entities frequently contradict each other's information and statistics with no repercussions.

In addition to its anarchist character, the central government is also big, inefficient and intrusive—characteristics that are hostile to a thriving economy and a vibrant society. While Iran's population has doubled since the 1979 revolution, the number of public servants has nearly quadrupled. And, while the government's general budget has increased 10-fold in the last decade, there has been no notable improvement in public services. Currently, the central government and semi-public agencies (state-owned enterprises, state-supported charitable foundations (*bonyads*) and public-dominated organizations) control nearly 70 percent of the economy. Despite being deplored and criticized in recent years and repeatedly targeted for downsizing in every five-year plan, the bureaucracy has been steadily on the rise. Parallel operations in the armed forces, the ministries and state enterprises abound, and they often operate at cross-purposes. There are at least three separate organizations in charge of energy, three of education and culture, five of economy, and two of labor and social affairs—all with inadequately defined duties and responsibilities. The Iranian bureaucracy, in short, suffers from insufficient respect for the law, lack of transparency, excessive centralization, inadequate fiscal discipline and significant inefficiency.

The lean and struggling private sector, involving mostly domestic trade and services, does not play a significant role in the economy's direction. Various privatization schemes initiated in the last 20 years, and a recent fundamental revision of Article 44 of the constitution toward de-nationalization, have not made more than a small dent in the giant structure. Of an estimated $120 billion in assets owned by state enterprises, some $40 billion have so far been disinvested. Assets valued at $22 billion have reportedly been "distributed" among the poorer strata as "justice shares"; another $7 billion worth has been paid to the Social Security and Employees Pension Funds in lieu of the Treasury's delayed debt; and $11 billion in shares has been sold to the public through the Tehran Stock Exchange, although in many cases these shares have been purchased by some parastatal organizations and thus are not really privatized. In all cases, too, the majority ownership and management of the "privatized" enterprises have remained in state hands.[10] The result has been a reduction of entrepreneurial efficiency and the undermining of a more rational use of business income.[11]

The Islamic government is also an all-intrusive behemoth. State interference in the economy covers a wide spectrum: wages, prices, exchange rates, trade and business, interest rates, and state-bank lending quotas in addition to direct industrial, agricultural and commercial control. The government also prescribes (and clumsily enforces) its citizens' daily lives: the way people are to eat, drink, dress, read, write, assemble, socialize, publish, preach and conduct their personal affairs. In this respect it surpasses other totalitarian (fascist and communist) regimes with which it shares most other characteristics.

The government also tends to regard political dissent as a threat to national security, and therefore subject to repression and, in serious cases, prosecution. Despite clear admonition by the constitution, civil liberties are routinely curbed by the authorities. People are arrested, incarcerated and denied access to counsel or courts for weeks and months with no explanation or charges. Reform-minded newspapers and publications are shut down. Movies, books and art exhibitions must obtain governmental permits prior to publication and display. Radio and TV stations are state monopolies. Freedom House's 2009 annual report on press freedom ranks the Islamic Republic 181 among 195 countries. Reporters Without Borders (Reporters sans frontières) calls Iran the world's largest prison for journalists.[12] All these restrictions and proscriptions, needless to say, impede the Perspective's optimum realization.

Economic fault lines

In the economic arena, the single most significant weakness now and for the next 15 years is Iran's unhealthy reliance on oil-export revenues as the mainstay of its economy. Although not the largest sector, oil accounts for more than 80 percent of annual foreign-exchange earnings and nearly 70 percent of annual state finances. While reduction and eventual elimination of this dependence has been mandated in every one of the past development plans, the reliance on oil has, if anything, actually intensified. The government's need for oil receipts has increased from $16 billion in 2001 to $41 billion in 2009. Recent oil-price volatility in the face of Iran's increasing heavy dependence on imports of essential capital and consumer goods (including such daily staples as wheat, rice, sugar and red meat) now presents an even more ominous threat. According to a recent IMF estimate, a protracted oil price below $75 per barrel may play havoc with Iran's economy. The Perspective's ultimate material success may, in fact, depend largely on the fate of Iran's gas and oil industries.

The national budget's lack of transparency is the second gravest economic threat. The annual budget document, approved by the Majlis usually after weeks of deliberation, is hardly ever faithfully adhered to. Always formally in balance at the time of approval, it invariably ends up in deficit[13] due to a paltry and inflexible tax base, recurrent losses of state-owned enterprises, poor tax collection and unaffordable public-welfare expenditures.[14] A shortage of funds in the current account is routinely made up by transfers from the development (capital-investment) portion. In recent years, one-fourth of the annual capital-investment budget has been diverted to regular expenditures, with the result that thousands of development projects remain unfinished due to lack of funds.[15] Budget deficits are routinely financed by the Central Bank, operating as the government's cash cow. Iran's endemic double-digit inflation, the highest in the region and among the eight highest in the world, is the result of this monetization of the public debt.

The budget's major black hole, on top of staggering employee compensation and fringe benefits, is across-the-board public subsidies. In addition to paying the highest energy subsidies among the 22 countries in the Middle East and North Africa—nearing 20 percent of GDP—the government also subsidizes the production, consumption, distribution and export of various products. Despite the lip service paid to the necessity of rapid production growth, the government's main concern has always focused on distribution rather than wealth creation—under the banner of Islamic "social justice." Nevertheless, current public subsidies, both explicit (budgeted) and implicit (foregone opportunity values), leave much to be desired in terms of fairness, efficiency and sustainability.

Anachronistic banking is another economic handicap. Iran's banking and financial sector, responsible for facilitating one-third of the total domestic product, is highly inefficient. The 11 major commercial and investment banks (controlling 90 percent of the sector) are state-owned and operate according to government directions. All state banks are financially undercapitalized; they suffer from too many money-losing branches and semi-idle employees, and too few initiatives. Under the country's so-called "interest-free" Islamic banking law, state and private banks have the unenviable task of fitting the twenty-first century's complicated modern financial services into the strait jacket of some seventh-century Islamic transaction modes. Interest rates paid on deposits and charged on loans are arbitrarily dictated by the government, often in total disregard of prevailing economic conditions. Since all state banks are under one corporate board composed of high government officials and are not required to publish their balance sheets, there is no way of knowing the true size of their nonperforming loans. The privately estimated figure amounts to $38 billion (or 20 percent of their total assets).[16] They are also indebted to the Central Bank to the tune of $22 billion,[17] as a result of making government-directed loans to various so-called quick-return enterprises that have proved delinquent in servicing their debts.[18]

Stagnant factor productivity is the third economic shackle. While some 2.5 percent of the 8 percent annual GDP growth targeted in the Perspective is supposed to materialize through increases in total factor productivity, the figure realized so far has been highly disappointing. According to private estimates, labor productivity in the last four years has risen by about 0.57 percent a year, but total factor productivity has been negative due to low returns on capital.[19] The reasons are not hard to find. Iran has one of the largest numbers of official holidays in the world. Lax supervision reduces government employees' productive daily working hours to a fraction of the norm. Inadequate wages in the face of rising inflation lead workers and state employees to work at two to three jobs a day. Many factories reportedly operate only three hours a day, due either to lack of input or to insufficient customers.[20] There is a significant mismatch between jobholders' skills and qualifications and their actual positions. There are also wide gaps between jobseekers' training and education, on the one hand, and basic national needs on the other. Iran's education system, at all levels, is both expensive and unproductive. It largely produces degree-chasing, desk-oriented graduates who, instead of forming a technically trained and economically productive work force, are certifiably unemployable. According to a recent police report, more than 6 percent of homeless people in Tehran have a university education!

Excessive waste of resources is the fourth problem. Topping the list is profligate energy use. Refineries and energy-based industries (steel, aluminum, cement, petrochemicals) use oil or gas at two to three times the world standard.[21] Due also to subsidized and dirt-cheap prices, per capita energy consumption is the highest among OPEC members and several times the world average.[22] The country's energy intensity (share of fuel in the final product) is three times the world's norm, using 16 barrels of crude oil to produce $1 million of final product, compared to three barrels in major industrial countries.[23] Only 3 percent of buildings in Iran are adequately insulated. By an official estimate, energy waste in Iran rises to as much as $30 billion a year.[24]

Poor management also is endemic. With the government controlling more than two-thirds of the economy, almost all key managers in state-owned enterprises, including oil and gas, heavy industry, commerce, transport, communications and charitable foundations, are government appointees. Their positions are based mostly on strict fealty to the regime and/or close blood relations with the ruling elite. Managers are frequently appointed or removed, not on the basis of performance, but on political and personal considerations. Turnover is frequent and demoralizing to the workforce. As a result, the country is deprived of the services of some of its best and brightest individuals, who routinely emigrate to the West and become successful business executives.

The last economic problem is the high cost of starting and conducting businesses. Obstacles include the tension-filled internal and external political climate, discriminatory and ever-changing laws and regulations, uncertainties regarding the state-determined foreign-exchange rate, an inadequate banking and financial market, an inefficient and tainted stock exchange, lack of protection for intellectual-property rights and, above all, a corrupt and politicized judicial and arbitration system. Domestic and foreign trade is dominated by a small number of public and private monopolies in the hands of a few clerical, military, security and other influential families—commonly dubbed the "economic mafia." The absence of a level playing field, and unfair competition by subsidized state-owned enterprises and *bonyads* discourage private entrepreneurship. The World Bank's 2009 international ranking of hospitable business environments ranked Iran 142 among 180 nations.[25]

Lack of economic freedom also hampers rapid economic growth, enhanced factor productivity and a hospitable business climate. The Heritage Foundation's 2009 report classifies the Islamic Republic as a "non-free" nation, placing it 168 out of 179 nations in terms of various freedom measures.

Technological shortcomings

Research and development in science and technology in the Islamic Republic faces dificulties. There are reports of notable advances in such fields as construction engineering, nuclear energy, space exploration and defense weaponry (armored vehicles, speed boats, drones, helicopters, ballistic missiles). There is also evident progress in medicine and biotechnology (organ transplants, stem-cell research, animal cloning), as well as in nanotechnology. Nearly all these advances, however, are borrowed and subject only to local adaptations. Iran has not been able so far to offer a single new and truly innovative technological model to the world.[26] With more than 100 years of immersion in the oil and gas industries, Iran has not yet registered a single patent under its own name. As a result, the bulk of the economy (agriculture, industry and transportation) operates at mid-twentieth-century technological standards. An average Iranian farm or industrial plant uses several times more energy, more workers, more material and more hours to produce a unit of final product than a similar entity in the West.[27]

A major reason is that research and development as such has never been institutionalized within the system. Research and development activities conducted by universities, think tanks and other entities in Iran are all financed, directed and supplied by the government. Demand for business innovations is scant. As a result, none of Iran's current industries can compete in world markets without subsidized imports and/or export "prizes." Their minuscule research budgets are generally wasted on costly, but inconsequential, conferences and seminars arranged by ambitious bureaucrats instead of serious scientific investigations. The annual brain drain, coupled with a large number of government-financed fellowship students abroad who decide not to return home, adds to the problem.

Sociocultural malaise

The sociocultural stumbling blocks to the Perspective's targeted objectives are numerous and complex. The country's spiritual and moral social fabric is under severe strain. Bureaucratic malfeasance, a near-total disregard of meritocracy in government employment, judicial capriciousness and wasteful distribution of the oil windfall have all reduced the credibility of Islamic social justice. The imposition of an antiquated Islamic moral code on a burgeoning young population enamored of Western dress, pop music and the Internet has damaged their spirit. The rapid rise of new privileged groups to fabulous fortunes through lucrative government contracts and access to enormous economic rents, combined with an ostentatious display of wealth, has made the *nouveaux riches* role models for the youth. Ironically enough, after 30 years of relentless religious admonition against crass materialism and conspicuous consumption, Iranian twentysomethings have never been as rapacious in the pursuit of the "good life" as they are now. Getting rich quick is their major goal. At the same time, this subculture has led to a reported annual exodus of more than 100,000 educated men and women in search of better and safer opportunities—placing Iran near the top of nations experiencing a brain drain. Adding to a long list of social ills are plagues such as the unusually high and growing rates of drug addiction, prostitution, divorce, runaway teens, youth suicide and juvenile crime.[28]

Adding to these factors is a new subculture of martyrdom and messianic anticipation promulgated by the incumbent administration. Elevating as this belief may be for ultimate spiritual salvation, it does not enhance mundane economic development or material rivalry with neighbors; nor is it of much help in competition with trading partners. The cult of personality—the supremacy and infallibility of the *vali-e-faqih*—is also clearly incompatible with the aspirations of free-thinking, innovative people. The sycophancy and mendacity spawned by this cult are likewise anathema to a dependable process of technological and material progress. Dependence by ordinary citizens on government handouts is another cultural negative. The harmful habit of seeking state solutions for all individual problems has now become an accepted way of life for the majority of the population. Self-reliance, individuality and mutual cooperation are further undermined by allowing people to submit their requests directly to the highest authority. Of the millions of officially claimed petitions presented to the president and his cabinet in their provincial tours, more than 90 percent reportedly involve demands for money to buy a house, pay debts, get married or make a trip to a holy site. This dependency has now become a highly charged political issue, as it encourages office seekers to outbid each other in promising a larger and larger government dole.

Jeopardizing the fulfillment of the Perspective's targets is also the plague of widespread and brazen endemic corruption, not only at the high levels of administration and state enterprises, but also in small routine daily transactions involving public services. Lucrative no-bid contracts given to the *pasdarans'* business entities, the sale of state-owned enterprises to favored groups at below-market prices, large and virtually unsecured loans made by state banks to privileged businesses or individuals, access to substantial economic rents in the purchase of goods and foreign exchange from government agencies, inside information available to certain parties about imminent changes in trade and exchange regulations, and petty bribes and kickbacks for routine public services are some examples. Transparency International places the Islamic Republic's position in terms of business ethics at 141 among 180 countries in 2009, down from 88 in 2005.

External drag

The Islamic Republic's recent belligerent and provocative foreign policies, particularly its hostile posture toward the West, denial of the Holocaust, threats to Israel and support for the "terrorist" groups on Washington's list, have poisoned the atmosphere for trade and investment transactions with the global community.[29] Combined with a series of provocations—launching a "spy" satellite, displaying thousands of new centrifuges for uranium enrichment, test-firing a surface-to-surface missile—this contentious stand presents a further major handicap. Iran's seemingly resolute intention to enrich uranium for avowedly peaceful purposes has been called into question by the West and resulted in a series of crippling economic sanctions. Without a mutually satisfactory resolution of this issue, the threats of more severe diplomatic pressure, more effective economic sanctions and even military action hang over the horizon. These existential threats would clearly impede Iran's efforts toward economic progress and prosperity. Further saber rattling by the Iranian government, even under the banner of defense and deterrence, is likely to be counterproductive. The four UN Security Council sanctions resolutions, combined with US bilateral sanctions, have so far substantially restricted the

Islamic Republic's access to global financial markets. They have raised foreign transaction costs and made dependence on volatile petroleum receipts the main source of external financing. With the realization of the Perspective's targets clearly dependent upon billions in foreign funds and direct foreign investments, anything short of a good-faith effort to resolve differences with Washington, Israel and the West would place the Perspective's final outcome in great jeopardy.

By most estimates, Iran needs some $25 billion of new investment each year for many years to come to provide employment for more than one million new entrants into the job market. Some 40 percent of this investment has to come from abroad.[30] Yet, the Islamic Republic's present lack of even minimal access to the world financial markets, coupled with a host of other impediments discussed elsewhere,[31] have placed it at the very bottom of countries attracting foreign-direct or even portfolio investments.[32] In the oil industry, where both capital and technology are badly needed, economic sanctions aggravated by a frustrating bureaucracy, long delays in decision making and unattractive "buy-back"[33] contract terms have further thwarted the realization of the targets set in the Fourth Plan and the Perspective. Nearly all Western oil and gas companies having the mindset, the technology and the capital for such investments have now stopped their new involvement in Iran. The Chinese, Indian and local entities that are replacing them lack most of the essential requirements. As a result, Iran is reportedly 11 years behind in getting its share from the South Pars gas reservoirs jointly owned with Qatar in the Persian Gulf, and seven years behind in the Salman gas field jointly owned with the United Arab Emirates. Tehran also has no share of the oil and gas exploited in the Caspian Sea by the other littoral states.[34] In the non-energy sectors, too, Iran has been woefully unsuccessful in attracting direct foreign investment due to the uncertain political climate, inadequate and ever-changing rules, bureaucratic hassles in starting a business, uncertainties about future exchange rates, and the unreliability of the judicial and arbitration systems.[35]

The brutal crackdowns—beatings, arrests, jailing, shootings and killings of peaceful demonstrators protesting alleged fraud in the June 2009 presidential elections—have further raised the level of worldwide indignation against the theocratic regime. This unprecedented repression has not only jeopardized Washington's declared intention of direct engagement with Tehran; it seems to have further postponed any conciliatory steps on the part of the European Union in restarting dialogue. The turmoil and its ensuing climate of increased anxiety and new uncertainties have more than ever jeopardized new domestic and foreign investments needed to foster growth and innovation.

A suggested rescue plan

Given the Islamic Republic's seventh-century ideology, non-democratic politics, socioeconomic flaws, skeptical worldview and other shortcomings, there is no possibility that the Perspective can reach its stated goals within the next 15 years. Nor can Iran become the number-one nation in the region in anything except perhaps the size of its population. Without drastic revisions of the current Constitution in both its domestic politico-economic stance as well as its global outlook, the Perspective's aspirations cannot even be approached. However, under certain conditions outlined below, some of its targets may perhaps be reached.

The most immediate need for the attainment of the Perspective's goals is to make up for the sub-par performance of the last several years and the baggage thus far accumulated. This burdensome legacy, as already mentioned, is manifested in (a) double-digit inflation, accompanied by widespread cost/price distortions; (b) double-digit unemployment[36] resulting from insufficient national saving and investment; (c) an overvalued national currency responsible for the country's current Dutch Disease and capital flight; (d) a highly indebted government with a nearly empty treasury;[37] (e) an unfavorable business climate and the absence of a level playing field between private and state enterprises; (f) declining management quality due to increased nepotism and growing intrusion of military and security forces into public enterprises; (g) stagnant factor productivity due to faulty investment, poor project design and a mismatch of skills and occupations; (h) a shortage of basic social amenities (housing, health clinics, recreational facilities) resulting from misplaced priorities and neglected maintenance; (i) increasing poverty and a widening gap between rich and poor;[38] and (j) international ostracism due the government's confrontational stance on nuclear and other foreign-policy issues.

With almost one-fourth of the Perspective's life expectancy already passed, the Iranian economy has to play catch-up to get back on track. With a relatively small percentage of the world's population and many times more than its share of natural and human-capital endowments, Iran's GDP is barely half of 1 percent of the world total. Iran's average annual exports (of which 80 percent are oil and gas) add up to only six-tenths of 1 percent of the global sum. Iran's share of the $1.9 trillion annual global foreign investments is about four-hundredths of 1 percent; its part of the $1 trillion worth of world tourism is even smaller. The national economy is currently faced with at least five major imbalances: (1) an international payments imbalance due to a highly overvalued exchange rate, increasing reliance on imports, lagging genuine non-oil-based exports, and a precarious and uncertain future oil-export market;[39] (2) a budget imbalance caused by rising expenditures in the face of stagnant and doubtful revenues; (3) a resource imbalance due to artificially low prices for water, power and fuels that encourage ever-expanding demand;[40] (4) a monetary and financial imbalance resulting from government-directed low interest rates, non-performing banking assets, rising defaults, and an increasing flow of savings into the informal market (the bazaar) and capital flight; and (5) a labor imbalance resulting from the rising work force, inadequate investment in housing and industry, and an anti-business labor code.[41]

There is no doubt that unless these imbalances are rectified, the Perspective's chances of reaching its grand objectives are nil. Every one of these shortfalls alone is capable of jeopardizing the ultimate goal. All of them together would ensure the Perspective's doom. The continuation of recent trends for the next 15 years is also likely to confront the government with 5 million new unemployed workers and billions in additional foreign debt.

The crucial task is to provide a stable climate for the conduct of normal trade and business. The quintessential requirements are a peaceful political environment, public confidence in the rule of law and the impartiality of the judicial system, and transparency on the part of state agencies. What is needed is a solemn and unwavering commitment by the government to abide by the business-sensitive clauses of the current constitution regarding the sanctity of private property and contracts, as well as the primacy of an independent and nonpolitical judiciary. Once these commitments are in place, the following challenges must be met.

Every one of the current imbalances is directly or indirectly influenced by the Islamic government's unfavorable standing in the world community. Due to a number of unwise political statements and actions by Iran's upper echelon in the last four years, Iran has suffered increasing worldwide and regional isolation. The first step in the Perspective's rescue efforts must thus begin with improvements in the Islamic Republic's external position and image. The central step toward the Perspective's salvation should involve a mutually satisfactory resolution of the nuclear issue and the country's pursuit of its legitimate uranium-enrichment program, resumption of negotiations with the United States and the EU, reduction of tension with countries in the region, and a de-linking of foreign policy from its Palestine-centric obsession.

Once the government is freed from external pressure, censure and other punitive measures, the climate may become receptive to new initiatives. The next step is to shift the economy's "commanding heights" from the state to the private sector, at least to the extent that the recent interpretation of the constitution's Article 44 permits. As part of this transfer, state involvement in the economy should become limited to (a) the design and enforcement of basic economic policies, (b) the construction and maintenance of major infrastructure, and (c) the provision of public goods (i.e., education, health and welfare). The government should simultaneously discard its romantic pursuit of economic self-sufficiency as a precondition for "political independence." No matter how it may hurt national pride, it should be recognized that Iran's physical, climatic and resource conditions do not allow the country to become self-sufficient in many consumer staples or industrial wares except at unaffordable costs.[42] The country's full economic potential can only be realized through integration into a well-regulated global economy, including early membership in the World Trade Organization. Full benefits from such integration may be reaped by specializing in areas where the country has a distinct strategic or competitive advantage. And since the ability to develop indigenous technology is the surest means of achieving genuine economic progress and acquiring a competitive edge, Iran will have to initiate and strengthen its own research and development institutes. Instead of relying almost totally on borrowed technology, the government has to envisage a major restructuring of its advanced educational curriculum and university programs, an area in which it has a long way to go. The first step in this direction is to change students' obsession with a university degree to a desire for productive and innovative skills. In no progressive country is the public's attachment to an educational title—even a bogus one—as intense as in Iran, where mushrooming private "universities" have now largely become commercial diploma mills.

National economic policies should then be directed toward removing the causes of existing imbalances. In the external-payments case, there is an urgent need for the adjustment of the foreign-exchange rate. The current parity, kept relatively stable in nominal terms in the last five years while domestic inflation has far exceeded that of Iran's trading partners, should be corrected as a matter of the highest priority. It should preferably be left floating and determined by daily inter bank transactions. Otherwise it should be regularly adjusted for differences between domestic and external price changes. Along with regular rate adjustments, the government should also reorganize the Oil Stabilization Fund to deal with unforeseen shortfalls in annual oil receipts and prevent the need for drastically reducing essential imports.[43] To supplement oil funds, the government also has to take necessary steps to attract direct and portfolio foreign investments, remove the incentives for domestic capital flight and seriously combat smuggling. Cutting non-essential imports and increasing non-energy-based exports should be seriously attempted.

The fiscal imbalance is harder to cope with, but its correction is critical to the Perspective's success since the budget deficit is largely responsible for many other economic disequilibria. The crucial corrective actions involve downsizing and reinventing the government, liquidating money-losing state enterprises, closing tax loopholes, reducing comprehensive tax exemptions, raising and expanding the tax base, and targeting the current across-the-board subsidies. The value-added tax system, already tried with dubious results, may not be the whole answer, nor are pending proposals in the Majlis for adjusting energy and other subsidies.[44] New thinking and new policies are needed.

The cost-price distortions are the result of years of populist and demagogic intervention by the Majlis, dating back to the Iran–Iraq War of 1980–88. Extensive and enduring price controls and minimum-wage legislation, designed to stem the tide of virulent inflation, have not only failed to achieve their intended goal; they have resulted instead in creating untold opportunities for abuse. Strong indications point to economic rents created by these controls, along with state-endorsed private trade monopolies, as the main source of *nouveau riche* wealth and related corruption.

The vexing imbalance in the money and banking sector calls for a radical shift in the government's thinking, expectations and demands. Of essential significance in this regard is the need to pass legislation endorsing the

Central Bank's independence and to reorganize the Council on Money and Credit. The Central Bank should be empowered to preserve the value of the national currency, control private liquidity and maintain relative price stability without interference or demands from the Majlis or the Treasury. The Council, as the main arm of the Central Bank, should be staffed with independent financial experts without vested interests—and not, as is currently the case, composed of government ministers and agency heads who are the main beneficiaries of increased liquidity. It should be given the sole responsibility of setting and enforcing monetary policy in the service of price stability and high employment. A large majority of state banks should be truly privatized and allowed to conduct their business without mandatory lending obligations and within prescribed monetary regulations.

The labor problem is the hardest nut to crack for a variety of reasons. First, due to a disastrous pro-natal policy adopted during the early years of the revolution (to "produce more soldiers for Islam"), Iran's youth (aged 15–29) now comprise more than one-third of the population and more than two-thirds of the unemployed—both ratios being the highest in the region and among the highest worldwide. The main concentration is among women 18 to 24 years of age. At the same time, education and training have left Iran's youth ill-suited for the country's economically viable jobs. Of the 100 different majors offered by Iran's state universities, only 10 are reportedly popular. But these 10 fields are capable of absorbing only a very small percentage of successful applicants in the annual university entrance exams. The other 90 fields are filled with those who simply want a university degree, those for whom free university attendance has zero opportunity cost, and those with the fewest job opportunities.[45] Although the current Fourth Development Plan has targeted new job creation at a minimum of 650,000 a year, the actual number in the last four years has reportedly been fewer than 300,000.[46] Creation of the targeted jobs has, in turn, required a 10–12 percent annual increase in aggregate domestic investment growth,[47] while the figures published by the authorities show the rate hovering at only around 5 percent.[48] Foreign direct investment, too, according to official figures, has averaged about $500 million a year from 2002 to 2008.[49] To employ all current job seekers and keep the current 12.9 percent unemployment rate from rising, 1.2 million new opportunities have to be created in each of the next two years—a virtual impossibility.[50] As already indicated, the lack of investment security, stifling bureaucratic regulations, a dearth of incentives for long-range commitments, and an uncertain political climate have been the major impediments to adequate job creation.[51]

The government's misguided policies in the last four years have also created another impediment to solving the labor imbalance. By mandating lower interest rates on bank loans to industrial and agricultural projects, the cost of capital has been reduced. At the same time, higher minimum wages and extensive fringe benefits have increased labor costs. The result has been increased use of capital-intensive projects at the expense of higher employment. Furthermore, the state banks' massive lending to so-called "quick-return projects" on government order has not only failed to make a dent in reducing unemployment, it has managed to increase liquidity to an unprecedented level and push inflation as high as 29 percent.[52] Youth unemployment will continue to be an albatross for some years to come.

A word of caution

None of these equilibrating measures is politically easy to adopt or quick to implement. Yet none is dispensable. If the Perspective's nirvana is going to be anything but a pipe dream, all corrective measures enumerated here would have to be followed simultaneously. But since faith-based and ideology-dominated regimes seldom achieve genuine socioeconomic progress, a fundamental change in the Islamic Republic's orientation and outlook is the essential condition for the Perspective's ultimate goals.

The momentous post-election events have now drastically altered Iran's political landscape and ushered in a new era of great uncertainty. With near paralysis at the top and obvious confusion on how to deal with the simmering revolt, reported rifts among military and security contingents, and vocal opposition to the reelected president's early actions by some of his former staunch supporters, the ruling elites will have increasing difficulty in rebranding the Islamic Republic as a stable, democratic regime. The stigma will, in turn, sap the government's ability to bargain with the West on disputed issues from a position of strength. And if the fight between the government and the opposition should go beyond the disputed elections and escalate into demands for drastic changes in the country's fundamental political structure, the Perspective's chances of approaching its goals will be in even greater jeopardy.

Notes

* First published in *Middle East Policy*, Fall 2009. Reproduced with permission.

1 For the Persian text of the document, see *Cheshmandaz-e Jomhoouri Eslami Iran dar Ofoq-e 1404* (Tehran: Jamal-al-Haq, 2006).

2 For detailed performance shortfalls from the plan's targets, see www.sarmayeh.net, June 21, 2009.

3 For a candid recognition of some of these barriers, see statements by Iran's ex-president Ali Akbar Hashemi Rafsanjani, available at http://emruz.net/ShowItem, November 9, 2008.

4 For details regarding this unique process, see Jahangir Amuzegar, "Iran's Theocracy under Siege," *Middle East Policy*, Vol. X, No. 1, Spring 2003.

5 For a recent reiteration of these tenets, see statements by the Islamic Republic's vice-president at www.jomhourieslami.com, May 18, 2009; see also www.iranmania.com, May 17, 2009.

6 A recent reiteration of this doctrine may be found in the statements by Supreme Leader Ali Khamenei before students of Kurdistan's university on May 17, 2009, available at www.jomhourieslami.com, May 17, 2009.

7 *Economics of Divine Unity* (1979–80); *Islamic/Marxist State Administration* (1981–88); *Postwar Structural and Stabilization Adjustments* (1989–96); *Islamic Democracy Rule* (1999–2004); and *Messianic/Populist Autocracy* (2005–09).

8 The outrageous and admitted fraud in the June 2009 presidential elections, resulting in the largest popular uprisings since 1979, is the latest proof of such indiscretions.
9 See Ahmad Tavakoli and Farshad Momeni at http://emruz.net, May 4, 2009 and May 12, 2009.
10 www.jomhourieslami.com, May 25, 2009.
11 For a discussion of how forced distribution of earnings as annual dividends to "justice shareholders" has undermined needed reinvestments, see www.sarmayeh.net, June 26, 2009.
12 See the statement by Reporters Without Borders (Reporters sans frontières), June 20, 2009.
13 In the last 27 years the budget has ended with a surplus in only four years. See *Iran Economics*, June 2009.
14 The shares of taxes in Iran's GDP and government revenue are 6 percent and 24 percent, respectively—one of the lowest in the world and the region and unchanged for over a decade. See www.sarmayeh.net, January 25, 2009.
15 According to a high-ranking Labor Ministry official, currently 9,000 development projects are unfinished and idle. Others estimate the actual number to be upward of 12,000, at a cost to the government of some $200 billion. See www.sarmayeh.net, January 19, 2009.
16 www.donya-e-eqtesad, May 16, 2009.
17 www.sarmayeh.net, May 17, 2009.
18 According to a private estimate, state banks' non-performing loans in the last four years exceed those of the last 100 years of Iranian banking and constitute the largest wave of rent-based gains in Iran's modern history. See www.sarmayeh.net, November 30, 2008.
19 See the statement by the minister of industries, available at www.sarmayeh.net, May 19, 2009; and *Iran Economics*, May 2009.
20 Statement by Secretary General of Islamic Engineers Association, available at http://emruz.net, September 23, 2008.
21 www.sarmayeh.net, May 12, 2009.
22 www.sarmayeh.net, December 13, 2008.
23 www.jomhourieslami.com, May 16, 2009.
24 For further comparison of energy consumption with world standards, see www.hamshahrionline.ir/News, January 14, 2009.
25 For details and comparison with prior years, see http://emruz.net, February 18, 2009.
26 See "Economic Model," available at www.donya-e-eqtesad.com, November 14, 2008.
27 It is estimated that, with current American technology, Iran's daily flared natural gas could generate four times as much electrical output as the Bushehr-type nuclear reactor. See *Nonproliferation Review*, March 2007.
28 While Iran's population has doubled since the 1979 revolution, the number of prisoners has increased more than 12 times, from 13,000 to 163,000, of which 45 percent are drug addicts. See www.iran-emruz.net, February 25, 2006; *UN Human Development Report 2007–2008*; and *Iran Times*, June 5, 2009.
29 Due to the Islamic Republic's current near-pariah status, it ranks 193 among 194 countries whose passports require visas for traveling abroad.
30 Some $50 billion are needed in the petrochemical industry alone in the next 15 years, and another $50 billion for developing the South Pars gas fields.
31 Complaining about the multiple and ever-changing bureaucratic and security steps required for the approval of foreign investment, the Chief of the Judiciary is reported to have said that "one must be crazy" to want to invest in Iran. *Kayhan* (London), February 12, 2009.

32 Iran's short- and long-run business risks have recently risen, according to *Business Monitor*. For comparisons with countries in the region and worldwide, see http://emruz.net, January 25, 2009.

33 Cf. Jahangir Amuzegar, "Iranian Oil Buybacks: A Formula No One Likes," *Oil & Gas Journal*, August 27, 2001.

34 www.sarmayeh.net, May 10, 2009.

35 According to a recent report, the Tehran Stock Exchange has received only $92 million in foreign investment in the last five years. See www.sarmayeh.net, May 17, 2009.

36 The definition and measurement of employment in Iran largely differ from global standards as students and housewives as well as those who had worked at least one hour in the previous month are considered "employed." See www.jomhourieslami.com, January 16, 2009, and May 13, 2009; and www.sarmayeh.net, April 15, 2009.

37 For the nearly 36 percent rise of government debt to the banking system (including the Central Bank) in the last four years, see www.sarmayeh.net, April 14, 2009.

38 The poverty line and its extent in Iran are subject to intense controversy. The Ministry of Welfare and Social Security refuses to offer necessary information. Private estimates of the "poor" range from 10 percent to 20 percent of the population, giving the actual number from 7 to 14 million. For the latest extensive discussions, see www.iran-emrooz.net, December 21, 2008; http://emruz.net, January 4, 2009; www.donya-e-eqtesad.com, April 7, 2009; www.hamshahrionline.ir, May 22, 2009; and www.sarmayeh.net, June 19, 2009.

39 While the nominal rial/dollar exchange rate has been kept fairly stable within a 5 percent range in the last five years, inflation has averaged more than 16 percent a year.

40 Annual price increases of public utilities and fuel products have been proposed by the government in every one of the last five-year plans, but the Majlis has often voted down such proposals.

41 For further details, see www.donya-e-eqtesad.com/2007, May 9, 2009.

42 For a discussion of such obstacles, see the statement by a former minister of agriculture at www.hamshahrionline.ir, October 15, 2008.

43 For an understanding of the correct functioning of the OSF, see Jahangir Amuzegar, "Iran Oil Stabilization Fund: A Misnomer," *Middle East Economic Survey*, November 21, 2005.

44 For details of these failed experiments, see Jahangir Amuzegar, "Iran's Major Economic Surgery," *Middle East Economic Survey*, November 25, 2008.

45 See statement by the Minister of Labor, who argues that closing most of Iran's public and private institutions of higher learning would be a boon to the economy and individual families. See http://emruz.net, February 10, 2009.

46 www.sarmayeh.net, May 31, 2009.

47 www.donya-e-eqtesad.com, May 9, 2009.

48 www.sarmayeh.net, June 18, 2009, and March 2, 2009.

49 *Iran Economics*, June 2009.

50 www.sarmayeh.net, May 31, 2009.

51 According to a private estimate, short-term trade and business deals have been 11 times more profitable than long-term industrial investments. See www.jomhourieslami.com, March 2, 2009.

52 For details regarding the cost of creating one new job and accompanying inflation, see www.sarmayeh.net, March 12, 2009.

6 Iran's Oil Stabilization Fund

A misnomer*

In Iran's presidential election last June, a factor that was deemed to have clinched the victory for Mahmoud Ahmadinejad was undoubtedly his seductive and crowd-pleasing promise "to put the oil manna on everyone's *sofreh* (dinner table)." Hinting darkly about an oil-sucking domestic mafia that was depriving the poor of their rightful share of the national oil wealth, he vowed to rectify the injustice. Ignored in his campaign rhetoric, and unchallenged by rival candidates, however, was the fact that the poor's dinner table had never been without the oil bounty. Inadequate transparency in the national budget and the balance sheets of state-owned enterprises does not permit an accurate assessment of the subsidies enjoyed by Iran's poor. Yet there is no doubt that the new president's core constituents have always been the beneficiaries of an estimated $6.5bn of explicit subsidies spent by the Treasury on consumer staples (bread, rice, sugar, cooking oil, cheese, and prescription drugs). The poor have also partially benefited from another $14bn of estimated implicit subsidies on energy and fuel products. And they have enjoyed government-supplied utilities (water, power, telephone, and urban transport) sold to them below cost—all courtesy of the oil revenues. On top of all this, thanks to the skyrocketing crude oil prices in the last few years, and a future-be-damned attitude in spending its proceeds, the government has not only used the oil-export receipts to finance more than 60% of its annual budget directly or indirectly, but has also profligately dipped into its national nest egg—partly to help the poor.

A rainy-day insurance scheme

The Islamic Republic's Oil Stabilization Fund (OSF) has been in existence for a brief period since 2000. Yet the impetus in other oil-exporting countries for setting up such funds dates back to the breakdown of the price-fixing power by the oil oligopoly. Ever since mid-October 1973, when Organization of the Petroleum Exporting Countries (OPEC) wrested the age-old control of price determination from the so-called Seven Sisters, oil price volatility has been a major economic and political concern for many OPEC members. Repeated cycles of oil boom and bust since then have played havoc with these countries' fiscal budgeting, domestic development efforts, and external payment obligations. And the search for a stabilization machinery has been one of their prime endeavors ever since. The economic rationale for creating an oil stabilization fund is based on three main considerations. First, there is the necessity and desirability of eliminating, or at least lowering, the costs of stop-go public expenditures associated with ups and downs of crude oil prices in the world markets. The second objective is to maintain fiscal discipline through decoupling public spending from oil price volatility so that planned levels of annual government expenditure would be maintained regardless of the behavior of world oil prices, or the size of export revenues. And third, there is the goal of avoiding excessive real appreciation or depreciation of the national currency resulting from fluctuations in annual oil exports receipts.

Despite a near consensus among development economists regarding the benefits of achieving these objectives, there is no unanimity among them as to whether oil funds are the proper instrument to accomplish the task. The expressed skepticism, simply phrased, revolves around three cogent arguments. First, if the fund is not integrated with the national budget, it is likely to create a dual machinery, and interfere with sound fiscal management. Second, these funds entail risks of fragmenting asset management, and reducing accountability and transparency. Third, they involve the thorny intergenerational issue of transferring funds from a possibly prudent and farsighted government that currently accumulates wealth to a possibly imprudent future government that could subsequently misuse this wealth. For these reasons, some economists believe that almost all the objectives of such funds could be accomplished by other means such as the use of financial instruments for hedging, accumulation of financial assets by investing budget surpluses in high-return projects, and the pursuit of a proper non-oil fiscal balance.

Iran's third plan initiative

Iranian development planners in the Islamic Republic, having had their fingers burned twice in 1986 and again in 1997–98 by an oil bust, decided to follow the examples of Kuwait, Oman, Norway and others in establishing an oil reserve fund. The goal was to smooth out the pattern of oil-dependent government expenditures, and to escape the so-called "resource curse." Reflecting this sentiment, Article 60 of the Third Five-Year Development Plan (2000–05) called for the establishment, with the Central Bank, of a "crude oil foreign exchange reserve account" for the purpose of stabilizing the government's annual budgets during the plan's life. According to the main provision of this article, all foreign exchange incomes received from crude oil exports over and above the figure specifically projected in the plan for each year, had to be deposited in that account. As of the beginning of the plan's third year, the Treasury could draw from the OSF account if the government's oil export receipts fell below the budgeted amount for that year. An amendment to the original plan law in November 2000, stipulated that 50% of the Fund reserves should be set aside for lending to domestic private entrepreneurs—in foreign exchange, and at low interest rates for "productive" investments in the third plan's priority sectors. The rial proceeds of OSF operations were to be placed in a Rial Reserve Fund for eventual budget deficit financing. While the principal objective of the OSF, like similar funds elsewhere, was to protect the economy from future oil price downfalls, and a sudden oil income crunch, the Iranian model has been unique in many respects. For example, it is different from the highly successful Norwegian Petroleum Fund that is an integral part of the Norwegian national budget. Moreover, while the latter fund is known for its cautious investing, observing distinct fiscal procedures, and investing its assets exclusively abroad in order to avoid domestic inflationary consequences, the Iranian scheme has no such safeguards. Iran's OSF is totally outside of the national budget, and is theoretically run by a seven-member Board of Trustees composed of senior government officials from various ministries under the chairmanship of the head of the Management and Plan Organization. Finally, while in Norway, a fiscal deficit in any year could be financed out of its fund resources, Iran's reserves are specifically earmarked to fill only the gap in foreign exchange shortfalls. The use of the OSF resources for making up the Treasury's inability to collect rials from tax and non-tax sources is strictly prohibited.

The OSF scorecard

The formal balance sheet of the OSF, despite a clear mandate by law, has never been submitted to the Majlis by its board of trustees, or published. The figures presented in this review have been collected and put together from different and conflicting statements by the Fund's secretary-general, Majlis deputies, and various government officials as well as occasional reports in the local press and periodicals. Collected data are in turn matched against fragmentary statistics provided by the Central Bank. The balance sheet presented here shows the Fund's receipts and payments in US dollars although its assets might be held in several foreign currencies. The picture shown here is rather unflattering because the Fund's revenues have fallen short of the planned target, and its expenditures have involved a breach of the planners' original intent. The total oil export revenues projected in the Third Plan amounted to \$56.7bn—based on expected oil prices between \$12 per barrel and \$19 per barrel. However, with Iran's oil prices rising during the period and averaging \$35 per barrel, the Islamic Republic's oil revenues in the five-year period went up more than twice the projected figure, and amounted to \$130.7bn. According to the law's provisions, the \$74bn surplus revenue had to be placed in the OSF. Instead, the total deposits in the Fund during the five years to March 2005 amounted to a mere \$29.1bn—as the Majlis increased the regular "oil share" of the budget each year beyond the Plan's targets. Meanwhile, the Fund's own interest earnings of \$1.1bn brought its total end-run assets to \$30.2bn. Furthermore, in addition to depriving the OSF of its entitled \$74bn, the Majlis, using its legislative prerogative, ignored the Fund's original purpose, by-passed the fund's Board, and authorized repeated withdrawals of nearly $17bn from even the short-changed $29bn reserves to finance a variety of projects. Of the total additionally legislated appropriations, some $7.6bn was paid to the Central Bank for losses incurred in foreign exchange unification, and $9.4bn was allotted to such "urgent" off-budget items as: relief to draught-stricken farmers, end-of-year bonuses to government retirees, payments for gasoline imports, expansion of the *basij* (volunteer militia) forces, grants to disabled war veterans, aid to Imam Khomeini's Relief Committee, supplements for short-funded subsidies on "essential" consumer goods, promotion of non-oil exports to Africa and Asia, purchase of new equipment for the police, provision of tourism facilities, disaster relief to earthquake and snow victims, and expanded rail and air transport facilities. None of these projects had anything to do with the main objective of the Fund.

In the meantime, some $11bn credit was set aside for loans to the private sector. This was nearly 31% of the mandated total instead of the mandated 50%. Of this allocation, however, the Fund trustees approved only $6.8bn for specific projects, of which only $3.7bn was disbursed by March 2005. Average length of these loans was eight years and the annual interest rate charged was 2% over the LIBOR's (or about 5.5%). For projects in "depressed regions" (e.g., Sistan), and certain enterprises in financial difficulties (e.g., textiles) the duration was extended to 10 years, and the interest rate reduced to 3%. In the case of cement that was badly needed in local construction, the length was exceptionally extended to 17 years. Of the total private sector credits, some 97% went to projects in the industrial and mining sector, and the rest was divided among transportation, technical services, and agriculture sectors. Industrial projects included such sub-sectors as autos, aviation, electric power, foodstuffs, machine building, petrochemicals, pharmaceutical, and textiles.

One of the reasons for the relatively small portion of the OSF being used by the private sector is believed to have been the relatively unattractive terms of the loans. The money borrowed by private enterprises was denominated in foreign currencies, and its use had to be exclusively for foreign purchases. The loans also had to be paid back in foreign exchange. Thus while the low 3–5% interest loans from the OSF seemed highly enticing compared to the prevailing double-digit rates charged by commercial banks, the ultimate borrowing costs could have run much higher due to changes in the exchange rates. With the Iranian rial steadily depreciating against foreign currencies, and no medium-term hedging facilities available in the Iranian financial system, the exchange-adjusted effective annual interest rate to be paid by private borrowers in many cases could actually reach 20%. In such cases, the latter rate was higher than the official 15% rate charged by the state banks for their rial-denominated loans. In sum, of the Fund's total assets of about $30bn, nearly $17bn was used in the public sector, and $3.7bn was paid out as loans to the private borrowers. By the end of the Plan period, the OSF assets consisted of $9.4bn cash, and $3.5bn of outstanding loans—for a total of $13bn.

Due to the larger-than-planned share of the public sector in the OSF allocation, and the preponderance of industrial projects in the private sector's share, the Fourth Development Plan (2005–10) law requires that the agriculture sector's share in the future OSF annual allocation be no less than 10%, and that the unutilized annual portion of the private sector's allotment in any year be added to the next year's figure for that sector so that the funds could not be used for public sector projects. In the current Iranian fiscal year (ending in March 2006) Iran's expected oil export income is expected to reach $45bn—on a notional average oil price of $28 per barrel. The 2005–6 national budget's ordinary share is set at $14bn. The rest of it is to be deposited in the OSF, and used in public and private projects. Although the budget law repeats the injunction against the use of the OSF fund for budget deficit financing, this objective is as usual achieved through off-budget appropriation out of the Fund. Thus, $9.13bn is set aside for three public categories: $4.6bn for completing unfinished public development projects; $1.6bn for repayment of exchange unification debt to the Central Bank; and $2.93bn to pay for additional gasoline imports. Another additional $1.1bn is also earmarked for setting up a new fund for helping the social needs of the youth. A total of $8bn is earmarked for loans to private entrepreneurs. According to press reports, some $5.3bn of the OSF has been used during the first seven months of the current year—a 74% rise over last year's withdrawals, and 16% above the authorized appropriation for the period.

A tentative appraisal

The skepticism expressed by economists regarding the effectiveness of oil reserve funds in improving fiscal management seems to have been fully confirmed by the Iranian experience. Stripped of all other considerations, the record shows that not only were all public sector withdrawals during the Third Plan in violation of Article 60, as well as the OSF charter's principles and procedures, but the sum total of these public projects even exceeded the government's 50% share—by 31.5%. In strict accounting terms, the Treasury's overdraft, and its debt to the OSF by March 2005, amounted to more than $6.5bn. More significant still, while both the letter and spirit of the legislation meant that the government could draw from the OSF only if oil revenue for the year fell below the budgeted amount and there was no possibility of financing the budget deficit through taxes or other means, the practice has been totally different. That is, the OSF that was initially established to come to the Treasury's rescue if the oil price dropped below $20 per barrel was in fact drawn upon even when the price of Iran's crude oil surpassed $54 per barrel in mid-2005. Flagrant violations of the original intent of the law have actually turned the OSF into a secure pot of gold, and a ready financing source, for the legislators to use it mainly for off-budget pork-barrel projects.

The Majlis' handling of the OSF has thus shown the futility, if not indeed the absurdity, of setting up a rainy-day fund if it can be freely used while the sunshine has never been brighter. Still further, a mechanism that was put in place for stabilizing the economy has been turned on its head, and has actually become a destabilizing force at times—and making the stabilization fund a misnomer. The reason is not hard to see. When the Majlis authorizes withdrawals from the OSF for domestic expenditures, the Central Bank has to add the withdrawn foreign exchange to its own foreign assets, and issue its rials equivalent to the Treasury. Therefore, instead of sterilizing excess foreign funds, the Central Bank is forced to increase the so-called "money base," and the result is increased overall liquidity and higher inflation.

Lessons learned

So far, the experiences of a half-a-dozen nations with oil funds, corroborated by Iran's case, show that this mechanism may be useful under certain specific circumstances, and not everywhere and not at all times. The totality of the lessons learned up to now indicates that an oil stabilization fund may work best as a stabilizing and balancing force where the country (1) is fairly rich, politically stable, and enjoys low inflation; (2) the national budget may alternate between deficit and surplus each year, but it is in balance over time; (3) the Treasury's credit for borrowing in the world capital markets is fairly high; and (4) foreign exchange surpluses earned during oil booms could be effectively sterilized by the Central Bank in order to contain domestic excess liquidity. By contrast, in a country such as Iran, with (1) low middle per capita income, perennial budget deficits reaching 5% of GDP in some years; (2) protracted double-digit inflation; (3) a bond rating of no better than a B+; and (4) a weak Central Bank subservient to the legislature, such a fund is at best inconsequential, and at worst an inflation ratcheting and destabilizing device. To wit: when the Islamic Republic is currently paying 8.75% interest rate per annum on its sovereign Eurobonds, the government cannot convince the legislators to accept the wisdom of keeping billions of foreign exchange assets in the OSF earning less than 4% a year. Or, where the budget is perennially in the red, and more than 15% of the people live below the poverty line, the government cannot persuade the men and women on the street that the OSF resources should not be touched—even for current urgent needs—because these funds are destined to be saved for future generations. Given political realities in a country like Iran, as long as there are unmet social needs on the one hand, and ready cash at the politicians' easy reach on the other, no government can resist political pressures to use the funds—unless there are additional provisions.

What Iran's case has taught us is that a country like the Islamic Republic that wishes to set aside some of its oil export revenues for future use might succeed in achieving its goal only if (1) the objective is clearly and inviolably written in its fund charter, and all ad hoc exceptions are disallowed; (2) the fund's management is composed of non-political individuals with long tenure, and who are totally independent of the legislature; (3) strict safeguards are in place to ensure transparency and accountability in managing the fund's resources; and (4) since the main purpose of the fund is to make up for the shortfalls in foreign exchange receipts from oil exports, the fund's assets should be invested exclusively in safe hard currency instruments, at the best obtainable returns. All other goals—including assistance to the private sector—should be pursued through other means, and carried out in the regular annual budgets and appropriations. Any mechanism short of these stipulations would be a dual budget, and another costly exercise in futility.

Note

* First published in the *Middle East Economic Survey*, November 21, 2005. Reproduced with permission.

7 Khatami's legacy

Dashed hopes*

Mohammad Khatami's presidency of Iran's Islamic Republic started with a deafening roar and ended in an unceremonious whisper. Chances are that his crisis-ridden eight-year tenure will be more favorably viewed in the future than is now the case with his disillusioned early supporters. While his administration was a mixture of some successes and certain setbacks—like all previous ones—the country that he left to his successor was in many respects freer, more prosperous, and more diplomatically respected that the one he inherited from his predecessor. The principal reason for his under-appreciated legacy may lie in the unbridgeable gap between his constituents' ever-rising expectations and his limited capacity to fulfill them. In other words, what was asked of him by the electorate was far more than the maximum he could possibly deliver, and what he did deliver was far less than the minimum his supporters were eager to receive.

The adage about "coming in with a roar and going out with a whisper" would perhaps find no better example than Muhammad Khatami's presidency in Iran. When this mid-level and little-known Shi'ite cleric was elected Iran's fifth post-revolution president in the spring of 1997, he was greeted as a national hero, and treated like a rock star. A female admirer later portrayed him as "our Napoleon with a book, instead of a sword, in his hand."[1] Yet, when he left office on August 4, 2005, no one but a handful of his dwindling supporters shed any tears over his departure. Justified or not, he is now also widely chastised as inadvertently responsible for the recent presidential victory of Mahmud Ahmadinejad—an obscurantist and demagogic technocrat who openly aspires to turn the country back to the early days of the 1979 revolution.

A thorough investigation of Khatami's presidential rise and fall may require several separate analyses. Psycho-historians may focus on his personality as a devout Muslim fascinated with Western democratic ideas; a pacifist teacher advocating patience, moderation, and prudence; and a utopian dreamer thrown by accident into the vortex of Iran's Byzantine politics. Divinity students and Islamic theocrats may dissect his novel concept of "Islamic democracy" in relation to both Shi'ite traditional theology as well as Ayatollah Ruhollah Khomeini's non-democratic concept of *velayat-e faqih* (rule by a jurisconsult). Clash-of-cultures theorists may scrutinize the significance and practicality of his proposed "Dialogue among Civilizations," and peaceful co-existence of East and West under different value systems. This article's limited goal is to examine the Khatami Administration's eight-year record regarding its promised tripartite goals of economic prosperity, pursuit of law and order at home, and establishment of amicable relations with the external world.[2] A discussion of Khatami's own personal fate and fortune as a leader and a reformer is offered elsewhere.[3] Accordingly, the following evaluation of his administration will be divided into three parts: the economy, internal sociocultural developments, and relations with the outside world.

A leap backward

The unexpected victory of Mahmud Ahmadinejad in Iran's presidential elections of June 2005 mystified the world, and caught Middle East pundits by surprise.[4] A virtually unknown revolutionary apparatchik, with a near blank resume as an appointed former governor of a fourth-tier province, and a hand-picked mayor of Tehran by a fundamentalist (*Ossulgra*) City Council, Ahmadinejad was the least known, least experienced, and least personally and professionally attractive of the seven candidates allowed to run by the Council of Guardians (out of a total of 1,014 aspirants). In all national polls taken shortly before the June election, he came out last. And yet, in the run-off election and final count, he beat Akbar Hashemi Rafsanjani—a Khomeini comrade-in-arms, a ten-year speaker of the Majlis, a two-time president of the Republic, the incumbent chairman of the powerful Expediency Council, and an all-out icon and stalwart of the regime. The lopsided margin was 61.7% to 35.9%.[5] More worrisome than the elected President's background and character was the content of his retrogressive and anachronistic populist agenda that backed a confrontation with the West and the United States on nuclear energy issues, called for the annihilation of Israel, advocated a return to a strict Islamic moral code, and promised economic measures reminiscent of the Mir-Hossein Musavi Administration's misguided war-time economic policies in the 1980s. Thus, just at the time that the country was beginning to recover from Musavi's misguided measures after 16 years of strenuous remedial efforts, and Iran seemed ready to move toward an eventual secular democracy, the new President has started speaking once again about building "a modern, progressive Islamic country" and making Iran a Shi'ite paradigm for "global Islam."[6]

The Khatami phenomenon

The stunning upset victory in Iran's 1997 presidential election of Hojjatoleslam Sayyed Muhammad Khatami was widely heralded at the time as a "turning point" for the post-1979 Islamic Republic. It was called a new phase in Iran's history, the dawn of a new era, and even a second revolution.[7] Hopes were raised that his administration would support political and cultural openness, solidify burgeoning democratic efforts, protect human rights, soften the stifling Islamic sociocultural restrictions, expand opportunities for women's employment and civic participation, liberalize the inward-oriented and state-dominated economy, fight rampant corruption, pursue peaceful relations with the rest of the world, and seek a respectable status for Iran in the international community. Prompted by these hopes, some 21 million voters—representing nearly 70% of the votes cast—flocked to the polling booths and made him the "people's choice."[8] The 80% voter participation surpassed all previous nationwide records, including Ayatollah Khomeini's 1979 referendum on a new Islamic constitution. In retrospect, five factors may be found to have been responsible for Khatami's surprise victory. First, the majority of voters were clearly disappointed and highly dissatisfied with President Rafsanjani's vacillating economic policies that had brought little benefit to the rank and file, while giving rise to a group of corrupt *nouveaux riches* (widely rumored to include his own family). Reconstruction and rehabilitation of cities ravaged by the 1980–88 Iran–Iraq War had not proceeded fast enough. Economic growth had been anemic, and per capita real income had barely increased. An attempt at the unification of the corruption-ridden 12-tier exchange regime had badly backfired, and had to be aborted due to its heavy socioeconomic cost. A privatization program had turned out to be a fiasco, and tainted with widespread manipulations and irregularities. Inflation and foreign debt levels had reached historic records. In short, Rafsanjani's administration had symbolized the "get rich quick" mentality that had been denounced by Ayatollah Ruhollah Khomeini, and repudiated in every weekly sermon by a coterie of Friday prayer imams.

Second, the yes votes for Khatami were partly no votes for his main rival—Speaker of the Majlis Ali Akbar Nateq Nuri—who was regarded as an arch-conservative cleric, belonging to the Islamic traditionalist right, and tacitly favored by Supreme Leader Ali Khamenei—the *rahbar.* Nuri's expected decision to strictly enforce Islamic legal and ethical codes in the government and society had particularly scared and alienated many women, young voters, and assorted liberals in and out of the clerical circles.

Third, despite Nuri's clever attempts to present himself as a moderate and statesman-like candidate, he was universally regarded as a status quo politician, following Rafsanjani's crony capitalism and disfavored agenda. By contrast, Khatami's main platform and campaign manifesto promised a totally new direction. His seductive agenda regarding human dignity, individual freedoms, social justice, the rule of law, equality of economic opportunity, a thriving civil society, and reduced tension with the outside world appealed to energized voters. Politically active students, pro-democracy intellectuals, rebellious and reform-seeking clerics, disadvantaged economic groups, disenfranchised women, religious and ethnic minorities, and human rights activists were all in Khatami's camp. His program particularly resonated with first-time voters as a symbol of hope, and a precursor of significant change.[9] Fourth,

Khatami's own personality had a lot to do with his victory. As a tall, elegant, good-looking and smiling clergyman, attentive to his mix-and-match attire, substituting Gucci shoes for the traditional *na'alayn* (strapless clerical footwear), dressing up for different occasions, and living a non-typical monogamous life for a well-to-do cleric, he could not present a greater contrast to his old-fashioned and unattractive rival. A mild-mannered man with a reputation for good humor, even temper, tolerance for opposing views, and preference for discussion and debates instead of fights and quarrels, he easily eclipsed his combative and garrulous competitor. His background as a secular college graduate who chose to be drafted into the Shah's army—instead of seeking legal exemption as a future seminarian—spoke well of his sense of discipline and devotion to duty. And, ideologically he was considered, judging from his published writings, an open-minded liberal.[10] Finally, Iran's post-revolution political dynamics, featuring alternative political pendulum swings from left to right and back, played an important role in the election. That is, after eight years of conservative Rafsanjani rule, time was ripe for the victory of a liberal and left-leaning administration in nearly the same fashion that Musavi's Islamic Marxist government was replaced by Rafsanjani's in 1989—and now Khatami's left-of-center tenure by Ahmadinejad's fundamentalist regime.

"A crisis every nine days"

On numerous occasions during his tenure, Khatami bitterly complained about his administration being plagued by "a crisis every nine days."[11] Yet, he never bothered to identify the origins and characteristics of these crises, their instigators, or the way he dealt with them. Crisis or not, however, Khatami's eight-year presidency involved a mixture of both pluses and minuses. Needless to say, some of the setbacks and successes of the Khatami Administration were due to exogenous forces and were beyond the President's own personal power and control. He therefore should neither be held responsible for all the bad and the ugly; nor should he claim credit for all the good and the blissful. Whether he wishes or not, however, the totality of his governance, and the results of his stewardship would, and should, be recorded as his legacy. The irony is that most of his major achievements were in the domestic economic field where he was least versed, initially least concerned, and even less adequately equipped to cope with. By contrast, his government's setbacks and failures were mostly in the internal political and social sphere that was the focus of his attention, and the core of his ideological value system. His record in foreign relations lies between the two.

Oil financed economic revival

In the opinion of his ardent supporters, the Khatami government's most splendid and significant achievements were in the economic arena.[12] By many significant indicators, the economy that Khatami left to Ahmadinejad was much better than the one he inherited from Rafsanjani—plagued with a low crude oil price, high inflation, large budget deficit, external payments imbalances, and a severe drought. Although Iran was not quite at the "take-off" stage in the summer of 2005 as the outgoing President boastfully claimed,[13] and the underlying economic conditions were far from healthy, the economy was not as "sick" as Khatami himself had called it in March of 1998.[14] Thanks to the unprecedented oil boom during 2002–05, and a number of other fortuitous conditions in the last five years of his administration, several major economic indicators showed noteworthy gains. According to published official data[15] real gross domestic product (GDP) rose by a modest but respectable average rate of 4.6% a year from 1997 to 2005—despite low oil prices, agricultural drought, and other unfavorable elements in the first three years. With population rising at a reduced annual rate of 1.6%, the real per capita income also rose during the same period by about 3.0% a year—from $1,550 to some $2,300. Thanks to substantial explicit and implicit consumer subsidies, plus various welfare assistances, equivalent to more than 20% of GDP, doled out from the oil bounty—combined with personal incomes rising faster than inflation in the last two years—absolute poverty was also slightly reduced. Thanks almost exclusively to surging crude oil prices, Iran's income from oil exports increased from $15.4 billion in 1997 to a record $36.3 billion in 2005. Non-oil exports went up from $2.9 billion to $7.5 billion. Exports of services surged from less than $1 billion to about $3 billion. Imports, paid for mainly by the oil windfalls, reached $36.6 billion from $14.1 billion—also a record. The consumer price index, however, remained high—showing an average annual rise of 15.8%, albeit following a downward trend from 17.3%. Although unemployment stayed at a double-digit rate throughout the period due to the influx of wartime baby boomers to the labor force, nearly twice as many job opportunities were created each year on average than in the previous eight years.[16] Despite the new Minister of Labor's acknowledgment that "there are no accurate unemployment statistics in Iran,"[17] it was claimed that joblessness had steadily declined from 15% to 11%. Total external debt that stood at $12.1 billion in 1997 climbed to $15.6 billion, but still constituted a much smaller percentage of GDP. The nation's foreign exchange holdings, replenished annually by the oil fortune, also neared $34 billion—a historic record. Labor, capital, and total factor productivity also improved, albeit imperceptibly.

At the micro and sectoral levels, the Khatami Administration could also justifiably claim noteworthy expansions in infrastructures, e.g., roads, railroads, air and seaports, irrigation dams, telecommunications, and access to the Internet. Highlighted by the President on numerous occasions have been advances in rural electrification, extension of natural gas lines to an increasing number of small towns, extensive housing construction, and beautification of the urban landscape. Self-sufficiency claimed in certain foodstuffs, new oil reserve discoveries and capacity expansion in crude output, successive activation of various phases of the South Pars natural gas fields, and noteworthy feats in the petrochemical industry (particularly at Assaluye) are also cited by various officials as other outstanding achievements. Although not fully elaborated in official reports, occasional statements by state officials, and published accounts by foreign analysts, also attest to considerable progress in the defense industry (and particularly in missile technology and nuclear energy development).[18] There are also reports of genuine progress in pure science research.

Praiseworthy as these accomplishments are, however, they had all been carried out as part of the reconstruction and development efforts started under Rafsanjani's presidency after Iran's war with Iraq. Some of the projects had designs going back to the Shah's time. What made the Khatami Administration's economic record clearly distinct from the past was a series of reforms to put the economy on the path to growth with sustained high employment and low inflation. Prodded by the International Monetary Fund (IMF) and the World Bank, the Khatami team, with the indispensable support of the Sixth Majlis, succeeded in instituting some needed reforms—despite considerable resistance by certain powerful vested interests. By far the boldest and most effective of these structural reforms involved the simplification of the multiple exchange rates, and the establishment of a unified managed floating system in March 2002, with reportedly no more than 2.5% inflationary consequences. In 2004, the Islamic Republic also accepted the liberal obligations of the IMF's Article VIII for the first time since Iran joined the Fund in 1945. Other major market-oriented reforms covered a vast area. In foreign trade, non-tariff barriers were replaced with tariffs, most export restrictions were eliminated, import licensing was streamlined, and tariff structure was rationalized. A pre-revolution statute for the attraction and protection of foreign direct investment was replaced by a revised version in 2002. Iran also joined the World Bank's Multilateral Investment Guarantee Agency. In the financial field, the Central Bank was granted some degree of independence. Mandatory bank credit allocations by the Majlis were reduced. State banks were given more flexibility in setting deposit and loan rates. Iran successfully issued two Eurobonds in 2002. Four private banks and two private insurance companies were licensed for the first time since the 1979 banking nationalization. In the fiscal area, a major tax reform was initiated in 2002, the Treasury issued participation papers (short-term bonds) to reduce direct reliance on the Central Bank, the budget transparency was improved, and charitable *bonyads* were legally subjected to greater oversight.[19] An Oil Stabilization Fund was established in 2000 to protect annual budgets from drastic oil price fluctuations. A National Privatization Organization was established in early 2001 to centralize, coordinate, and more efficiently conduct the government's privatization policy.[20] To this list should be added the far-reaching and innovative interpretation by the Expediency Council of Article 44 of the Constitution, allowing privatization of many nationalized industries.[21] A number of bills aimed at targeting subsidies, introducing a value-added tax system, risk-based banking supervision, capital market regulation, and anti-money-laundering were also prepared by various state agencies and submitted to the Majlis for ratification.

Despite these clearly recognizable pluses, Iran's economy in 2005 compared unfavorably in some notable respects with the one in 1997. Notwithstanding repeated pledges by President Khatami and his economic team to downsize the bureaucracy, privatize state enterprises, reduce budget dependence on oil income, replace the unfair and ineffective across-the-board subsidies by a means-tested system, increase the share of taxes in government revenues, tame the renegade *bonyads*, fight corruption, and improve national economic welfare, the final result missed these goals in every single respect. When Ahmadinejad assumed the presidency in August 2005, the Iranian public sector was larger than ever. Privatization was mired in bureaucratic turf battles. The budget was more dependent on oil income. The Iranian rial had lost more[22] than half its exchange value. Subsidies still favored higher income strata. The share of taxes in budget revenues had actually decreased. *Bonyads* still scoffed at government laws and regulations. Corruption was more pervasive. Overall national welfare lagged behind the 1997 level. Flight of capital and brain drain intensified despite Iran's dire needs for both talent and investment funds.

Published official data show that between 1997 and 2005 the public sector's debt to the banking system quadrupled while government efficiency and its responsiveness declined considerably.[23] Large state-owned enterprises that numbered about 400 in 1997 reached 523 in 2004 during a period where privatization topped the list of the government's major reforms.[24] Only a fraction of the projected privatization revenues during the eight-year period materialized.[25] The budget reliance on oil income rose from about 42% to 63%.[26] The highest 10% of income earners still enjoyed the lion's share of subsidies on consumer goods.[27] The share of taxes in the total government revenues actually fell from 27.7% to 25.6%, and the budget deficit rose to 16% from 5%.[28] One US dollar that bought 3,007 rials in March 1997 was worth Rls 8,900 in June 2005. The pernicious influence of opaque *bonyads* and mafia-type business interest groups continued unabated.[29] While Iran's absolute poverty, according to the UNDP ranking, slightly improved from 34 to 31, a World Bank report finds some nine million people (14% of the population) still living under the poverty line.[30] And while the Management and Plan Organization (MPO) claims that rising per capita income, accompanied by a fairer income distribution, resulted in enhanced social welfare, a joint UNDP/MPO study in 2005 shows that the Gini coefficient of income distribution has not changed in the last decade.[31] Anecdotal evidence in fact shows that the income gap between social classes actually widened. The ostentatious display of opulence and wealth by the regime's grandees and their offspring—children of the revolution who were supposed to follow Imam Ali's ascetic life—has been regarded as a major source of the growing anger and resentment among the rank and file, and a reason for their support of Ahmadinejad. Iran's Human Development Index (HDI), broadly representing national welfare, deteriorated from 95 to 99 during Khatami's tenure.[32] Although comparable data for all economic indicators between the beginning and the end of the Khatami Administration do not exist, a raft of statistics in some areas show a lack of palpable progress. According to the Heritage Foundation's Index of Economic Freedom, Iran in 2005 still remained a "repressed" country with a score of 4.16 (out of 5.00 as the least free) compared to 4.7 in 1997. In both years, the country remained 148th among 150–55 countries.[33] The Fraser Institute's Index of Economic Freedom for 2005 ranks the Islamic Republic 111th among 127 countries with a numerical category of 5.6 (out of 10 as the freest) and 0.5 worse than the previous year's. Other scattered data also show a rather unflattering picture of the economy after eight years of partial improvements. Local and foreign press report about thousands of Iranians taking billions of dollars out of Iran for investment abroad. If true in number, and correct in method of calculating costs, the data compare quite unfavorably with Iranian workers' yearly remittances of a paltry $1.1 billion back to the homeland.[34] Transparency International's 2005 Annual Report finds Iran's corruption rank among 159 countries steadily worsening from 78 in 2003 and 88 in 2004 to 93 in 2005. The institute gives the country a rating of 2.9 out of 10—with 1 being the most corrupt, and 10 totally honest. A report on the same subject presents a dismal and shameful picture of the country.[35] Other reports place the Islamic Republic in 2005 108th among 155 countries in terms of facilities for private business activities; and presenting more investment risks than 72 countries in a universe of 168.[36]

Law and order at home

Despite some notable economic achievements, Khatami's presidency will in all likelihood always be remembered for its disappointing domestic sociopolitical record. In his presidential campaign, the candidate's domestic agenda promised the dawn of an Islamic democracy where the theocratic concept of the *velayat-e faqih* would be reconciled with modern-day popular participation in decision-making. Supporters and critics both concur that the first two years of the Khatami Administration were the golden years of the Islamic Republic in terms of political liberalization and sociocultural openness when the country became clearly a freer and more tolerant place to live since 1979. In the domestic sociopolitical field, Khatami supported relative relaxation in the Islamic morals code (e.g., dress, music, social contacts), increased openness in political discourse (e.g., newspapers, private news organizations, liberal periodicals, films, and use of the Internet), and greater attention to women's rights and their access to university education, employment, travel, and political participation.[37] He is, thus, rightly credited with an emphasis on human dignity, establishment of political participation as both the citizens' right and privilege, tolerance toward the loyal opposition, the growth of nongovernmental organizations (NGOs), holding nationwide municipal and village council elections, and democratization of political power.

Yet, during the Khatami Administration, the government's efforts to enforce Iran's constitutional guarantees of human rights and civil liberties were severely hampered by hard-line institutions, corrupt and partisan judges, rogue elements within the security forces, and vigilantes supported by fanatical clerics. The "rule of law" was thus never effectively established. Human rights and civil liberties were flagrantly violated.[38] Several political dissidents were physically eliminated through the so-called "serial killings." Student dorms were savagely invaded, and self-appointed vice squads called *Ansar-e Hizbullah* frequently disrupted public lectures by Khatami supporters. Upward of 100 newspapers and periodicals were banned one after another. Scores of reporters, lecturers, and audacious Majlis deputies were arrested and jailed. Attorneys defending political dissidents were disbarred. Political prisoners were subjected to mental and physical tortures in a Stalinist fashion.

In short, there was hardly any fundamental improvement in human rights protection by the end of the Khatami Administration. In Freedom House's 2005 annual report, entitled *Freedom in the World*, the Islamic Republic's rank in political rights and civil liberties remained the same between 1997 and 2004. In both years, Iran was placed in category 6 on a scale of 7—with 7 representing the lowest level of freedom. The country as a whole has been classified as "non-free." Reporters Without Borders (RWB, Reporters sans frontières), which had previously called Iran the largest prison for journalists, places Iran in its October 2005 report at 164th among 167 countries in terms of press freedom[39]—down from 122nd out of 139 in 2002. In the last year of Khatami stewardship alone, according to the RWB, 17 journalists were arrested and imprisoned, 20 publications were banned or censored, two foreign correspondents were expelled, and 65 reporters were interrogated, threatened, or abused.[40] According to reams of official and private statistics, such social scourges as drug addiction,[41] affliction with AIDS, violent crimes, teenage prostitution, dysfunctional families, rising divorce rates, child abuse, runaway youngsters, and mounting[42] suicides among the youth all increased—dotting the social landscape.[43] Iran's theocratic oligarchy, which was supposed to be replaced by Islamic democracy, gradually but methodically slouched toward a form of Islamic fascism—with the *rahbar* assuming extra-constitutional power. By the time of Khatami's departure, clerical hegemony seemed absolute, and for the time being, secure.

Joining the world on Iran's own terms

In his campaign oratories, Khatami's détente policy stressed the need to defuse tension with the outside world, and establish normal relations with all countries on the basis of mutual respect and equality. Temperamentally, intellectually, and politically, the President harbored an enlightened and essentially pragmatic attitude and outlook toward the outside world. Tacitly refuting the hardliners' views of "Western cultural onslaught," he dared to regard Western civilization as intellectually, ethically, technologically, and politically challenging. He argued that all civilizations can and should influence each other. Since the West's current dominance and entrenchment could not be ignored, Islam and Iran had to study it, judge it objectively, and learn from its achievements while rejecting its defects. Misunderstandings, disputes, and quarrels with other nations should be resolved not by guns and rifles, but through dialogues and negotiations.[44] Acutely aware of Iran's isolated, if not pariah, status in the world community when he assumed office, Khatami had to move fast to tear down "the wall of mutual distrust," as he called it, with other nations on several fronts at once. A tenuous relationship with the European Union (EU), unconcealed suspicion by Sunni Muslim countries regarding the Islamic Republic's propagation of Shi'ism in the region (e.g., Lebanon, Bahrain, Saudi Arabia), the need for a final peace treaty with Iraq, and sporadic disputes with neighbors (e.g., Pakistan, Turkey, Azerbaijan, the Taliban's Afghanistan, and the United Arab Emirates—UAE) were all formidable challenges to his foreign policy agenda.

Following the *rahbar*'s tripartite principles of Iran's foreign policy based on "dignity, rationality, and national interest," Khatami began his diplomatic maneuvers with due diligence. His election to the presidency of the Organization of the Islamic Conference (OIC) in December 1997 gave him a triumphant start. Soon after, a rapprochement was reached with Saudi Arabia after years of mutual recrimination and name-calling. Relations with other Arab countries in the Persian Gulf and the region (e.g., Bahrain, Qatar, the UAE, and even Iraq) palpably improved. Ties with Turkey and Pakistan were strengthened. Friendship with Russia and China intensified. Traditional closeness with the EU, which had been shaken in the recent past, was measurably restored. His more notable diplomatic coup came with the acceptance by the United Nations of his suggestion to declare 2001 the year of "Dialogue among Civilizations." He further claimed credit for improving Iran's image in the world by signing international treaties against chemical and biological weapons, and winning world-wide acclaim for the fight against drug trafficking. His warmly welcomed and relatively fruitful trips to countries on both sides of the old ideological divide in five continents enhanced Iran's independent and "non-aligned" position.

However, as relaxed sociocultural restrictions began to be reversed, and disregard of civil liberties gradually intensified, the UN Human Rights Committee along with other Western governments resumed the condemnation of the Islamic government's human rights violations. Iran's initially brightening image began to darken.[45] Khatami's foreign policy initiatives in the region also proved to be short-lived. Agreement on the division of Caspian Sea resources was never reached despite interminable negotiations and conferences among the littoral states. Relations with Egypt and the UAE remained strained. From April 2001 onward, the European Community changed its ongoing "constructive" dialogue with Tehran back to the previous "critical" talks. Conflict with the EU intensified when it was discovered that Iran had clandestinely engaged in a uranium enrichment program with nuclear bomb-making potential for 18 years in violation of its obligations under the Non-Proliferation Treaty (NPT). After President George W. Bush described Iran's nuclear weapons aspirations as "unacceptable" to Washington, a

French–British–German effort got underway to convince Tehran to freeze sensitive nuclear programs in exchange for a range of economic, security, and technological incentives. Khatami's strong stance on Iran's rights under the NPT to engage in uranium conversion for peaceful purposes, and his firm resistance to the demands and offers by the US-EU coalition also somewhat sullied his early laudable initiatives and accomplishments—eventually forcing the EU trio to side with Washington.[46] Finally, the "Dialogue among Civilizations"—Khatami's unique claim to global fame—followed a slow and uncharted course toward becoming mainly an expensive international debating society.

The Khatami Administration's fence mending with the outside world was, however, always effectively undermined by the difficulties of engagement with Washington, and continued unconcealed enmity toward Israel. The Islamic Republic's hostility toward the United States and the Jewish state had its origin in Ayatollah Khomeini's writings and foreign policy speeches regarding Zionism, and the necessity of following a "neither East nor West" foreign policy. However, interpreting Khomeini's latterday dictum that the Islamic government's interest[47] (*maslehat-e nezam*) overrides all other considerations—even primary Islamic edicts—Khatami's predecessor, Hashemi Rafsanjani, had already sought friendship with the East (Russia and China) as a counterpart to Washington's dual containment policy. Shortly after his election, Khatami began to issue conciliatory statements toward the United States. He began by reiterating the long-standing official line that relations between the countries should be based on mutual respect, common interest, and non-interference in each other's internal affairs, free from domination and hegemony, and grounded in clear recognition of Iran's independence, sovereignty, and equality of status. In a press conference at the time of the OIC meeting in Tehran in December 1997 he expressed hope for "a philosophical and historical interchange with the American people." And in a subsequent interview with CNN in January 1998, he could barely conceal his willingness to open a new chapter between the two governments.[48] For its part, Washington cautiously opened a small window for informal contacts. In June 1998, both President Bill Clinton and Secretary of State Albright delivered encouraging statements. Although still requiring Tehran to prove its trustworthiness on some hot-button issues (i.e., terrorism, weapons of mass destruction, the Arab–Israeli conflict, and domestic human rights), they conveyed Washington's willingness to "test the possibilities for bridging the gap between the two nations."[49] In March 2000, Secretary Albright went as far as deploring Washington's role in the 1953 Anglo-American coup against Mossadeq's elected government. Yet the gap between the two countries' demands was too wide to be bridged by such perfunctory gestures. While there was pragmatic interest on the part of both the Khatami and Clinton administrations to improve relations, some powerful interest groups in and out of the US Congress, and in and out of the *rahbar*'s office, successfully blocked any positive move. Name-calling, demonization, and hostility between the two countries intensified on both sides during Bush's Administration when the Islamic Republic was placed on the "Axis of Evil" along with Iraq and North Korea. Meanwhile, sanctions against the Tehran government were routinely renewed each year. The Islamic Republic also topped the list of terrorist-sponsoring governments year after year in State Department reports, and was routinely accused of restricting religious freedom.

Despite all this, the Khatami Administration's foreign policy record has been rather positive. When Khatami was elected president, the Islamic Republic had Syria as its only friend in the whole world. Pakistan officially represented Iran's diplomatic interests in Washington, but maintained a tenuous relation with Tehran. The EU was the largest beneficiary of Iran's trade, and while acting as occasional diplomatic critic, it was still Tehran's only refuge against Washington's attacks. Russia and China were also fair-weather bedfellows. Israel and the United States were the only declared enemies. And the rest of the world seemed fearful, suspicious, or indifferent. By the time Khatami left office, Cuba, North Korea, and Venezuela had joined Russia and China as Iran's steady supporters against Washington. Iraq and Afghanistan had far better relations with Iran, and despite the presence of US troops, approached Syria's category. India joined Pakistan in coveting Iran's energy resources, and became its new fair-weather friend. And most members of the 115-nation Non-Aligned Movement, angry with Washington over many global issues, became somewhat sympathetic to Tehran's position—even occasionally on the nuclear energy issue. In retrospect, by redirecting Iran's friendship, commerce, and cultural ties from the West to the East, the Khatami Administration succeeded in changing the Islamic Republic's image from a friendless nation in the international community to a valiant champion of national sovereignty, and a carefully watched major player on the global scene.[50]

The fault lines

Truth be told, there was little doubt from the beginning that the Khatami presidency was not destined to enjoy smooth sailing. In an analysis shortly after his rise to power, the odds for success in establishing his promised politico-economic order were given no better than 50–50 at best.[51] The reasons were convincing then as they proved incontestable later on for a number of foreseeable weaknesses.

The first element in the Khatami Administration's overall sub-par performance had to do with the President's own temperament and value system. Like most well-meaning and reform-minded but idealistic and wishful thinkers, Khatami seemed to believe in the ubiquity of compromise in life. He saw, for example, no unbridgeable gap between *velayat-e motlaqeh faqih* (absolute rule by a jurisconsult) and democracy's rule of law. He identified his concept of civil society with *madinato-nabi* (Prophet Mohammad's city). His novel theme of Islamic democracy—considered oxymoronic by many—looked to him as rational and attainable. Censorship of books and pictures that went beyond the theocratic "red lines" was perfectly legitimate to him in an Islamic regime.

Blinded by a vapid and simplistic philosophy, he thought of his mission as a bridge builder between Islamic theocracy and participatory democracy. This misconceived and hollow messianic agenda ultimately turned his presidency into a subservient appendage of the *rahbar* and the conservative clerical establishment—a position that he was forced to admit shortly before the end of his eight-year tenure. Second, his domestic and foreign policy agenda was Delphic, abstract, and largely wishful and impractical in the Iranian political context. In the domestic sociopolitical area, his overarching emphasis on the rule of law, a strict observance of the Constitution, the need for the Majlis' exercise of supervisory power over state and parastatal organizations, and the necessity of developing a vibrant civil society were all rational, democratic, and essential ingredients of good governance. But, if strictly implemented, they would have shaken the 19-year-old Islamic Republic to its roots. For example, the President's law and order pledge was bound to put an end to the state agencies' frequent disregard of statutes or court orders. Partisan or corrupt judges would have been unable to ignore constitutional prohibitions against unlawful search and seizure. Wayward municipalities would have been prevented from ignoring zoning regulations. Charitable *bonyads* would not have been free to flout government tax and tariff laws. Religious vigilantes would not have dared to harass the public. And Islamic militia (*pasdaran* and *basijis*) would not have been allowed to engage in certain clandestine and extra-legal economic and political activities. The new administration would also have been able to encourage the formation of political parties, allow free labor unions, promote secular professional associations, protect a free press and political expression, and welcome the rise of non-governmental organizations. In short, Khatami's governance would have put an end to the Khomeini-style Islamic regime that had been in place for the previous 19 years.

On the economic front, Khatami's platform equally suffered from considerable contradictions, ambiguities, and lack of concrete plans. As its basic mantra, he reiterated the Khominiist line that economic development should be tempered with social justice. Yet in the same breath, he emphasized that growth should not be slowed down in the name of equity. In answers to a local newspaper questionnaire, he presented a strange mixture of interventionist measures along with a raft of market-oriented proposals side by side. Thus, he spoke of guiding national economic development through central planning, wage and price controls, state involvement in job creation and low-cost housing construction, and support for the cooperatives to eliminate middlemen. Shortly after, however, his Finance Minister, addressing the joint annual meetings of the IMF and the World Bank in September 1997, reaffirmed the Khatami government's intention to abide by all provisions of the 1995–2000 Second Economic Development Plan[52] that called for the privatization of most state economic functions, business deregulation, trade liberalization, sale of state enterprises to the public, unification of the multiple exchange-rates regime, and gradual wage/price decontrols. The contradictions were too profound to be dismissed as a nuance. Marketization and state intervention had to go hand-in-hand—with the result that neither one effectively did.

On foreign policy, the contrasts and contradictions were again glaring. Khatami called for the reduction of international tension through dialogue, and declared his presidency devoted to a "detente with the outside world" based on national "principles and values."[53] He would seek reconciliation with all countries based on "mutual respect." His global peace and security, however, had to be cognizant of each country's legitimate rights and interests, rather than one based on hegemony and force—a more polite version of "global arrogance" (a.k.a. *pax Americana*). In a typically even-handed manner, he distanced himself from xenophobic clerics by praising Western civilization to which Iran must look without prejudice while declaring that the West's political system was not flawless.

The third factor in the Khatami Administration's lackluster performance was the relatively limited power of the President in the Islamic Republic's constitutional hierarchy. Although Khatami had the votes of some 21 million citizens behind him, he had to take all his critical cues from the Supreme Leader. He had neither the authority nor the independence to deliver on his promises without the *rahbar*'s consent and approval. Furthermore, he lacked the trust and confidence of the traditional Islamic right and religious hard-liners who controlled entrenched national institutions (e.g., the Council of Guardians, the judiciary, the Expediency Council, and the Experts Assembly). Still further, he had to cope with a number of informal but powerful power centers (e.g., the bazaar, the *bonyads*, assorted post-revolutionary Islamic organizations, and a range of private-vested interests). And, in the first three years of his presidency, he had to contend with the uncooperative Fifth Majlis whose solid majority had supported Nateq-Nuri's candidacy, and elected him as speaker. Shortly before leaving office, he derisively called Iran's president a *tadorak-chi* (logistics manager) of the regime.

Fourth, Khatami lacked an identifiably independent popular base of his own. His main organized supporters for the presidency consisted of several disparate groups with diverse domestic and foreign policy agendas. The three main factions consisted of the modern Islamic left, *Majma-e Ruhaniyun-e Mobarez* (Combatant Clerics' Society) a splinter group of which Khatami himself was a founding member; the traditional Islamic left and remnants of the anti-Shah movement—*Mojahedin-e Enqelabe Eslami* (Warriors of the Islamic Revolution); and the modern Islamic right—*kargozaran-e sazandegi* (Agents of Reconstruction)—the technocrats beholden to ex-President Rafsanjani. The only reason for these diverse groups' coalition was that none could come up with a candidate of its own capable of challenging Nateq-Nuri's seemingly unstoppable victory. Once they succeeded in electing him, each group expected him to protect and promote its own parochial interests and agenda. He, for his part, having won their endorsement, persistently refused to create a distinct political party or even head a clear political movement—preferring to act as the president of all the people. His faint endorsement of his younger brother's unofficial Islamic Iran's Participation Front (*Jebhe Moshasekat-e Iran-e Eslami*) served neither of them any good. As a result, by taking the high moral ground, and refusing to establish a Western-style political party of his own with nationwide party cells and coverage, he repeated Mossadeq's fatal mistake that ultimately cost both of them prestige and popularity.

Fifth, and finally, despite all evidence to the contrary, Khatami on numerous occasions described his cabinet as a cohesive, harmonious, innovative, experienced, and capable team, ready to fulfill their religious, revolutionary, and national obligations.[54] The reality, however, was different. In an awkward attempt to reward the three main factions that supported him in the elections, he started his administration with an incongruous, incompatible, and nondescript cabinet charged with attaining conflicting objectives. And to the end of his tenure, he was never able to put together a team of like-minded, competent, balanced, popular, and loyal aides. The first cabinet that he presented to the conservative-dominated Fifth Majlis was anything but fresh, promising, innovative, or reformist. All of its members belonged to the Islamic Republic's exclusive, and relatively fixed 200 or so, *nomenklatura*. There were no new faces on the roster, and most conspicuously, no woman minister—despite women's crucial role in his election. Five of his 22 cabinet members and two of his seven vice-presidents were Rafsanjani loyalists, and former members of his team. Four were left over from Musavi's wartime cabinet. He also kept the Central Bank Governor who belonged to the Rafsanjani faction. Furthermore, in the selection of individuals for sensitive ministries (e.g., intelligence, defense, and foreign affairs) he had to make notable concessions to the entrenched establishment, and most eminently to the *rahbar*. More baffling still, he appointed as his top advisor Mir-Hossein Musavi, the wartime Prime Minister, and the architect of nearly all of Iran's subsequent economic woes: i.e., overflowing population, overvalued exchange rate, overburdening subsidies, and over-regulated trade and business. As a result, while the Rafsanjani loyalists were bent on deliberate marketization and economic deregulation, the other two left-of-center factions pushed for continued state intervention in the economy, larger subsidies, foreign exchange controls, and trade restrictions. The almost perpetual, and often public, quarrels among the Minister of Finance, the head of the Management and Plan Organization, and the Governor of the Central Bank provided rich fodder for the liberated press and the capital's chattering class.[55]

A lasting image

History may be kinder to Muhammad Khatami than his contemporaries—including those millions of people who twice elected him their president, and later witnessed his eclipse into political irrelevance with utter insouciance. Several reasons were given here for his unceremonious exit from the political scene. Other factors may be pointed out by other analysts now or discovered in the future. Yet in the final analysis, the main reason for his loss of public confidence and support is not much of a mystery. By all evidence, a crucial disconnect between his own rather limited ambitions and the voters' unbound expectations did him in. That is, based on his lofty campaign promises, what was expected of him by the electorate was far more than the *maximum* he could possibly deliver, and what he did deliver was far less than the *minimum* his hurried and hopeful constituents anticipated. Yet he never acknowledged that fact. To the end of his last days in office, he stubbornly clung to his controversial thesis that sustained economic development is contingent upon, and impossible without, prior cultural and political development—allegedly neglected during Rafsanjani's two-term presidency.[56] In other words, Rafsanjani's *perestroika* had failed because it was not preceded by Khatami's *glasnost*.

True to this ideological fetish, Khatami and his Islamic-leftist followers directed their primary efforts toward emphasizing the sanctity of human rights, primacy of the rule of law, significance of political freedoms, importance of the free press, the useful role of NGOs, the propagation of Islamic democracy, and the need for dialogue among cultures. While these issues were philosophically and ideologically important, they were the type of values of special appeal to a tiny intellectual and affluent minority, and especially privileged classes in the country. They had little or no relevance to what the majority cared for: steady jobs, livable wages, affordable prices, low-cost housing, fruitful education, access to health care, and social security. Khatami's presidency transformed Iran's social, political, and economic landscape beyond any doubt, but largely failed to install solid and permanent institutions capable of preventing a leap backward. Iranian society after eight years of Khatami tenure was more than ever polarized, alienated, and cynical. It was less confident, secure, and hopeful. Strangely enough, if it is true that Ahmadinejad won his presidency not by guaranteeing freedoms of speech and assembly, but on his popular ticket of reducing poverty and putting the oil money on everyone's dinner table, then Khatami surely proved Muhammad Reza Shah right in insisting on his much vilified thesis that, for the poor and undereducated, *economic* well-being precedes *political* liberties. In other words, when poverty rules, freedom cannot prosper.

The irony of all ironies, however, is that Khatami—a well-meaning, optimistic, and hopeful man of God—finished his earthly mission by dashing all hopes for salvation among the disillusioned post-revolution generation. His eight-year presidency demonstrated that the anachronistic and retrogressive Islamic Republic could not be deconstructed and reshaped from within. And all other alternatives now look unthinkably ominous.

Notes

* First published in *Middle East Journal*, vol. 60, no. 1, Winter 2006. Reproduced with permission.

1 *Iranmania News*, January 5, 2002.
2 For an assessment of Khatami's first four years see Jahangir Amuzegar, "Khatami's First-Term Presidency," *SAIS Review* (Winter/Summer 2002); and "Khatami's Economic Record: Small Bandages on Deep Wounds," *Global Dialogue* (Spring/Summer 2001).
3 See Jahangir Amuzegar, "Khatami: Folk Hero in Search of Relevance," *Middle East Policy*, Summer 2004.
4 For a reference to foreign and Iranian pundits ignoring him as a viable candidate, see Karl Vick, "Hardliner in Iran Runoff," *Washington Post*, June 19, 2005 and "Class is Pivotal in Iran Runoff," *Washington Post*, June 24, 2005; Abbas Milani and Michael McFall, "Cracks in the Land of the Ayatollahs," *International Herald Tribune*, June 17, 2005; Michael Slackman, "Iran Moderate Says Hardliners Rigged Election," *New York Times*, June 19, 2005.
5 *Iran Times* (Washington, DC), July 1, 2005.
6 Patrick Seale, "Iran's Election May Provide an Islamic Role Model," *Daily Star* (Beirut), July 17, 2005.
7 "Moderate Leader is Elected in Iran," *New York Times*, May 25, 1997; "Khatami Promises a Fresh Start," *Middle East Economic Digest*, June 6, 1997; R.H. Curtis, "Khatami's Election May Be a Turning Point," *Washington Report on Middle East Affairs*, August–September 1997; and S.C. Fairbanks, "Iran's Democratic Efforts," *Middle East Policy*, September 1997.
8 For the breakdown of the election results, see Wilfried Buchta, *Who Rules Iran* (Washington, DC: Washington Center for Near East Policy, 2000). For Khatami's detailed platform and promises, see Jahangir Amuzegar, "Iran Under New Management," *SAIS Review* (Winter–Spring 1998).
9 See John Lancaster, "Iranians Voted for New Ideas, Not a New System," *Washington Post*, May 26, 1997.
10 For a portrait and a list of his writings, see David Menashri, "Whither Iranian Politics," in *Iran Under Khatami* (Washington, DC: Washington Institute for Near East Policy, 1998).
11 For a sample, see *The Iranian* (Washington, DC), December 15, 2002.
12 See *Iranian Student's News Agency (ISNA)*, July 19, 2005; and www.donya-e-eqtesad.com (Tehran), August 3, and October 21, 2005.
13 The President's report to the Majlis, available at www.hamshahri.ir (Tehran), August 2, 2005.
14 *Iran Focus* (UK), April 1998.
15 Data released during Khatami's presidency by the three principal economic agencies—the Central Bank, the Management and Plan Organization, and the Ministry of Finance—on the same subjects are conflicting and contradictory. They should, therefore, be treated with a great deal of caution.
16 See www.donya-e eqtesad.com, May 24, 2005.
17 See www.hamshahri.ir, October 25, 2005.
18 "Khatami's Third Plan Report to the Majlis," available at www.emrouz.info/Show, June 3, 2005; and extracts from *Nature* at www.radiofarda.com/Iran, May 21, 2005.
19 *Bonyads* are parastatal charitable foundations, owning and operating mostly the assets confiscated from people and institutions associated with the Pahlavi regime.
20 For more detailed discussion of these reforms, see *Islamic Republic of Iran—Staff Report for the 2003 Article IV Constitution* (Washington, DC: IMF, August 4, 2003); and Jahangir Amuzegar, "Iran's Third Development Plan: An Appraisal," *Middle East Policy*, Fall 2005.
21 Cf. www.emrooz-info/showItem, August 3, 2005.
22 *Economic Trends* (Tehran: Central Bank) No. 13 and 39; and *Governance Matters IV* (Washington, DC: The World Bank, 2005).

23 See www.hamshahri.ir, October 25, 2005.
24 See www.hamshahri.ir, January 18, 2005 and April 9, 2005.
25 *Economic Trends*, No. 13 and www.hamshahri.ir, April 9, 2005.
26 Press conference by the Minister of Welfare and Social Security, *ISNA*, July 2005; President Khatami himself considered the inability to target subsidies his administration's greatest failure. Available at www.hamshahri.ir, May 20, 2005.
27 *Economic Trends*, No. 13 and www.hamshahri.ir, April 9, 2005.
28 Statement by the Khatami government's spokesman, available at www.emrouz.info, August 3, 2005.
29 www.radiofarda.com/Iran, September 24, 2005. See also www.hamshahri.ir, November 9, 2005.
30 The claim is that the income ratio of the highest 10% to the lowest 10% of income receivers declined from about 19 times to nearly 16 between 2000 and 2003. See www.mp.org/irakhbar/84-6-14-2htm, October 2, 2005. For the conclusion of UNDP/MPO study see www.donya-e-eqtesad.com, November 23, 2005, and www.Iran-emrouz.net, November 25, 2005.
31 *Human Development Report* (New York: UNDP), 1999 and 2005. In the HDI ranking 1 is highest and 157 lowest. For a similar conclusion see www.hamshahri.ir, December 14, 2005.
32 For the components of complete freedom (scores of 1.00–1.99), methods of calculation, and ranking of countries, see the Foundation's annual reports for 1997 and 2005. The Foundation ranked 150 countries in 1997 and 155 in 2005.
33 www.hamshahri.ir, September 11, 2005.
34 www.hamshahri.ir, September 11, 2005. See "Nothing Can Be Done in Iran without Bribes," available at www.bbc.co.uk/persian/business, December 24, 2005.
35 See www.hamshahri.ir, September 10 and 16, 2005.
36 See "Iran Report," *Radio Free Europe/Radio Liberty*, August 9, 2005.
37 "UN Condemns Tehran on Rights," available at www.thestar.com, December 16, 2005.
38 "Iran—2005 Annual Report," *RWF*, www.rsf.org/print. For rankings in different years, see *Kayhan* (London), October 27, 2005.
39 Cf. www.emrouz.info May 7, 2005. For Khatami's admission of censorship in Iran, see "*Vedae Khatami ba nahadhay-e madani*" ["Khatami's Farewell with Civil Societies"], www.donya-e-eqtesad.com, August 1, 2005.
40 The UN World Drug Report for 2005 lists Iran as the country with the highest rate of opiate addicts in the world.
41 For a fuller discussion of social ills, see Jahangir Amuzegar, "Iran's Theocracy Under Siege," *Middle East Policy* (Spring 2003).
42 For a window into his thinking, see his *Beem-e Mowj* [*Fear of Wave*] (Tehran: Simay-e Jawan, 1995); *Az Donya-ye Shahr to Shahr-e Donya* [*From the World of the City to the City of the World*] (Tehran: Nashr-e Nay, 1997); and *Hope and Challenge* (Binghampton, NY: SUNY, 1997).
43 For the background of these events, see Geneive Abdo, "Days of Rage in Tehran," and Jahangir Amuzegar, "Iran's Future," *Middle East Policy* (October 1999).
44 See Trita Parsi, "Europe's Mendacity Doomed Iran Talk to Failure," *Financial Times*, August 30, 2005.
45 For Khomeini's decree see *Ettela'at* (Tehran), January 7, 1998, and *Kayhan* (Tehran), January 7, 1988. For Rafsanjani's interpretation, see David Menashri, *A Decade of War and Revolution* (New York: Holmes, 1990).
46 *IRNA*, December 14, 1998, and January 7, 1998.
47 US Department of State Press Statement, June 17, 1998; and Daily Press Briefing, June 18, 1998.

48 See www.emrouz.info, August 10, 2005.
49 See Jahangir Amuzegar, "Iran under a New Management," *SAIS Review* (Winter–Spring 1998).
50 For details of the agenda, see *Iran Times* (Washington, DC) June 13, 1997; and www.hamshahri.ir (Tehran), August 5, 1997.
51 For the full text of answers, see US Foreign Broadcast Information Service (FBIS), June 9, 1997.
52 IMF and World Bank, Press Release No. 10 (Board of Governors Annual Meetings), September 23–25, 1997.
53 The *Economist*, May 31, 1997; "Khatami Becomes Fifth President," *Iran Times*, August 8, 1997.
54 See, for example, *FBIS-NES*, August 18, 1997.
55 For a candid admission of these intramural turf battles, see the interview with Khatami's vice president for parliamentary affairs at www.donya-e-eqtesad.com, October 21, 2005.
56 "*Khoda Hafezi ye Khatami dar Otaq-e Bazargan*i" ["Farewell to the Chamber of Commerce"], available at www.donya-e-eqtesad.com, July 19, 2005.

8 Sanctioning the Islamic Republic

A new global wave*

The year 2010 has so far been Iran's *annus horribilis*. In addition to a number of domestic political turmoils, economic setbacks, and social crises, the "year of the tiger" has witnessed a concerted diplomatic censure. Prompted by a new and highly critical report on Iran by the International Atomic Energy Agency (IAEA), the United Nations Security Council (UNSC) issued its fourth round of sanctions on 9 June due to Tehran's refusal to abide by previous nuclear and missile-related resolutions. Soon after, a number of countries, led by Washington, introduced additional unilateral penalties of their own. All these sanctions were initiated and imposed on the assumptions, hidden or otherwise, that: (1) the Islamic Republic—despite its repeated denials—intends to develop nuclear weapons in order to intimidate and dominate its neighbors; (2) whether or not Iranian bombs should pose an existential threat to Israel or elsewhere, they will induce a costly and dangerous nuclear arms race in the region; and (3) even if Washington provides a protective atomic shield to Iran's neighbor to prevent such an arms race, nuclear devices might fall into the hands of rogue elements, terrorists, and Jihadist warriors.

UN Security Council action

The UNSC Resolution 1929, passed on 9 June 2010, was the culmination of three previous ones—Resolution 1737 of 23 December 2006; Resolution 1747 of 24 March 2007; and Resolution 1803 of 3 March 2008—in accordance with Article 41, Chapter 7, of the UN Charter. The 1929 resolution flowed from a new international effort to punish Iran for expanding its uranium enrichment program in defiance of the previous UN resolutions. After months of protracted negotiations between the five permanent members of the Council, the latest much watered-down resolution: (1) calls for a ban on sales of conventional military hardware (tanks, airplanes, missiles) to Iran and restricts Iran's missile development activities; (2) blacklists some Iranian shipping companies and calls on nations to inspect ships suspected of transporting contraband cargo; (3) asks countries to deny financial sources for firms suspected of trafficking in nuclear proliferation items; (4) adds 40 new companies to the list of entities involved in sanctioned activity; and (5) asks countries to "exercise vigilance" over transactions involving Iranian banks. There are, however, only limited restrictions on Iran's energy sector (where both Russia and China—the two veto powers of the Council—have keen interests and substantial involvement). None of these imposed sanctions bans the export and sale of Iranian oil and gas—thus continuing to provide the Islamic government with a powerful means of resisting, and combating, imposed restrictions. The resolution contains a pledge to assist Iran's civilian nuclear program financially and technologically provided Tehran suspends uranium enrichment.

United States measures

The Obama administration and the US Congress, considering the latest UNSC resolution not aggressive enough to upend Iran's nuclear efforts, immediately began to draft their own unilateral measures with more bite. Washington was particularly disappointed that: (a) the UN resolution did not blackball Iran's major transportation companies engaged in procuring equipment for its nuclear program; (b) there was no international ban on Iran's access to global financial markets; (c) no blacklisting of Iran's Central Bank; and (d) no reference to the energy sector as the mainstay of Iran's economy. A concerted bipartisan effort to remedy the situation thus got underway in both houses of the US Congress.

A new sanctions law, passed almost unanimously by the US Congress, and signed by the president on 1 July 2010, supplements some 19 previous US presidential and congressional sanctions—going back to 1981 in the aftermath of the American hostage crisis. The Comprehensive Iran Sanctions, Accountability, and Divestment Act of 2010 thus: (1) bans from the US market foreign companies that work with Iranian businesses charged with aiding the Islamic Republic's nuclear programs; (2) cuts off from the US financial system any foreign bank dealing with Iranian entities that are blacklisted by the United Nations or Washington; (3) sanctions Iranian entities or individuals accused of suppressing moves towards democracy in Iran, and targets foreign firms that provide technologies to the Islamic government to repress political dissent; (4) denies US government contracts to any foreign firm doing business with any sanctioned Iranian companies or entities, including those related to the Islamic Revolutionary Guard Corps (IRGC); (5) bans the sale of gasoline and other refined products to Iran of more than $1mn each time, or more than $5mn altogether in a year; (6) bars foreign travel by named Iranians; (7) closes loopholes in the Iran-Libya Sanctions Act of 1996 targeting international firms investing more than $20mn a year in Iran's oil and gas sector; and (8) provides the president with only limited waiver power on national security grounds. Companies found in violation of the US law risk being barred from the US market and financial system. Under a special executive order signed by President Barack Obama on 29 September 2010, a separate, targeted set of sanctions was imposed on some top Iranian government officials for their alleged violations of Iranian citizens' human rights after the country's disputed 2009 presidential elections.

Shortly after the bill's ratification, Washington proceeded to blacklist a large number of Iranian military leaders, firms connected with the IRGC, certain "charitable" foundations and their various front companies, in addition to some 17 specific Iranian banks. At the same time, a concerted effort has been made by Washington to press the international commercial companies to withdraw from Iran in order to enhance its isolation. US officials have been visiting East Asia, Latin America, and the Middle East region to garner support for tightening Iran sanctions. They have particularly implored foreign governments not to allow their companies to fill the vacancies created by Western entities.

The European Union sanctions

On 27 July 2010, the 27 members of the European Union (EU) imposed a raft of new sanctions on the Islamic Republic. These measures went far beyond the sanctions voted on by the UN Security Council several weeks earlier, but they were still nowhere near as harsh as the US sanctions. Briefly highlighted, the EU: (1) bars European investments in, or technical assistance to, Iran's oil and gas sectors including the supply of equipment and technology; (2) imposes stiff financial restrictions—prohibiting insurance for Iranian trade, and forbidding Iranian bond sales in Europe; (3) prohibits all Iranian cargo aircraft to land in European airports; (4) forbids the sale of equipment or technology that could contribute to uranium enrichment, even if there is a dual use; and (5) extends travel bans and asset freezes to a number of named IRGC officers and government officials. The EU communiqué acknowledges Iran's legitimate rights to the peaceful use of nuclear energy, and emphasizes that its aim was to rebuild international confidence in the exclusively peaceful nature of Iran's nuclear program.

Shortly after the EU action, a number of other countries, including Australia, Canada, Japan, Malaysia, Norway, and South Korea supplemented the UN's June resolution on their own in various degrees of intensity and coverage. Most others, however, pledged to abide by the UN measures, but no more. Turkey and Brazil, which had voted no to the latest UN resolution, promised to follow suit.

Tehran's reactions

The Islamic regime's reactions to these measures were predictable. Sanctions are not new to Iran. The Islamic Republic, since its inception, has been faced with international censure, isolation, pressures, and a hostile foreign environment. Iran is currently one of the world's most sanctioned countries. So far, however, Tehran has always found a way to get around these punitive measures. According to a recent US Government Accountability officer, for example, some 41 foreign companies are still active in Iran's energy sector in 2010 despite the 1996 Iran–Libya Sanctions Act. A dozen foreign car companies are still assembling their autos in various parts of the country. Scores of smaller banks around the world still transact with their Iranian counterparts. Many countries supply the Islamic regime with its needed gasoline and other essential imports.

As a result, the Islamic Republic response to the nearly universal sanctions has ranged from enthusiastic welcome and embrace, to dismissal and ridicule, and ironically threats of retaliation and revenge. At various occasions, the Supreme Leader, the president, and other high officials have welcomed the sanctions as a spur to Iran's greater self-reliance and enhanced domestic ingenuity. Supreme Leader Ali Khamenei has called the sanctions a sign of Iran's growing clout and "increasing power of awakening Islam." He has described the penalties as a "potential opportunity" and a "blessing"—promising to get around them successfully and triumphantly. President Mahmoud Ahmadinejad, calling the latest UN resolution a "used napkin" destined for the "garbage can," has vowed not to make "one iota of concession" to the West, and to push forward with building four new nuclear reactors. Declaring the efforts of past sanctions "pathetic," he has said even "100 times more sanctions" will not have an impact on the Iranian economy. Using some intemperate language in describing the West's actions, he has declared his determination to turn the impositions into opportunities for self-reliance through belt-tightening and resistance. The finance minister has claimed that Iran is now much stronger because of sanctions. The head of Iran's Central Bank has stated that sanctions may result in reduced imports of non-essential goods and services, thus helping to increase foreign exchange reserves. The health minister claims that Iran's pharmaceutical industry has become 96% self-sufficient due to sanctions. An Iranian defense department official boasts that despite the UNSC Resolution 1747 of 24 March 2010 (prohibiting the sale, export, supply, or transfer of arms) the Islamic Republic is now exporting military equipment to some 40 countries.

Hand in hand with these welcomes, there also have been some defiant voices. Two days before the EU sanctions were issued, President Ahmadinejad threatened swift retaliation for any measures aimed at Iran, adding that any nation joining the Americans in their anti-Iranian agenda would be considered "hostile," and treated as such. On another occasion, he threatened to withdraw Iranian financial assets from any country engaged in sanctions. He also warned that if sanctions were voted on, there would be no further negotiations on the nuclear issue with the 5+1 group (five permanent members of the UN Security Council plus one). Responding to the last UN resolution, Iran's ambassador to the United Nations said: "No amount of pressure and mischief will be able to break our determination to pursue nuclear energy." Then he added: "Iran has never bowed and will never bow to hostile actions." And, soon after the UN sanction resolution was issued, the president announced that Iran would send a man into space five years earlier than the 2019 planned date.

These defiant gestures were then followed by expressions of revenge. In late July 2010, the Majlis passed a law requiring retaliatory seizure and inspection of cargo ships or planes belonging to countries that might subject Iranian means of transport to UN sanctions. And when US officials and others began to claim that the latest international sanctions had succeeded in weakening Iran's resolve in pursuing its nuclear ambitions, the Islamic Republic's spokesman, in mid-August 2010, unveiled a new law mandating the production of higher enriched uranium, and curtailing cooperation with the UN atomic energy watchdog. Simultaneously, the head of Iran's Atomic Energy Organization announced that Tehran would begin the construction of its third enrichment plant by early 2011.

In addition to the verbal assaults and defiant posture, Tehran has also been quietly moving to meet all eventualities. Anticipating new US and Western sanctions, the groundwork has been laid to resist such punishments, or deflect their influence through: (1) stockpiling of gasoline (albeit at 25% over market prices); (2) increasing domestic gasoline production to the point of claimed "self-sufficiency"; (3) amassing some 2,800 kg of low enriched uranium and 22 kg of material enriched to 20% ostensibly to provide nuclear material for its old medical research reactor; and (4) replacing the United Arab Emirates, its closest and most active trade and financial partner now facing increasing banking restrictions, with Turkey and Armenia.

Lingering doubts

Many analysts still believe that the recent sanctions are not aggressive enough to force the Iranian leadership to abandon its nuclear program—for several reasons. First, due to the lack of progress so far in finding a mutually satisfactory solution to the domestic uranium enrichment, the matter has now become one of honor, prestige, sovereignty, and independence for the Islamic regime, and a case of "inalienable right" for the indoctrinated rank and file. Without a respectable face-saving device and a convenient fig leaf, no Iranian administration—of any color—might be expected to budge. Second, the entrenched ideological commitment to pursue minimum uranium enrichment at home overrides any rational cost/benefit analysis of the West's stick-and-carrot approach. Third, Washington's inability or reluctance to impose sanctions on Russian, Chinese, and other security-sensitive foreign companies which are ignoring the US sanctions is likely to undermine significant pressures on the Islamic regime. Fourth, efforts by Washington and Brussels to build a united front to bring Tehran to the negotiating table through stiff sanctions have faced increasingly bold resistance from the BRIC group (Brazil, Russia, India and China), Turkey, and some other Muslim countries. The BRIC coalition has, in fact, talked about submitting a resolution to the UN General Assembly banning any unilateral sanctions beyond those approved by the UNSC resolutions. Fifth, though sanctions have forced a large number of Western energy and industrial companies to stop doing business in Iran, other firms have attempted to fill the void. Massive smuggling has also kept the country well supplied with essential goods. Finally, the Tehran government, coping with sanctions for years, has learned how to bypass and neutralize them. To wit, the names and ownership of blacklisted Iranian ships have frequently been changed faster than the US Treasury can update them. There is also evidence that a sanctions-busting industry has emerged with new firms specializing in helping penalized entities to overcome the restrictions—at a hefty price.

A new scenario

There are currently strong reasons to believe that a confluence of several factors makes the impact of the new sanctions this time vastly different from the past. First, not only are the sanctions' intensity and scope unprecedented, but also the participants constitute a much broader coalition of governments and their private sectors. Second, the imposition of the new sanctions comes at a time when the Ahmadinejad administration intends to implement four unpopular and hazardous domestic economic policies: a value-added tax system; a drastic subsidies reform; increased import restrictions; and possibly a rial revaluation—all in the midst of both rising inflation and stubborn unemployment. Third, internal political solidarity and cohesion within the top leadership circle has for the first time been badly shaken by open disputes between President Ahmadinejad and the heads of the legislative and the judicial branches. There is also a much publicized recrimination between the president's chief of staff and the head of the Iranian armed forces. Fourth, there are increasing dissatisfactions expressed by some grand ayatollahs in Qom regarding the government's conduct of business. As a result of these heightened political tensions, there have been protracted labor strikes, bazaar boycotts, suspicious industrial accidents, and turbulence in the gold and foreign exchange markets.

Assessment of difficulties

Matching the ease of identifying the sectors impacted by the sanctions is the difficulty of measuring their tangible impacts. To wit, palpable evidence already shows that Iran's energy sector, banking and insurance operations, air and maritime transport, foreign trade, and access to foreign technology and capital markets have all been more or less affected by recent sanctions. Yet when it comes to assessing the damage, the difficulties arise either because required data are not available to outsiders, or the losses are not practically calculable.

The Islamic government undoubtedly knows, or can assess: (a) the foregone value of its declining daily oil output due to the lack of access to Western technology; (b) greater transaction costs of banking and insurance in its foreign trade; (c) higher prices paid, and longer waiting time involved, in purchasing prohibited goods on the black markets; (d) higher interest rates paid for borrowing abroad or floating its own bonds; and (e) losses involved in delayed implementation of the country's development projects—all due to the sanctions. Yet, almost none of the data are available to outside investigators.

Oftentimes, however, the figures are not assessable even by the government itself. Such factors as the inferior worth of second-hand technology, lower quality of imported goods and services, scientific knowledge denied Iranian students in certain fields at Western universities or research centers, and—above all—the value of lives lost in airplane accidents due to the lack of access to spare parts, are totally out of reach, or extremely difficult to determine by anyone.

Signs of impact

Despite these difficulties, some early indications of the sanctions' effectiveness can be detected from various private and semi-official quarters. Open sources such as trade publications and company statements reveal that: (1) dozens of Iranian-flagged ships transporting gasoline, crude oil, and other products have been denied insurance coverage, and thus refusal of entry in most ports; (2) a number of European energy suppliers have halted gasoline sales to Iran, and almost all European oil giants (Total, Shell, Eni, and Statoil) have stopped or curtailed their business with Iran; (3) a score of multinational industrial companies—European, Japanese, and South Korean—have announced publicly that they have reduced or eliminated their business ties to Iran in order to maintain their more lucrative US market share; (4) while sanctions do not apply to Iran's oil and gas exports, there seem to be mounting difficulties in selling the crude as major European and Middle Eastern banks have all but stopped issuing letters of credit to Iranian financial institutions; (5) Iran's liquid natural gas ambitions are now considered a clear casualty of sanctions due to exiting of European partners; (6) the EU has vetoed any Iranian gas participation in the Nabucco pipelines being built to carry the Caspian natural gas across Turkey to Europe; and (7) the Obama administration has for the first time sanctioned Switzerland's Naftiran Intertrade Company, a wholly owned subsidiary of National Iranian Oil Company (NIOC) for financing energy projects inside Iran, and the European–Iranian Trade Bank AG in Hamburg, Germany.

Private analysts and lower echelon government officials also point to other palpable sanctions' impacts. Many in the bazaar and the private sector, and almost all of the informed public, now admit that the fresh rounds of noose-tightening are taking an increasing toll on the domestic economy. A former president of the Tehran Chamber of Commerce and Industry, for example, attributes 35% of the total costs of domestic consumer goods to sanctions because a number of dual-use items must now be purchased at much higher prices in the black market. A former oil ministry official recently told a local news agency that the cost of the country's energy projects had doubled due to the difficulties of finding needed supplies, technology, and capital. Another former NIOC director believes that the Islamic government's inability to obtain badly needed new technologies in the West, lack of access to the major world capital markets, and failure to place its own energy bonds abroad are seriously threatening the fate of Iran's oil and gas industry.

A blessing in disguise?

The scope, intensity, and speed of the new measures, and the strength of the international community's resolve, seem to be increasingly felt by the Iranian top leadership. In fact, at no time since the earlier years of the revolution has the Iranian society been so polarized and divided with respect to its increasing global isolation. While the current sanctions are not yet "crippling" Iran, they are seriously complicating its efforts to do business around the world—a fact that is constantly pointed out by the opposition, and not disregarded by many in the administration. Reactions to the sanctions are also seen as causing increasing splits within the Iranian top ruling elite. Ex-president Hashemi Rafsanjani has publicly called on the current Iranian leadership "to take the sanctions seriously and not to dismiss them as a joke"—arguing that international sanctions on Iran had never been as stiff and extensive.

At the same time, while all sanction resolutions have explicitly or otherwise emphasized that they do not intend to impose undue hardship on the Iranian people, and are only meant to punish the regime, there is no doubt that the fresh rounds of economic restrictions appear to have put pressure on the ordinary people. Higher costs and lower quality of consumer goods, restrictions on foreign exchange purchases by the public, Iran Air's difficulties in refueling in many European airports—threatening the main lifeline for Iranians with the outside world—and the deteriorating domestic business climate, are all palpably felt by the rank and file. President Obama has already acknowledged his "concern" for the Iranian people, but believes that they have to blame their leaders for their plight. The opposition to the Ahmadinejad government claims that sanctions can only hurt the most vulnerable social classes in Iran—a fact that is not disregarded by the rank and file. It is argued that the impositions are in fact a gift to the ruling powers by providing them with a pretext for cracking down further on political dissidents, and equating them with foreign enemies. It is also argued that the powerful IRGC can manage to circumvent the sanctions, and even profit from the embargo, by engaging in wholesale contraband.

Due to the rising popular discontent, and repeated criticisms by the struggling but still vibrant opposition, there are indications that the regime—despite its continued defiance and audacious bravado, may be induced to start new negotiations with the 5+1 group towards finding a mutually satisfactory solution of the nuclear issue. Recent conciliatory statements by Iran's foreign minister may be a clue. If such a scenario ever materializes, then the enhanced sanctions might be considered a blessing in disguise.

Note

* First published in the *Middle East Economic Survey*, November 1, 2010. Reproduced with permission.

9 Iran

The rial saga*

During the last 12 months, and particularly since January 2012, the erratic and unhinged behavior of the Iranian currency, the rial, has been added to the Islamic Republic's other thorny and protracted economic woes. After nearly a decade of relative stability in both the official and free market, the rial experienced a precipitous plunge in late December 2011, and subsequently lost nearly half of its value within a short time. With far-reaching effects not only on external trade, but also on domestic prices, interest rates, savings, investments and capital flows, the rial's value has become the Mahmoud Ahmadinejad administration's biggest daily economic headache.

While the explanations, reasons, and guesses so far offered for the upheaval have ranged from the probable (e.g. deteriorating business climate and political uncertainties) to the bizarre (e.g. sabotage by government "enemies," manipulation by local currency dealers, and the administration's own stratagem to make up for budget deficits), the real reasons are more numerous and far more complicated. This review attempts to seek the underlying causes of the recent events in a number of deeper-rooted and interrelated phenomena that have not so far been sufficiently scrutinized.

The unfolding drama

The fall of the rial's value has a long history. On the eve of the 1979 revolution, Iran's domestic exchange rate for the US dollar was IR 70.6. The revolution's subsequent economic disasters—the bureaucracy's massive upheaval, wholesale nationalization of banks, industries, and commercial enterprises, the exodus of nearly all experienced industrial managers, and massive capital flights exerted relentless daily pressure on the rial. The ruinous 1980–88 Iran–Iraq war and the drastic fall in Iran's annual oil exports, accompanied by lower oil prices in the mid-1980s, imposed further heavy burdens on the Iranian currency. A series of misguided economic policies followed by Mir Hossein Musavi's left-center government during the 1980s, designed to control prices and wages, resulted in the rise of a multiple exchange rate system. So, by the end of the war, the Islamic Republic had 12 different official exchange rates for the US dollar. Subsequent attempts by the postwar government of President Hashemi Rafsanjani designed to cope with rent-seeking activities, spreading corruption, and economic injustices gradually reduced the exchange number to four. Under President Mohammad Khatami's "reformist" government, the last four exchange rates were finally unified in 2002.

During 1978–2002 the rial lost its foreign exchange value steadily year after year. While the official dollar rate—announced by the Central Bank of Iran (CBI) under its so-called "managed float" system—started weakening from \$1 = IR70 in 1978 to \$1 = IR1,750 in 2001, the free market rate rose from \$1 = IR100 to \$1 = IR7,920 during the same 23 years. As the free market rate had reached \$1 = IR8,000 by 2002, the new unified rate was set at \$1 = IR7,950 and was periodically raised by small increments.

In the meantime, the free market rate's difference from the official rate was virtually eliminated until September 2010 when a relatively modest difference of about IR1,300 began between the two rates, and repeated attempts to eliminate the daily difference were not successful. On 7 June 2011, the rial unexpectedly crashed on the open market and traded near \$1 = IR11,800. The CBI, moving to eliminate the difference and unify the two rates, raised the ongoing official rate from \$1 = IR10,590 to \$1 = IR11,740—a 10.5% devaluation. In a matter of days, due to the CBI's massive market interventions, a new stability was established. In order to minimize future rate differences, the CBI opened a "secondary" exchange window designed to deal with dollar demands for services (e.g. travel) at a third rate between official and free.

In early November 2011, while the foreign political climate became cloudier, the dollar rate in the secondary and free markets registered IR12,800, and IR13,300, respectively, while the official dollar rate was fixed at IR10,850. By 30 November, while the official rate was \$1 = IR10,900 the free market rate climbed to \$1 = IR13,300. In the third week of December 2011, the free market rate climbed to \$1 = IR14,300 and by 30 December it had reached \$1 = IR15,480. On 2 January 2012 the US currency sold at IR18,000 and climbed to \$1 = IR22,100 by 24 January. A series of panicked reactions by the CBI (e.g. frequently adjusting the official rate up and down) were of no avail, and market volatility intensified. Failing to calm the situation through monetary interventions and a sizeable injection of dollars in the market, the government resorted to a coercive policy. The Majlis passed legislation forbidding street venders (i.e. unlicensed money changers) from selling foreign currencies, ordering licensed dealers to sell dollars at no more than the specified rate, and blocking websites that reported hourly dollar prices. The judiciary chief threatened to execute currency manipulators.

On 18 January 2012, failing to stop the currency's continued decline, the Central Bank lowered the official rate by 8.5% to \$1 = IR12,260, and promised to offer unlimited dollars for current transactions. Then the Council on Money and Credit on 25 January 2012 changed its long-held policy of fixing deposit interest rates, allowing both government and private banks to set their own competitive rates. While the official rate was kept unchanged, the rial continued to slip and slide in the free market as the CBI was not prepared to meet all daily dollar demands. Powerless to maintain parity between official and free market rates, the CBI finally sanctified the coexistence of the "dual markets" on 14 March 2012, and let private money changers handle dollar demands for "non-essential" imports. The free market rate in late March 2012 fell to $1 = IR19,000, or about 55% of its 2002–11 value. Five months after the previous high in January, the dollar rate was ranging between IR17,000 and IR19,000, surpassing $1 = IR20,000 for a brief period. It has hovered around $1 = IR19,000 since, with no particular direction and responsive mainly to current political events.

Leading causes

The official explanations of the rial's turbulence are few, far between and occasionally even bizarre. Despite reams of theoretical proofs, and decades of practical evidence to the contrary, President Ahmadinejad has linked the currency upheaval to a conspiracy between private exchange dealers, opposition politicians and the hostile press. The Central Bank governor has called it the reflection of a mob mentality, and the product of a "defective exchange market" where "hoarders, smugglers and soulless speculators" are trying to create "a false demand" for dollars as a "venue for investment."

An objective and realistic look at the recent events, however, seems to show that the real factors behind the precipitous fall in the rial's exchange value should be traced to: (1) a mistaken belief in the high value of the national currency as an economic *desideratum*; (2) a series of wrongheaded economic policies pursued by the Ahmadinejad administration to deal with both inflation and unemployment; (3) the perseverant pursuit of a national nuclear power policy, inviting the West's wrath and resulting in a series of hardening economic sanctions; and (4) significant loss of public confidence in the government's ability to support the official exchange rate in the face of external pressures.

The "strong currency" myth

The strength of the national currency and the high exchange value of the rial has always been more of a political, rather than a monetary or market phenomenon, in Iran. A strong rial, in the eyes of both the man in the street and the seasoned politicians, has always been a clear sign of economic vigor, and a symbol of political power and prestige. The intensity of faith in this myth has also been related to the believers' economic literacy. Keeping the dollar/rial rate deliberately (and artificially) low, while one of the clearest economic policy mistakes of the past decade, is still widely demanded and revered. A current Persian website—Asr-e Iran—nostalgically laments that while the Iranian national currency unit—the *Shahi*—was equal to one shilling or one-twentieth of the English pound in the 16th century, the value of today's rial is officially equal to 1/19,500 of the British pound and its free market rate is as little as 1/30,000.

Due to the pervasive influence of this myth, there were neither any effective business demands, nor any urgent political will, to adjust the exchange rate to its proper level after the 2002 rate unification—although all leading economic indicators warranted such realignment. There were faint voices of advice by private economists, and desperate pleas by disadvantaged exporters for the rate adjustment. The first group was contemptuously ignored by the authorities, and the second was partly silenced through the so-called "export prizes" and subsidies.

Neglecting realities

Handicapped by the nostalgic feeling about the high national currency value, and obsessed by certain "out-of-the-box" economic convictions, President Ahmadinejad began his tenure in 2005 by following a populist and welfare-oriented economic policy, promising to "put the oil money on everyone's table." His economic agenda included: (a) an expansionist fiscal policy aimed at "eradicating poverty"; (b) a distinctly overvalued rial to reduce import costs; (c) a mandatory low interest rate policy to minimize capital costs of business; and (d) the use of bank loans, bond issues, and the sale of state enterprise to finance budget deficits—instead of tax hikes or more efficient tax collection.

The expansionist binge began with: (i) extensive and poorly supervised loans to the so-called "quick-return projects" in order to increase employment; (ii) an immense nationwide housing project (*maskan-e-mehr*) to increase home ownership; (iii) hundreds of half-baked local development projects to satisfy the crowds who greeted the president on his countrywide tours; and (iv) a "subsidies reform program" involving monthly cash payments to nearly the entire population to make up for higher energy and bread prices. As a result, the national budget rose from IR1,590 trillion in 2005 to IR5,100 trillion in 2011—or more than three times in seven years. With annual budget deficits running at more than 4% of gross domestic product (GDP) each year, total liquidity rose from IR921 trillion in 2005 to IR3,720 trillion in 2011, or nearly fourfold.

Protracted budget deficits and liquidity expansion during 2005–11 caused the average official cost of living index to rise by nearly 17% a year—with the most conservative private estimate showing 22%. During the same period, Iran's main trading partners had price increases of 2–4% a year. By a simple calculation, the difference between Iran's cumulated inflation during the seven-year period compared with those of its trade partners would have warranted some 90% devaluation of the Iranian rial. In actuality, the exchange rate only rose from $1 = IR9,025 in 2005 to $1 = IR10,445 before the December crash, or a total correction of less than 16%. Thus, the government not only ignored the facts; it also violated the clear mandates of both the Fourth and Fifth Economic Development Plans, requiring annual adjustments of the rial's exchange rate in line with the differences between domestic and foreign inflation rates. Curiously enough, in December 2010, while announcing his subsidies reform program, President Ahmadinejad asked the head of the CBI to come up with a new and "realistic" exchange rate in view of Iran's "ample foreign exchange reserves"—an order which some of his aides at the time interpreted to mean revaluing the rial towards $1 = IR5,000!

The same incongruous treatment greeted the government's regulations of bank interest rates. During the first six years of the Ahmadinejad administration, the authorized interest rate on short-term savings deposits frequently trailed the annual inflation rate, eroding the net value of the depositors' wealth. The maximum interest rate (called "profit share" to comply with Islamic principles) payable by commercial banks on short-term (less than five years) deposits during 2005–10 averaged 13% per annum, while the corresponding inflation rate registered 17–22%. In the highly inflationary year 2008, the negative spread reached 10%. As a result, there was a steady decline in the growth of savings deposits during the entire period. Despite these warning signs, however, and even ignoring the mandates of the Fifth Economic Development Plan (2010–15), requiring periodic adjustments of the deposit rates in line with the inflation rate, the Council on Money and Credit, chaired by the president, refused to budge. Even when faced with continued turmoil in the exchange market in early January 2012, the Council (in the absence of the president) allowed interest rates paid on savings deposits to be left at the individual bank's discretion (in order to divert liquidity from gold and dollars markets). The decision was vetoed once the president returned from a foreign trip. It was only after strong public pressures that on 25 January 2012 the president finally approved the rate adjustments.

President Ahmadinejad's third gamble with the teetering economy was to fight a virulent and cumulative inflation with the wrong weapon. Instead of controlling consumer prices through conventional means, e.g. balancing the budget, raising interest rates, reducing bank borrowings, controlling liquidity, or raising factor efficiency, he chose the easy way. Blessed by the best six years of oil export receipts from Iran's 106-year-old oil industry, he opened the import floodgates. Iran's revenues during the first six years of the Ahmadinejad administration reached $560bn, compared to only $433bn by all the eight previous governments since the 1979 revolution. In the same six years, imports amounted to $330bn—three times those of the Khatami and Rafsanjani administrations. Yet, during the same six-year period, the government debt to the banking system rose from IR113 trillion to IR403 trillion—or nearly fourfold. The pernicious policy of trying to fight domestic inflation through cheap imports required the rial to be kept highly overvalued.

Sanctions as catalyst

The Islamic Republic's nuclear development program has been the third factor in the exchange rate drama. Widespread suspicion in the West regarding the ultimate objective of Iran's uranium enrichment activities initially led the United Nations Security Council to issue four consecutive sanctions resolutions. And the move was subsequently followed by the US, the European Union and others. Thus, the original "targeted" and "smart" penalties gradually morphed into the current "crippling" restrictions. They currently consist of stiff and extensive restrictions on travel, trade, banking, finance, shipping, insurance, investment, and transfers of nuclear technology involving hundreds of individuals, businesses, and agencies associated with the Tehran government. Their sole objective has been to dissuade Iran from pursuing its nuclear program—a program which Tehran claims to be for purely civilian energy research and production, but the "sanctioneers" suspect it to involve certain military objectives and possibly even nuclear weapons ambitions.

Although the current sanctions have not targeted the exchange rate in any direct way, their indirect impact on the rate's movement has been notable. While the rial's equilibrium exchange rate was due for a substantial correction and for a long time, the plunge would not have occurred without a catalyst. The currency could still have remained out of equilibrium for a while thanks to rising oil export earnings. The trigger for the precipitous plunge was supplied by the news of forthcoming new crippling American and European sanctions in early December 2011—particularly the oil embargo. The exchange market was visibly rattled. And, on 31 December, when US President Barack Obama signed into law the new (and unprecedented) sanctions involving Iran's Central Bank, the exchange dam burst, and the downward movement began.

In the same vein, while negative interest rates on bank deposits were not unique to the Ahmadinejad administration, and never a lever for a game change, two specific factors related to sanctions heralded a dynamic change. The first was a shift in the investment climate, shaken by the threatening sanctions. Prior to 2010, when there was relative political calm, the real estate market was flourishing, and rising liquidity would flow into land, apartment building, and the Tehran Stock Exchange. With the news of ominous times ahead, the funds started to invade the gold and foreign exchange markets as far safer and better havens. The second factor was a bewildering and untimely decision by the Council on Money and Credit, aimed at compensating the effects of sanctions, to lower short-term interest rates from 16% in 2008 and 13% in 2009, down to 11% in 2010 and 10% in 2011, at the very time that consumer prices had begun to rise from 12% towards 22%!

Loss of market confidence

The fourth factor in the rial's declining value has been the loss of people's confidence in the CBI's ability to cope with the crisis. The bank officials' frequent empty promises, inadequate determination to follow declared policies, insufficient action to deal with the crisis, and inadequate supply of dollars to stem the growing speculative demand have all been major sources of popular disappointment. To wit, when the free market rate for the dollar dropped by more than 10% in less than a day in late December 2011, the CBI governor responded with a firm promise to bring it back even below the official rate. Yet nothing happened. On 5 January 2011, the bank ordered private exchange dealers to charge no more than IR14,000 for the dollar. The order was totally ignored. And the rate offered by the street vendors jumped to $1 = IR16,250. The governor said he had firm plans to stabilize the market, but it was not in the public interest to reveal them. On 25 January 2012, the governor said the four demerged exchange rates (reference, official free, travelers, and open market) would be unified in 48 hours, and there would be no limitation in the dollar supply for various current transactions. It proved to be an empty gesture. And there was mistake after mistake. For example, one of the reasons for the people's rush to buy dollars in the first days of the new year was their lack of confidence in the CBI's claim of ample gold and dollar reserves. Yet, instead of reducing this skepticism by showing resolve to meet all dollar demands, the Central Bank on 6 January 2012 cut the travelers' ongoing $2,000 allowance down to $1,000—thus reinforcing the people's conviction that the bank was running out of dollars. As a result, the public was convinced that due to hardening sanctions, Iran's oil exports would be drastically reduced, and higher oil prices caused by global tensions would not be enough to compensate for total receipts, thus, sooner or later, forcing the CBI to ration foreign exchange sale.

The ideal exchange rate

The hottest current economic issue in Iran is the proper exchange value of the rial in terms of the US dollar. In the absence of an objective determinant of the equilibrium exchange rate, suggestions about the right number abound. Private analysts, on the basis of rapid inflation and sluggish exchange rate adjustments in the last few years, argue for a rial devaluation towards the current free market rate of about $1 = IR19,000. Government officials, aware of the devaluation's effect on import costs and further domestic inflation, favor the opposite course and hope to bring the free market rate down towards the official rate. Traders are also divided on the basis of strict self-interest. Exporters and domestic producers of tradable goods are demanding a lower rial rate in order to become more competitive abroad. Importers, on the other hand, argue that since the bulk of Iran's imports consist of raw materials and semi-processed goods, a strong rial is in the national interest as it keeps down producers' costs. Anti-devaluation groups also argue that since Iran is dependent on imports for 30% of its food consumption, any upward adjustment of the exchange rate would add to the already high domestic consumer living costs. They similarly allude to the low price elasticity of both Iran's exports and imports as a significant disincentive for devaluation.

Private market analysts also argue for substantial devaluation, pointing to the fact that due to cheap dollars, Iran's imports have increased from $18bn in 2001 to more than $64bn in 2010 (not including payments of $19bn for services, and an estimated $20bn in smuggling). The latest imports roster, mostly from China, comprises items that have never been on Iran's import list. As a result, not only have traditional exporters been unable to compete in foreign markets due to the overvalued national currency, domestic producers have also lost their competitive power, gone bankrupt, or become packagers and handlers of foreign articles. Domestic industry has become increasingly hallowed.

Determining the right rate of exchange for the Iranian currency, however, is difficult due to the country's heavily oil-based economy, and the unpredictable effects of sanctions. Iran's oil industry—responsible for more than 85% of the country's annual foreign exchange earnings—is state-owned. The government is the sole arbiter of daily oil extraction, and the sole dispenser of oil export receipts (i.e. injection into the economy). The government's decision to sell more or less oil thus influences the exchange rate automatically. The small "free market" plays only a marginal role. In such a case, where the main provider of the foreign exchange is the treasury, and the major users of the foreign money are state enterprises, whatever rate the Central Bank might set would be arbitrary and not necessarily the "equilibrium" rate. The rate that is determined in the "free market" by private importers, travelers, students, smugglers, and capital movers is marginal. The free market's difference with the official rate at any given time is only indicative of the fact that the official rate is "out of range" and that the government is not willing (or able) to meet the entire "discretionary" demand.

Searching for the right exchange number

Already five months into the Persian New Year, there is still no clearly declared exchange rate policy by the CBI, and the dollar rate is drifting up and down with no clear direction. On 27 July 2012 the deputy director of Iran's Export Promotion Organization announced a "consensus agreement" among the CBI and other government agencies to divide the entire imports list into 10 main categories, with the first five (comprising a list of specific consumer staples and industrial necessities) eligible to receive dollars at the official rate, and the other five (discretionary and luxury items) supplied with the dollars earned from non-oil exports and other free market sources. The secondary market is closed, and foreign exchange at the official rate will now be sold only for travel to religious destinations.

A successful and orderly administration of such a complex exchange regime is highly difficult in normal times. It would be extremely complicated and hazardous in the present domestic economic conditions. Under the strain of biting sanctions, Iran's economy is experiencing an unprecedented anemic economic growth, disturbing double-digit inflation, worsening youth unemployment, falling oil output, reduced oil exports, and lower oil prices. GDP growth this year is estimated to be no more than 1%. Unemployment among 18–25-year-olds is officially 29.1%, with many analysts estimating much higher rates. Press reports point to a large portion of the production sector operating at half-capacity, with a wave of bankruptcies and business closures. The latest CBI data show wholesale prices up by 33.4% and the consumer price index by 22.4%, with certain food items (e.g. chicken, red meat, and milk) up by a staggering 30–80%. The Organization of the Petroleum Exporting Countries and other sources report Iran's daily oil production (the economy's lifeblood) at 2.9mn b/d, down from 3.9mn b/d last year. Oil exports (the country's main foreign exchange source) are reportedly at 1.2mn b/d, compared to 2.3mn b/d prior to the oil embargo. Oil export earnings (the annual budget's major source of income) are reduced considerably due largely to the European oil embargo, and partly to lower oil prices (from the record $126 per barrel in March to $96 per barrel in June). According to reliable estimates, the Islamic Republic needs a $117 per barrel price to finance its current fiscal budget, while market prices have lately been running at $105–111 per barrel.

The sanctions' role in these setbacks is coming to light as days go by. After years of defiantly denying the stiffening results of universal restriction, and in fact welcoming them as a spur to national self-sufficiency, a chorus of influential voices is now openly showing concern. Supreme Leader Ali Khamenei himself still remains defiant, and claims that Iran is currently "100 times stronger" than before, and that "Westerners" themselves have "vaccinated" the country against sanctions through their 30 years of censure—arguing that an oil-less, and knowledge-based economy could well resist any sanctions. But a growing group of top civilian and military leaders, Majlis lawmakers, and even high-ranking clergy show clear signs of unease and openly bemoan current economic hardships. President Ahmadinejad has recently acknowledged the serious financial impact of what he called the "toughest" measures ever imposed on the Iranian economy. The Minister of Industry and Trade has called them "devastating." The Majlis speaker has acknowledged the sanctions' share in the current plight.

The insoluble dilemma

The Central Bank's latest de facto acceptance of a multi-tiered official exchange regime has now reopened the old Pandora's Box of economic rents, appropriation of cheaper dollars to insiders, and widespread corruption—reminiscent of the 1980s as a major source of ill-gotten wealth for the Islamic Republic's current financial moguls. There are already press reports regarding industrial producers complaining about lack of access to the official rate, the necessity of bribing bank officials to receive cheaper dollars, and the growth of under-the-table deals. The current IR7,000 difference between official and free market rates, if continued, would promise to generate billions of new "rent" to materialize in the next few months sure to be grabbed by insiders.

However, despite strong verbal objections to the current multiple exchange system by certain influential groups in and out of the government, and strong popular demands for the return to currency unification, the dilemma continues insoluble. An early return by the CBI to a single rate around the current official rate would seem out of the question without prior easing of the crushing sanctions, e.g. the oil embargo and Central Bank operations. On the other hand, a more logical realignment towards the free market rate would also be nearly impossible at this juncture without first taming the intolerable high domestic inflation.

What seems certain is that in the next few months and beyond, the Islamic Republic is going to face its toughest and most troublesome economic challenge since the end of Iran–Iraq war, with unprecedented major headwinds. The fate of the rial also will, by more than any other factor, be directly tied to the course of Tehran's relations with the 5+1 group, and the resolution of the nuclear issue.

Note

* First published in the *Middle East Economic Survey*, August 6, 2012. Reproduced with permission.

10 Iran

The subsidy dilemma*

Iran's current "targeted subsidies," in effect monthly cash payments to almost all Iranian families, have led to a deficit of IR100 trillion ($3bn) over the last three years. The deficit continues to grow, and reform is urgently needed.

The issue of subsidies has once again become front and center for the Islamic Republic. Both the "moderate" Rohani administration and the "conservative" Majlis deputies have come to the conclusion that a substantial overhaul of the program is in order.

While the program's actual financial balance sheet (i.e. total income and expenditures) and the exact number of registered (and phantom) cash recipients are still murky and in dispute, its deficit is real and transparent.

According to a senior official in the Rohani administration, the program's current monthly payment obligations amount to IR35 trillion while its total revenues come to no more than IR18 trillion—with the shortfall being made up from other sources.

Background to reform

Iran's 2010 Subsidies Targeting Act (MEES, May 31, 2010) aimed at ending the 30-year-old across-the-board and costly practice of selling government-supplied energy, water, power, and other items to the public at below cost—often at as little as 20–25% of their international prices. This cost the treasury more than $25bn annually in cash, and close to $90–110bn in opportunity value. The law called for the gradual raising of prices to international levels over five years. Some 50% of the resultant savings to the treasury were to be paid back to consumers according to need in order to compensate for their higher expenditures; 30% was to go to energy-intensive industries to encourage innovation, and partially make up for their higher cost outlays; and the remaining 20% was to be kept by the treasury to cover the program's administrative cost.

Trouble from day one

The cash subsidy program's deficit started almost from day one. This outcome was not hard to predict, but it had not been anticipated for two basic reasons.

First, the actual cost of the program was grossly miscalculated in all its components: the potential number of welfare recipients; the magnitude of monthly cash payments to each individual; and the scope for potential cheating and fraud. Due to the statistical difficulty of identifying various income groups, and the relatively small number of rich people who voluntarily excluded themselves, the program's basic concept of "welfare for the poor" became a universal handout.

Similarly, while the monthly cash payment to individuals was rather meager at IR455,000 (compared to the legal minimum monthly wage of IR4.9mn), the total magnitude of cash outlays was not accurately assessed, and in retrospect, it was set too high. The number of potential recipients was also uncontrolled.

"Phantom" beneficiaries

The Rohani government has found that the number of current monthly welfare recipients is 77,000 more than the entire Iranian population of 77mn! These "phantom" beneficiaries—thought to include Afghan refugees, Iranians living abroad, and owners of forged identity cards—have received a total of IR56 trillion over the last three years.

The actual number of current "fake" recipients, however, must be more than 77,000 since the 77mn-plus reported recipients obviously still exclude a sizeable number of voluntary "unregistered" families and individuals choosing to be excluded, and a whole gamut of other "non-recipients" (e.g. homeless people and inhabitants of remote villages).

The second miscalculation involved the size of potential revenues from higher food and fuel prices. The income estimate was based on a set of static and symmetrical assumptions, with no regard to underlying demand elasticity. Thus, while average prices for all energy products, water, power, bread, and some other items were raised much higher than allowed by the statute, or expected by the legislature, the projected new revenues were still grossly overestimated. It was implicitly (and wrongly) assumed that higher energy and food prices would have little effect on consumer demand—ironically at the same time that higher prices were aimed at reducing waste and profligacy!

As the outlays grew larger, and the deficit mounted while revenues proved inadequate, the shortfall was temporarily financed by borrowing from the Central Bank of Iran (CBI) in the hope it would be "repaid" from subsequent higher receipts. Failing to receive the expected income, the share that was to have gone to the government (20%) was eliminated, and the industry share was drastically cut from the intended 30%. Faced with continued revenue shortfalls, consumers finally became the sole beneficiaries of the program in the second and third years of operation. The shortfall has been made up from various other sources including the sale of a state enterprise.

An interim assessment

The Subsidies Targeting Act of 2010 aimed at achieving both social justice and economic efficiency. As it turned out, it did neither. In actual implementation the new law was merely a change in form from universal commodity assistance to partial cash payments to all—a fact which again brings into question the rationality of involving the entire population in the government's largesse.

The program has also been presented to the public and the world as one recommended and endorsed by the World Bank. In reality neither the World Bank nor the International Monetary Fund recommended a specific program in their annual consultations with the Iranian authorities, but rather a general guideline. Based on the libertarian principle of "consumer sovereignty" these organizations' advice was that if you are going to give a person welfare assistance, it is more effective in the form of cash rather than commodities because the recipient will have total discretion as to how it is spent.

The current subsidy program, however, follows this theoretical principle only in name and not in spirit. In the program, the targeted cash recipients do not individually enjoy the intended "sovereignty" because the IR455,000 monthly assistance to each member of the family is placed at the disposal of the family head. Individual members (wife, children, and other dependents) have no "sovereign" control over their share. And there is no guarantee that the family head will behave in the best interest of his members. In fact, with some 2.5mn officially estimated drug addicts in the country, the chances of some being the head of a family (and therefore not competent to handle the family assistance) cannot be ruled out. The same would be the case with a family head being a gambler, a drunk, or suffering from similar afflictions.

The more deplorable aspect of the program, however, has not been its large deficit or its distributional shortcomings but its failure to achieve any of its major objectives: ending wasteful energy consumption, increasing energy efficiency, a fairer distribution of Iran's oil and gas bounty, improving industrial technology, reducing fuel smuggling, ending gasoline imports, and improved environmental protection.

Demand unrestrained

A cursory look at Iran's current consumption pattern shows that while fuel use was temporarily reduced after the initial price increases, no further reduction has occurred, and gasoline consumption is now back to its previous level. There has been no increase in industrial efficiency as the share of savings slated for industry was not fully paid. The poorest 20–30% of the population's share of national income may have slightly improved at first as a result of monthly cash receipts, but subsequent increases in inflation have erased the early benefits. Smuggling has returned. The environment has been further degraded: an international environmental protection ranking has seen Iran fall 36 places to 114 (of 132 countries) in the last few years.

The nearly $38bn spent on monthly cash payments over the last three years could have been used: (1) to complete 10,000-plus unfinished development projects, in particular in crucial natural gas exploration in the Persian Gulf; (2) to set up educational and training workshops to raise productivity; or (3) to establish an effective social safety net.

Tough remedy choices

To deal with the accumulated deficit and prevent further monthly shortfalls there are only two alternatives: either (1) cut the program's expenditure commitments (the size of monthly cash payments and/or the number of recipients), or (2) further raise the program's revenue source (fuel and food prices). However, cutting the number of cash welfare recipients would be politically hazardous, as it would undoubtedly lead to protests by those losing out. With nearly 40% inflation and close to 20% unemployment, new price increases would also be economic folly. That is why both the Ahmadinejad and Rohani administrations have refused to raise energy prices, although the 2013–14 budget law permits a 38% rise in order to deal with the deficits.

Leaning towards the second choice, the Majlis on 23 October voted in principle to eliminate the top 30% of subsidy recipients at the start of the 2014–15 Persian new year (in March 2014). The law gives the government three months to identify 23mn well-to-do cash recipients to be eliminated. This, however, has proven easier legislated than accomplished. The original Subsidies Targeting Act also required individual income categorization. And the task was attempted through several different measures—self-declaration of income, answers to income questionnaires, visits by state agents to individual residences—all to no avail. The government saw no other solution but a uniform monthly cash payment to all, including thousands of top-rated professionals and corporate executives with an annual income of half-a-million dollars or more!

Income categorization: mission impossible

Nothing has changed since. And income categorization remains a mission impossible. The magnitude of individual wealth and income in Iran has never been surveyed or known. Nor can it be easily and accurately ascertained.

In a country with no enforced income tax returns, no other reliable sources of income data, or easily assessable individual assets, the categorization and classification of cash recipients are an impossible task. According to a consensus among statisticians and accountants, the current sources of information at the government's disposal are in no way helpful in identifying the rich one-third. Current data collected by the CBI are focused on families' expenditures rather than incomes.

The identification of a limited number of rich people could of course be made on a case-by-case basis: high-salaried government employees, owners of prime real estate, drivers of luxury cars, CEOs, banks' key account holders and frequent travellers abroad, for example. But, the number will not reach 23mn. And, snooping into some of these sources of income (e.g. bank accounts or lifestyle) may involve gross violations of personal privacy.

Facing these difficulties, President Rohani, in submitting the 2014–15 budget to the Majlis on December 8, told the deputies that his administration has lost no time studying the flaws in the current welfare system, and that he intends to come up with a new plan for the management of subsidies in a comprehensive bill to be presented to the assembly next year. In the meantime, and until the new plan is put into operation, the current system will continue. Accordingly, the proposed 2014–15 budget appropriates IR388 trillion to pay IR455,000/month now to some 74mn citizens.

Rational alternative needed

By most criteria Iran is not an egalitarian society. The officially claimed Gini coefficient of around 4 indicates relatively acceptable income distribution, but all other evidence shows a different picture. In a recent Gallup poll, some 50% of Iranian respondents considered themselves "poor," i.e. not being able to feed their family from time to time. According to Iran's High Council of Elders, there are now 6mn old people in Iran of which 30% (1.7mn) live below the poverty line and are assisted by various charities. Another private study shows that the third of the population at the bottom of the income pole consumes only 15% of the national product, while the top third enjoys 60%—four times the share!

In a modern, civilized society facing this type of inequality, it is taken for granted that the clearly deprived segment of society—the real poor—should be helped through what is generally referred to as a social safety net. The Islamic government's across-the-board subsidies, in either price discount or cash payment forms, fail to meet the universal criteria of efficiency and equity. They also present many flaws from both a political and a psychological perspective.

From an equity standpoint, the inclusion of middle and high income earners in any subsidy program makes no sense. While a payment of $45/month or so to the truly poor (i.e. 50¢/day over the absolute poverty line) would presumably be of some help, an equal sum to the rich and the well-to-do may not even pay for a day's dog food! On efficiency grounds, across-the-board cash subsidies needlessly encourage increased consumption, and are patently wrong-headed in a country with relatively meager national savings and in desperate need of substantial investment to reduce unemployment. Encouraging increased consumption is also ideologically incompatible with a constitution which emphasizes frugality and parsimony as man's principal guide in life—a country whose leaders have been trying to establish an "Islamic" and frugal "consumption model" for years.

Across-the-board and indiscriminate cash distribution is also fraught with great political hazards. While the initiation of small monthly payments would receive a lukewarm welcome from recipients, their reduction or termination would be fought tooth and nail. The government can always give; but it can seldom take anything back. In fact, the greatest challenge for the Rohani government is how to cut, and ultimately to end, the current program. From a socio-psychological viewpoint too, equal monthly payments to the entire population would initiate, promote, and perpetuate a culture of dependence on the state instead of encouraging self-reliance and hard work. Creating one new, even minimum-wage, job for one family member would be more beneficial than giving 10 members a monthly welfare check.

A better alternative?

The past three years' experience with the Subsidies Targeting Program has clearly shown that the initiative, no matter how well-intentioned, has been neither equitable nor cost-effective in dealing with the basic problems of poverty and financial inequity. The program's equal treatment of rich and poor people has had no welfare or distributional merits. A program which was thought to be not only self-financing but also income generating has turned out to be a money-losing fiasco. Its burden on the treasury, substantial addition to inflation and high administrative costs have been far too high a price to pay for an arguably slight improvement in the absolute poor's living conditions.

Second phase

The program's "second phase"—slated to start in the Persian new year (2014–15), presumably after a satisfactory resolution to the current financial and distributional problems, should hopefully begin with a better outlook, structure, and financial support. To begin with, since the drastic devaluation of the rial over the last few months has once again widened the difference between domestic and world prices to pre-2010 levels, the current statute's provisions are already outdated, and a new price adjustment program must now be tried.

Under any such new scheme, the current gaps could be closed over the next five years by means of a 20%/year price hike. The proceeds from new higher prices could have two distinct and separate outlets.

The first portion could be earmarked for direct subsidies to the real poor at the exclusion of the majority of current beneficiaries. Currently, some 12mn people in Iran are considered poor. Of these, an estimated 6mn are now under the partial umbrellas of various welfare agencies (The Imam Khomeini Relief Committee, Behzizty Organization), or charitable *bonyads* (Mostazafan, Shaheed). They can easily be identified and included among the new subsidized groups.

The other 6mn eligible recipients for public assistance would be those who by sworn affidavit declare themselves to be below the official poverty line—under the threat of heavy legal penalties for false claims. These 20% lowest income earners should then be given the equivalent of $2/day in cash, or kind (food stamps, shelter coupons, etc.) as long as they remain in the "poor" category.

Broader safety net

A larger portion of the expected revenues could be earmarked for broader safety net projects.

With unemployment, underemployment and low wages being the main causes of poverty and deprivation, priority could be given to such endeavors as a more accommodating education system, labor training workshops, higher minimum wages, adequate unemployment insurance and more effective labor mobilization. Physical and mental impairments being other causes of poverty, a comprehensive health insurance system, adequate mobile health units, day care centers and accessible rehabilitation centers could receive priority. Pension funds should also be strengthened given rising numbers of old and infirm. Adult literacy classes to target the estimated 14% who are illiterate and improved public transport are other candidates.

These measures would be much more effective, less costly, more equitable and by far superior to the current monthly welfare checks.

Note

* First published in the *Middle East Economic Survey*, December 7, 2013. Reproduced with permission.

11 Ahmadinejad's legacy*

On 3 August 2013, the controversial and crisis-ridden eight-year tenure of President Ahmadinejad came to an end—leaving a sad legacy behind. This review intends to trace this legacy to its major causes.

Of the six politicians who served as president of the Islamic Republic between 1979 and 2013, none has been so mercilessly vilified by a multitude of his detractors, or so admiringly praised by his worshipful friends and acolytes, as Mahmoud Ahmadinejad. There is also no doubt that he has been both patriotic and well-meaning. What he did to the country and the economy clearly reflected the best of his knowledge and intentions. He was a true supporter of the poor and underprivileged. Yet his decisions and actions damaged the Iranian polity, society, and economy more than those of any other leader of the Islamic Republic.

A self-made man from a large working-class family with brief civil service as a provincial governor and a controversial tenure as the mayor of Tehran, he won a stunning presidential victory in 2005—trouncing four political giants, including a former two-times president and a pillar of the 1979 revolution.

This darkest of all dark horses managed to win another term in 2009, defeating a former wartime prime minister and a former speaker of the Majlis. The second victory, however, was marred by widespread accusations of vote-rigging and fraud. Massive street demonstrations protesting his election resulted in bloodshed, incarceration of peaceful protesters and the house arrest of his two main rivals. Facing this havoc, he still struck an arrogant, defiant and combative attitude, calling the protesters "weeds and debris." His second term also turned out to be crisis-ridden as he tangled openly with the Majlis speaker and the judiciary chief, was overridden by the Supreme Leader on several occasions, and steadily lost the full support of conservative Majlis deputies and hard-line newspapers.

As it ultimately turned out, he was to be the wrong man for the job. He lacked the proper dignity and maturity to handle his position, mismanaged the country's delicate and vulnerable economy, and adopted a needlessly belligerent and defiant position toward the West.

Personal values

As a product of hard-scrabble roots and a self-styled crusader for the poor and the disenfranchised, Ahmadinejad perceived economics as a handbook for distributing assets and income rather than primarily a source of income and wealth creation. A pious Muslim, he rejected all non-Islamic economic systems—capitalism, socialism and communism—as unjust, exploitative and oppressive. Consequently, he found the current personal and regional distribution of wealth and income in the global as well as the Iranian economy unfair, unjust and distorted. He also harbored an irrational personal and ideological grudge against banks and bankers, wishing to abolish interest payments and encourage non-interest banking institutions (*Qarzol-Hassaneh*). He distrusted big business, favoring small production units. He regarded inflation a result of higher production costs rather than a monetary phenomenon. Believing money to be the answer to every social and economic problem, he undertook an unprecedented expansionary monetary policy. He believed that the reform and reconstruction measures undertaken by his two predecessors had benefited some privileged segments of society and bypassed the masses. In particular, he thought that the oil money had been unjustly distributed. An ardent Iranian chauvinist and an Islamic zealot, he believed that the West's "geopolitical hegemony" (called "arrogance" in the Islamic Republic's lexicon) has to be challenged for both political and religious reasons.

Having caused a sea change in Iranian politics by besting four better-known, more experienced, more attractive, more qualified and more promising contenders, he was naturally expected to show a certain humility and to exhibit respect for the defeated elders and a willingness to consult with them. Instead, he took a defiant, condescending and dismissive attitude, repeatedly bragging about his more than 20 million votes and claiming to have a mandate for drastic change.

Management style

As a political neophyte with little managerial knowledge or experience but a huge ego and unbounded self-confidence, he confronted his formidable presidential tasks with a naive abandon. He adopted an informal, down-to-earth manner but micromanaged behavior, often in clear violation of statutory requirements. Convening cabinet meetings periodically in all of the country's 31 *ostans* (provinces), making hundreds of personal trips to different cities, answering millions of petitions from the rank and file, approving thousands of small development projects on the spot during his provincial trips exemplify his populist style.

The arbitrary selection of staff and bureaucratic cadres was another hallmark of his administration. Instead of considering expertise, experience and professional qualifications as criteria for choosing the government's top officers, he chose professional affinity, personal loyalty and total obedience. True to form, he methodically dismissed the technocrats assembled by his two predecessors and replaced them by commanders from the Islamic Revolutionary Guard Corps (IRGC) and the *basij* militia. At one time, 12 of his 18-member cabinet were from these two organizations; and when his administration ended, six ministers were still former military and security officers. By one estimate, the share of the IRGC in the economy increased 10 times during his tenure.

Adulation was his second major criterion for personnel selection. For example, a mid-level functionary who described him as "the third century's miracle-maker," and his *maskan-e-mehr* housing project as "the finest undertaking since Adam,"[1] was promoted to first vice president. A director of Iran's Tourist Organization who called him "Iran's golden opportunity," whose "audacity has now become universally recognized,"[2] became his chief of staff and number-one advisor. A professor in one of Iran's third-rate universities was made a cabinet minister, as he had supervised the president's doctoral thesis on traffic management. Ahmadinejad's dictatorial tendencies were another hallmark of his eight-year administration. Unquestioned acceptance of his decisions and faithful execution of his orders were prerequisites for holding major state positions. Failure resulted in quick dismissal.[3] A score of administrative and economic councils in charge of auxiliary decision making were dismembered in the first few months of his administration. And, most significantly, the Planning and Budget Organization, the purveyor of Iran's five-year development plans and preparation of fiscal budgets, was abolished and its duties transferred to the president's office.

Issuing ministerial decrees contrary to established Majlis statutes, refusing to execute legislation, hasty and ad hoc decisions with no prior preparation e.g., approving some 100 small projects in two hours on one of his provincial trips) and other such actions demonstrate his governing style.[4] One of his dismissed cabinet ministers describes him as an egotist who dismisses his critics, feels answerable to no one, places blame on others and belittles everyone around him.

He and his disciples have frequently bragged about his international reputation. One of his ardent devotees has called him "a unique and incomparable global leader."[5] He himself once said about his trips to various countries, "Everyone is eager to hear the Iranian people's message. The world is rapidly becoming Ahmadinejadized."[6] In a sense, no head of a government of the size and significance of Iran has been so well-known and talked about around the globe. He was the butt of jokes on late-night American comedy shows and a gift from heaven to cartoonists.

Economic approach

With the exception of Ahmadinejad himself and his small circle of friends and admirers, there is no analyst inside or outside of Iran who does not believe that the Iranian economy was grossly mismanaged, if not permanently damaged, during his administration. The extent and dimensions of this mismanagement, however, are hard to assess due to the official data that are deliberately withheld, camouflaged, doctored, falsified or contradicted by the agencies involved.[7] A recent report by the Majlis' Research Center refers to most of the 2005–13 official data as defective and misleading.[8] A Majlis deputy has asked for an independent governmental commission to review all data presented by the administration.[9]

After publishing cryptic and questionable data on basic economic indicators in his first term, the administration stopped releasing figures in 2008 on national income (GDP growth). Figures on inflation and unemployment released by the Central Bank and the Statistical Center have been contradictory and dubious. Figures on foreign-exchange reserves are labeled "confidential" and not published. Budget deficits are routinely camouflaged by counting borrowing as revenue. Due to these shortcomings, all arguments and conclusions made here must be treated with caution and are subject to necessary correction.

Ahmadinejad's eight-year economic record may be said to represent the soul of his presidency. He began his tenure with lofty rhetoric. Slave to unnecessary details, the new president initially announced four transcendental values, 14 basic objectives, and 58 specific proposals to improve the Iranian economy, the main popular concern.[10] True to his campaign promises, these values included justice, empathy, service to the people, and improvements in the country's material and spiritual conditions. The main objectives, however, included essentially justice: fighting against poverty, corruption, discrimination and nepotism; progressing toward an Islamic society; and observing justice, peace and dignity in international relations.

His repeated slogans of "justice, compassion, fairness and integrity" promising fair income and wealth distribution, increasing economic opportunities, and fighting corruption were welcomed by a large segment of the population. Passing as a champion of the poor and working classes, he called himself the people's "servant" (*nokar*) and defender of the "oppressed" (*mazloom*); both words signify a humbler and sharper connotation in Persian. He specifically promised to fight the "oil mafia," put oil money on everyone's dinner table, restore full employment within two years, and reduce the size of the government.

A confessed economic illiterate and proud of it, he once said, "Thank God that I do not know about economics."[11] He embarked on a number of misguided policies, ignoring all advice from independent economists and relying on his personal and ideological tendencies. Influenced perhaps by his austere childhood and regarding money as the key to every economic problem, he began with a highly expansionary program: increasing the fiscal budget, revving up the Central Bank's printing press, expanding bank lending, and removing every administrative barrier to his plans. He dismissed several Central Bank governors who abstained from monetizing the government's debt. According to a newspaper report, some 500 trillion rials were printed and put into circulation during Ahmadinejad's tenure.[12] At the same time, the government debt to the banks and the private sector during his tenure reached 1,800 trillion rials ($72 billion).[13]

The annual budget went up 5 percent above the inflation rate, from 1,590,000 billion rials in 2005 to 7,280,000 billion in 2013—4.5 times—with a deficit every year. Corresponding total liquidity increased from 92,000 billion rials to 5,300 billion—5.75 times. During the same period, the state sector's debt to the banking system went up from 236 trillion rials to 1,152 trillion. A fortuitous rise in oil-export receipts gave his administration some $700 billion, compared to $440 billion received by all previous administrations since the revolution, and five times the receipts between the discovery of oil in 1906 and the end of the Pahlavi regime in 1979.

Faced with protracted double-digit price rises from perennial budget deficits and rising debt to the banking system, Ahmadinejad decided to combat this demand-caused economic disequilibrium by focusing on the supply side. Thus, instead of trying to raise revenues or reduce wasteful expenditures, he chose a crowd-pleasing, short-term policy of controlling costs, with scant regard for its harmful long-term implications. To keep household and business expenses in check, the government proceeded to hold three vital cost factors—exchange rates, interest rates and basic energy prices—in check through government diktats. The outcome was a near disaster in all three areas.

Regarding a strong national currency as a symbol of affluence and prestige, the president pushed to keep the Iranian rial artificially high against the US dollar and other foreign exchanges when every economic indicator required the opposite policy. Keeping the exchange rate artificially overvalued in order to hold import costs down led to a number of troublesome consequences: (a) reducing domestic producers' ability to compete with foreign suppliers; (b) bringing down domestic production capacity of import-competing industries by some 30–40 percent; (c) idling thousands of workers with each additional billion dollars of imports; (d) worsening Iran's non-oil trade balance; and (e) giving hefty subsidies to foreign farmers and manufacturers. The overvalued exchange rate also resulted in increased national dependence on the world economy (even for essential food items) and capital flight. Thus, with the imposition of tough new sanctions on Iran's oil exports and its Central Bank operations, announced in late 2011, the Iranian rial lost two-thirds of its value against the dollar and other foreign exchanges. The subsequent era of exchange instability was ensured. Strangely enough, toward the end of his tenure, when the US dollar value of the Iranian rial was fixed by the Central Bank at around 10,000 rials and the inflation-adjusted equilibrium rate was estimated to be 24,000 rials, the president wished to bring the rate down to 5,000 rials.

The government's extensive interest rate regulation and mandatory lending was the second policy mistake. Holding interest rates on savings deposits below the inflation rate and keeping bank charges on commercial and investment loans below free-market levels in the bazaar inflicted immeasurable damage to the economy. Low (and negative) returns on deposits discouraged individual savings, stifled productive investments, and led savers to move their funds from bank accounts to outlets such as real estate, precious metals and US dollars. Losing savings deposits led the commercial banks to steadily borrow from the Central Bank for their voluntary as well as state-mandated loans. As a result, commercial bank debt to the Central Bank rose more than 13 times.[14]

Government-dictated loans to favored, but money-losing, projects have been a main cause of the banks' skyrocketing nonperforming assets—from a mere 70 trillion rials in 2005 to 700 trillion rials in 2013. Sizeable differences between mandated bank interest rates and the rates prevailing in the bazaar, combined with small penalties for late repayments of loans, induced some well-connected businessmen to borrow money from the state banks at rates in the low 20s, lend the borrowed sum in the bazaar at percentage rates in the 30s, and postpone repayment of the loans for years at an annual penalty of only 6 percent! Poor and unprofessional assessments of borrowers' proposed projects and the concentration of bank loans on a few selected mega borrowers were other causes of the banking system's problems. Nearly 8 percent of total bank loans are now reportedly in the hands of less than 12 percent of active businessmen.

Keeping energy prices artificially down for years resulted in profligate energy consumption, the continuation of energy inefficiencies, the rise of energy intensive industries vulnerable to external shocks, and a growing need for energy imports, severe air pollution and a clear rise in energy smuggling to neighboring countries.

The outcome of this rank mismanagement has been well reflected in the behavior of the main economic indicators. The GDP growth of 6.9 percent in 2005 gradually tapered off year after year, ending the last two years of the Ahmadinejad administration (2011 and 2012) in negative territory, at –1.7 percent and –5.4 percent, respectively,[15] for an average annual growth of 3 percent during the whole period. Even this modest growth was achieved at a very high cost. For each 1 percent of growth during the Khatami administration, the government had invested $5.4 billion,[16] while the Ahmadinejad administration spent $8.2 billion.

Data on various aspects of employment (and unemployment) are among the least comprehensive and reliable published by the administration. The official unemployment rate reportedly rose from 11.5 percent in 2005 to 12.2 percent in 2013, with more than 3 million people out of jobs. The figure for the 15–24 age group was at the critical level of 27 percent. Unofficial figures indicate 20 percent of the total labor force looking for work; with 5 million youths entering the job market now, the country will soon be faced with 8 million seeking employment. Official figures from the Statistical Center further show that participation in the labor force declined from 41 percent in 2005 to 37.3 percent in 2012. In short, only about 68,000 jobs were created each year from 2005 to 2012; about 34,000 annually have been added to the unemployed.[17] Despite the president's officially expressed sentiment regarding women (e.g., the first president to nominate three women for his cabinet), women's participation in the labor force was at best 17 percent. Female unemployment actually doubled during the period, in addition to women being subject to discrimination in wages, promotion and tenure.

The official consumer-price index of 10.4 percent in 2005 began to rise steadily year after year, surpassing 40 percent—the world's third highest—in the summer of 2013, when Ahmadinejad's term ended. Private estimates of the price rise were consistently higher. Significantly responsible for the steady rise in liquidity and consumer prices were the president's three signature projects—financed primarily by the Central Bank's new money creation: (1) loans to the so-called "quick returns" projects to create 2 million jobs; (2) low-cost housing in the periphery of large cities; and (3) the controversial cash-payment-based subsidies reform.[18] All three are considered failed schemes. The housing project alone, according to the current housing minister, has been responsible for 40 percent of the new liquidity.

To combat inflation, instead of balancing the budget, reducing bank lending and controlling liquidity, Ahmadinejad opened the import gates for cheaper competing products. Thus, of the nearly $700 billion in oil-export revenue received during his eight-year tenure—63 percent of all oil income during the last 108 years—some $440 billion was spent on imports, raising yearly purchases from $36 billion to $60 billion. The outcome, while benefiting low-income groups through decreasing prices, was the destruction of domestic industries. At the same time, precious foreign exchange received from the export of a depleting resource, instead of being reinvested to produce new wealth, was squandered in the import of petty consumer goods.

The government claims that, as a result of its populist projects, the Gini coefficient of income distribution improved. Although denied by other reports, even if it were true, relative poverty did not diminish, and still over 20 percent of the population languished in poverty.

On top of these policy errors, Iran's economy experienced a sea change during Ahmadinejad's tenure in the direction of economic militarization—comparable to the Indonesian and Egyptian cases. Already suffering from a large and inefficient state sector, it moved further in that direction, despite earlier promises to reduce it. Initiated and supported by Ahmadinejad himself, the IRGC rapidly took over an increasing segment of the Iranian economy.

The Khatamol-Anbia Corporation, and its sister, Khatamol-Ossia, the engineering arms of the IRGC, gradually became the largest and richest domestic contractors, spreading their wings over such sectors as oil, gas, petrochemicals, industry, mines, road building, irrigation and dam construction, Curiously enough, as the UN, US and EU economic sanctions primarily targeted the Corps, they all inadvertently helped it to grow by overtaking the work of foreign contractors and by becoming the country's number-one smuggler.

And, despite frequent promises to reduce the government's role in the economy, and the budget's reliance on oil revenues, the opposite occurred in both cases. Recent information shows that the much-trumpeted program of privatization during Ahmadinejad's tenure was really a sham: only 17 percent of the state enterprises were sold to the true private sector, and 83 percent were taken over by the semi-public agencies.[19]

Foreign relations

In the foreign arena, just as Western frustration with the slow pace of negotiations on Iran's nuclear program was building, and the Islamic Republic needed an experienced and astute leader to handle the situation, the opposite occurred. A narrow-minded Islamic fanatic, who had never traveled outside Iran and was reflexively anti-Western, took the helm. Although not directly involved in the conduct of nuclear negotiations with the P5+1 group, his attitudes inflicted irreparable damage to Iran's position. By being combative and provocative, and by repeatedly denying the Holocaust, he raised the ire of the civilized world and made it impossible for the Islamic Republic to pursue a serious foreign policy. Oddly enough, toward the end of his tenure, he called his blatantly and damaging statement about Holocaust one of the "greatest achievements of his presidency"; he had raised "a taboo topic that no one in the West allowed to be heard" and thus "broke the spine of the Western capitalist regime"![20]

Enormously ambitious and highly self-confident, though a novice in diplomacy and foreign policy, Ahmadinejad lowered the international prestige of Iran had gained during the Khatami administration. He forged an unholy alliance with a number of small, poor and wayward countries in Latin America and Africa against Washington, further contributing to Iran's isolation and negative image. His fruitless confrontational pronouncements caused irreparable damage to Iran's national interest. And, by assuming the role of Western "provocateur-in-chief" pursuing confrontation with Washington, the EU and the UN,[21] he triggered one economic sanction after another, undermined Iran's global standing, and ultimately turned it into a pariah state. Meaningless statements like "we do not need the world, the world needs us" caused nothing but problems. Iran's relations with Bahrain, Yemen, Lebanon and Saudi Arabia badly deteriorated due to Tehran's support of Shia minorities in those countries.

A Sui Generis phenomenon

By all indications, Ahmadinejad is intelligent, informed and politically astute. He often brags about his advanced education and his doctorate. He writes and speaks eloquently in Farsi. He is a master of debate.[22] Yet some of his statements and proposed projects not only defy explanation,[23] but also smack of delusion:

- The Holocaust did not happen; it was a pretext by Western governments to justify the establishment of the Zionist regime.

- The September 11 tragedy in Washington and New York was orchestrated by Washington to combat US economic recession, a fact accepted by the majority of American people and most nations around the world.
- The West created HIV in order to plunder Africa.
- Our Western enemies are preventing rain-bearing clouds from coming our way, causing drought.
- One of our 13-year-old students has been able to generate nuclear power in her basement. We have a sorcerer who, getting inspiration from the saints, can point to various mines by looking at the grass.

Equally astonishing have been some of his pet proposals. In a country with scant rainfall, frequent drought and water rationing, he proposed to give every citizen 2,000 meters of land for a vegetable garden to grow vegetables and sustain himself. When he was reminded of the paucity of water for such a venture, he said, "God never created a land without enough water for it!" In a country already importing 30 percent of its food, he proposed that Iran's prize-winning population-control program be abandoned and that the government encourage every family to have four to six children, as the country could afford to sustain 150 million people.

A sorrowful finish

Ahmadinejad's administration came to an end without even a whisper. There were no celebratory parties, no appreciative demonstrations, no praise of his tenure. Members of the new government have taken turns to point out his misdeeds. At a birthday party organized for him a few weeks after leaving office, only 70 people showed up. He has shunned public speaking since then. The only faint praise of his services has come from Supreme Leader Khamenei, who had backed him all along and found the ex-president's ideas close to his own. At the last meeting of his cabinet with the *Rahbar* in mid-July 2013, Ayatollah Khamenei did praise his government for its "accomplishments", particularly for propagating and illuminating "revolutionary slogans."[24]

Ahmadinejad's spectacular fall from grace is best portrayed in his treatment at the hands of the most conservative newspaper, *Kayhan*, which normally reflects the views of the Supreme Leader. The lead editorial, which had initially labeled his administration "the most beloved government" since the Islamic revolution, changed its tune. On Tuesday, April 23, 2013, it called the outgoing president "a coward, a bluffer and insincere."

Notes

* First published in *Middle East Policy*, Vol. XX, No. 4, Winter 2013. Reproduced with permission.

1 *Kayhan* (London), July 17, 2013.

2 *Kayhan*, May 8, 2013.

3 www.radiofarda.com, August 3, 2013.
4 A long list of specific examples may be found in Radio Farda's Persian broadcast, August 3, 2013.
5 *Kayhan*, May 8, 2013.
6 Inter Press Service News Agency, November 30, 2006.
7 www.jomhourieslami.com, September 21, 2013.
8 www.jomhourieslami.com, August 30, 2013.
9 www.radiofarda.com, July 22, 2013.
10 For the full list, see *Iran Economics*, September 2005.
11 Vision of the Islamic Republic of Iran Network (TV), August 14, 2006.
12 www.radiofarda.com, October 4, 2013.
13 http://payvand.com, October 23, 2013.
14 www.radiofarda.com, October 24, 2013.
15 www.radiofarda.com, September 7, 2013.
16 www.jomhourieslami.com, October 14, 2013.
17 www.radiofarda.com, September 28, 2013.
18 For detailed discussions of this program, see the *Middle East Economic Survey*, May 31, 2010, June 20, 2011, January 30, 2012, and December 14, 2012.
19 www.jomhourieslami.com, November 7, 2013.
20 Speech quoted in *Iran Times* (Washington, DC), July 12, 2013.
21 His reckless rhetoric denying the Holocaust and casting doubts about the perpetrators of the September 11 attack induced Washington to marshal a universal condemnation of Iran's position.
22 For a fuller description of his character, see Jahangir Amuzegar, "The Ahmadinejad Era," *Journal of International Affairs* 60, no. 2 (March 2007).
23 For a list of these and similar statements, see radiofarda.com, April 20, 2013.
24 www.radiofarda.com, August 1, 2013.

12 Nuclear Iran

Perils and prospects*

On April 11, 2006, Iran's president, Mahmoud Ahmadinejad, proudly and triumphantly announced that the Islamic Republic had joined "the club of nuclear countries." Calling it "a very historic moment" of epochal significance, he said that Iranian scientists had succeeded in enriching uranium in a pilot test, thus paving the way for the enrichment process to proceed on an industrial scale. God willing, he added, Iran would soon be self-sufficient in nuclear fuel for its power plants.[1] Worldwide reporting of this claim within hours was the culmination of the global media's almost daily coverage of Iran's nuclear activities over the last three and-a-half years. Since the summer of 2002, when the world learned for the first time that the Islamic Republic had a secret nuclear plant to enrich uranium, stories about Iran's "nuclear ambitions" have been a regular feature of world news. One upmanship in getting tough with the Islamic Republic has transcended US neocon think tanks and pro-Israeli action committees to become a campaign issue for potential Democratic and Republican candidates in the 2008 presidential race. President Ahmadinejad's colorless attire and colorful fulminations against the United States and Israel have provided additional fodder for commentators. Yet the Tehran government's real motives for its nuclear program, its ultimate ability to pursue advanced nuclear technology and the program's potential consequences remain unknown, not only to the public at large, but also to the monitoring agency's seasoned experts.

Iran's nuclear dossier, currently before the UN Security Council for ultimate resolution, contains a tangled web of bilateral and regional issues involving mainly Washington and Israel, with some peripheral global implications. This paper attempts to (1) trace the background of Iran's nuclear program; (2) review Iran's dealings with the International Atomic Energy Agency (IAEA) and the Security Council; (3) explore Iran's presumed motives for seeking nuclear weapons; (4) underline the international community's objections to a nuclear-powered Iran; (5) gauge the time frame deemed necessary for Iran to acquire a deliverable bomb; (6) identify the Security Council's options in dealing with a defiant Tehran government; and (7) evaluate the "ultimate recourse" to deal with Iran's nuclear capability. The last section will try to highlight the real and hidden agenda behind the issue and possible hopes for its resolution.

From alliance to enmity

Despite its diverse aspects, Iran's "nuclear case" is essentially a dispute instigated, developed, orchestrated and brought before the UN Security Council by Washington on behalf of itself and Israel. In its barest essence, Iran claims that it is legally entitled under the Nuclear Non-Proliferation Treaty (NPT) to enrich uranium for civilian use and that nuclear-powered electricity would release its oil and gas reserves for higher value-added purposes. Washington claims that Iran's program is a cover for making a bomb and that, on a small scale, nuclear energy would not be cheaper. Above all, since Tehran has for nearly two decades deceived the nuclear watchdog agency about its activities, it has lost whatever legal rights it once enjoyed. President George W. Bush has declared the Islamic Republic part of "an axis of evil," and a "great national security concern" for the United States, but also a regime "bent to destroy our ally Israel."[2] In a March 20, 2006 speech in Cleveland, the president said, "Iran's stated objective is to destroy our strong ally Israel; it's a threat, in essence, to a strong alliance. I made it clear, I'll make it clear again, that we will use military might to protect our ally, Israel."[3] The influential Senator John McCain told the Brussels forum in late April 2006 that "the United States would not stand by and let Iran wipe out Israel."[4] Secretary of State Condoleezza Rice has said, "We may face no greater challenge from a single country than from Iran whose policies would be 180 degrees different than the Middle East we would like to see developed."[5] The US National Security Strategy issued on March 16, 2006, identifies Iran as the "single country" that may pose the biggest danger to the United States.[6] The supreme irony in Washington's spirited objections to Iran's nuclear program is that Tehran is now being castigated for trying to master the very same art that the United States encouraged the shah's government to acquire. Iran's initial nuclear program started in the mid-1950s, when Mohammad Reza Shah signed a civilian "atoms for peace" agreement with the Eisenhower administration and later received an American research reactor for the Tehran Nuclear Research Center. The shah's government signed the NPT in 1968 and ratified it in 1970. Iran's subsequent intention to establish a nuclear-energy capability for electric-power generation, in turn, dates back to the aftershocks of the 1974 oil-price explosion, when the shah argued that oil was a "noble" commodity worthy of use in higher-value products. Iran's Atomic Energy Organization was created with the explicit task of replacing oil and gas for power generation. In the same year, an American firm, the Stanford Research Institute, was hired by the Iranian government for assistance in the design and construction of nuclear plants. The monarch wanted to construct 20 nuclear power stations capable of producing 2,000 MW of electricity by the year 2000.

The current program was thus born nearly 50 years ago with the full consent and support of the United States, not only endorsed but encouraged by Washington. President Gerald Ford offered the shah a full nuclear cycle in 1976. The Ford team—including many senior officials in the present Bush administration who are now opposed to even a limited uranium-enrichment capacity—reportedly approved the deal for a complete nuclear fuel cycle. US companies offered atomic reactors capable of regenerating fissile materials on a self-sustaining basis to the shah's government for sale, albeit without the uranium enrichment capabilities sought by Tehran today.[7] As the first installment of a 20-MW power grid, a light-water reactor was started at Bushehr on the Persian Gulf with the help of Germany's Siemens AG in the late 1970s.

After the revolution, the Bazargan government hastily abandoned the program as costly and wasteful. Ayatollah Khomeini's supporters now claim that he believed weapons of mass destruction were "immoral." By 1987, for reasons that remain unclear, the wartime Mussavi government decided to restart the project. The unfinished plant, however, had been badly damaged by Iraqi bombardment, and Germany declined to resume the work or even supply the original blueprints. Tehran then approached Moscow for help. Russia agreed to undertake the job of finishing the plant by 1995, including initially a centrifuge unit with fissile-material capabilities. The Russian deal called for supplying the Bushehr plant with nuclear fuel for ten years and required Iran to allow the IAEA to monitor and observe the safeguards protocol. The 30-year-old plant is still unfinished.

A trust needing verification

After the resumption of nuclear development in the late 1980s, the Islamic Republic's top leadership openly, repeatedly and unequivocally stated that Iran's sole objective is to enrich uranium at low levels to obtain fuel for its nuclear power plant. Supreme Leader Ayatollah Khamenei and ex-presidents Rafsanjani and Khatami reiterated that nuclear weapons were against Iran's political and economic interests, as well as its Islamic beliefs.[8] President Ahmadinejad, in his turn, has added that "a cultured, learned, rational, and civilized" nation such as Iran "does not need nuclear weapons; only those who want to solve all problems by force do."[9] Washington, however, has insisted all along that Iran's "peaceful" program is in reality a cover for the ultimate development of nuclear weapons and a threat to its interests in the region as well as Israel's security and survival.[10] In August 2002, the National Council of Resistance—officially, a front for the outlawed exile opposition group Mojahedeen Khalq but, in fact, the recipient of information from anti-regime groups in the region—stunned the international community. It claimed that the Islamic Republic had a secret "nuclear weapons" facility at Natanz, 150 miles southwest of Tehran. Satellite photographs in December 2002 subsequently confirmed the existence of the site. To assuage suspicion about Iran's nuclear ambitions, Tehran invited IAEA inspectors in February 2003 to examine all nuclear facilities for an extended period, and succeeded in obtaining a report in November 2003 stating that the nuclear watchdog agency found no evidence of nuclear-arms activities. Furthermore, in December 2003, Iran signed the Additional Protocol to the NPT, allowing unannounced and more intrusive inspections by IAEA agents. In June 2004, a mysterious laptop, allegedly stolen from a targeted Iranian asset, reportedly showed a test shaft and drawings tangentially related to missile modifications and a nuclear weapons program, but without any reference to such a plan. Tehran called the documents forgeries, and there was no independent authentication.[11] However, further investigations revealed that, as far back as 1987, Iran had started clandestine negotiations with Pakistani nuclear scientist A.Q. Khan for the purchase of nuclear equipment, drawings and centrifuge components.

The Bush administration found these startling revelations to be a golden opportunity to demand that Iran's violations be referred to the Security Council as a threat to international peace and security. Failing to muster a consensus for the move, Washington reluctantly agreed to let a European trio—France, Germany and the United Kingdom—carry out the task of persuading Iran to cease its suspicious nuclear activities. As part of the understanding with the Europeans under the so-called Paris Agreement of November 2004, the Tehran government agreed to voluntarily suspend all uranium enrichment and related activities while negotiations were in progress. On August 1, 2005, the United Kingdom, Germany and France offered their "package" of incentives, including their own security assurances, further economic cooperation, and a guaranteed supply of fuel for electricity reactors. In exchange, Iran had to forego permanently production of fissile material used in nuclear weapons.[12] The Tehran government immediately rejected the so-called "implementation document" as vague and embellished with minor incentives to be exchanged for Iran's permanent abandonment of an "inalienable right." Shortly afterward, Iran announced the resumption at Isfahan of uranium conversion, i.e., turning yellow cake into a gas that could be further purified and used as a fuel in nuclear reactors and ultimately converted into nuclear weapons. As the face-off with the EU-3 continued, President Ahmadinejad's fiery speech before the UN General Assembly on September 17, 2005—mentioning a "nuclear apartheid" and insisting that Iran would develop fuel-cycle technology regardless of the West's concerns—brought the confrontation to a boil. An informal bill of indictment by three European foreign ministers, published as an op-ed in the *Wall Street Journal*, tried to demonstrate Iran's unacceptable behavior since the Paris Agreement.[13] On September 24, 2005, the IAEA board of governors found Iran in violation of the NPT and voted to report it to the Security Council, ending Tehran's relentless efforts to prevent such a move. The resolution cited "the absence of confidence" that Iran's program was exclusively for peaceful purposes. There were 21 votes in favor, one against and 12 abstentions, including most prominently Russia and China, at whose insistence the actual time of referral to the Council was left open. Tehran denounced the decision as part of the political vendetta initiated by Washington,[14] and, as had already been threatened, the IAEA ordered its inspectors to remove agency seals from the nuclear-enrichment facility at Natanz. The move thus virtually ended the agreement Iran had voluntarily signed with the European trio 16 months earlier.

An IAEA report issued at the end of January 2006 said it had found evidence suggesting a link between Iran's officially peaceful nuclear-research program and its military work on high explosives and missiles under a so-called Green Salt Project.[15] The report was the first such declaration by the agency, which had repeatedly refused to back Washington's claim that at least some of Iran's nuclear activities had links to a military project. Furthermore, in late January 2006, Iran turned over a raft of documents requested by the IAEA for years, including a 1987 offer from A.Q. Kahn detailing the use of nuclear-weapons components. Iranian officials told UN inspectors that the 15-page document was part of the Pakistani network's package and that Tehran had made no use of its contents.

Iran's abrogation of its voluntary agreement with the EU-3, the breaking of IAEA seals and removal of its cameras, and the reopening of its enrichment plant at Natanz resulted in Washington's call for an emergency meeting of the IAEA board of governors. Ahmadinejad's inflammatory speeches calling the Holocaust a "myth" and wishing to "wipe Israel from the world map" stoked international fury and united the West against Tehran. On February 4, 2006, a solid majority of the governing board of the IAEA decided to report Iran's 16 specific NPT violations to the Security Council. The decision marked the end of years of calculated efforts to avoid being referred to the Security Council, thanks to the new government's belligerence.[16] The European-drafted and carefully worded February 4 resolution was passed by a vote of 27 to three with five abstentions. Only Cuba, Syria and Venezuela voted against it. The resolution was particularly welcome by Washington because it had the signatures of both Russia and China, which had abstained in September 2005. In the resolution, Iran was directed to take three actions to avoid potential sanctions: (1) resume its suspension of all enrichment and reprocessing activities (i.e., shut down its centrifuge facility at Natanz); (2) ratify the Additional Protocol to the NPT and give IAEA inspectors free rein for spot inspections; and (3) fulfill pending requests of the IAEA inspectors regarding documents, workshop visits and interviews with Iran's atomic scientists. In addition, the Islamic Republic was asked to "reconsider" its plans to build a heavy-water reactor at Arak. The Security Council, however, was to take no action until after the IAEA director general delivered a new assessment of Iran's cooperation, to be done by March 6, 2006. The IAEA board's nearly unified stand was reached after days of deliberations and a series of delicate compromises on the part of the 35 members. The final statement underscored a consensus between Washington, which had campaigned for nearly three years for an early and immediate referral, and the long-standing Sino-Russian resistance to any involvement by the Council, as well as to what President Vladimir Putin called "rash or erroneous moves."[17] Yet, while Secretary of State

Condoleezza Rice afterwards kept using the word "unity," Washington's victory was at best partial, if not Phyrric. For one thing, at Chinese and Russian insistence, Iran's dossier was *reported* and not *referred* to the Council, signifying a simple transfer of the case on an informational basis rather than a referral for possible immediate consideration and action. The Russians also blocked the resolution from including the word "noncompliance" by Iran, a phrase that under the IAEA's statute would imply specific legal consequences. Furthermore, Washington had to back down and accept a clause in the resolution referring to the goal of a nuclear-free zone in the Middle East (implicitly questioning Israel's nuclear weapons status).[18] Finally, the resolution delayed for another month any action by the Security Council until receipt of a new progress report by the agency's director general (before March 2006).

Prior to the February 4 resolution, Iran's chief nuclear negotiator asserted in a letter to the agency's director that a referral to the Security Council would mean the end of all voluntary compliance.[19] He also informed him that the government had decided to build 50,000 centrifuges at Natanz and begin full-scale production of enriched uranium if the case were referred to the Security Council. Faithful to this and frequent previous warnings, the Tehran government announced immediately after the IAEA vote that it would no longer observe the Additional Protocol.[20] In a televised speech commemorating the twenty-seventh anniversary of the Iranian revolution, President Ahmadinejad even darkly hinted of the possibility of Iran withdrawing from the NPT.[21] In a February 27, 2006, report to the IAEA board of governors, the director general said the agency "has not seen any diversion of nuclear material to nuclear weapons or other nuclear explosive devices." Yet, he added, the agency was not "in a position to conclude that there are no undeclared nuclear materials or activities in Iran."[22] The report listed a number of specific violations of the NPT by Iran, mainly failures to inform the agency about its nuclear work as required by the treaty. For example, Iran gave IAEA inspectors access to its Lavizan-Shian site only in January 2006, two years after the buildings were demolished, the site leveled and the earth moved. Tehran never allowed the agency to see all requested documents, visit workshops, interview scientists and operators involved in the programs, or visit certain buildings on its detailed list. Iran also declined to address or discuss matters related to the procurement of dual-use technologies, the design of missile-reentry vehicles, or documents related to centrifuge technology.[23] On the basis of this report,[24] the 15-member Security Council unanimously adopted a nonbinding statement on March 29, 2006, calling on Iran to suspend its nuclear-enrichment program within 30 days and return to negotiations with the IAEA. However, the first unified statement on the issue, considered by Washington as a breakthrough, did not commit the United Nations to any action against Tehran. Iran did not immediately offer a formal response, but declared that it did not accept "pressure or intimidation."[25] Despite its mild tone of apparent consensus, the agreement masked the persistent disagreement among the Council's five major powers: Russia and China wanted the issue to be handled exclusively by the Vienna watchdog agency, and the other three wished to bring the United Nations into action.[26] Two weeks later, Tehran openly defied the Council by announcing that its enrichment decision was "irreversible."

Iran's "nuclear ambitions"

Notwithstanding the Islamic government's repeated and emphatic denial of any intention to develop nuclear weapons, the IAEA's refusal to give Tehran a clean bill of health has now convinced more than two-thirds of the world that the Iranian nuclear program is a clandestine military nuclear scheme.[27] A reported statement by Iran's former chief nuclear negotiator that the lengthy talks with the European trio were, in fact, intended to "dupe" them while Iran completed the Isfahan facility added fuel to the fire.[28] The French foreign minister, Philippe Douste-Blazy, representing a country with long-standing and sizable commerce with Iran, expressed his concerns in the bluntest terms: "It's very simple: No civilian nuclear plan can explain Iran's nuclear program. Therefore, it's a clandestine military program."[29] Echoing his exasperation, Germany's chancellor, Angela Merkel, said, "We must prevent Iran from developing its nuclear activities."[30] Moscow and Beijing also talked on various occasions about the world's lack of confidence in the Iranian nuclear activities.[31] President Putin emphasized that Russia has a "very close position with England and the United States" in objection to Iran's nuclear bombs.[32] After years of silence, some Persian Gulf states also expressed worries about a nuclear Iran and called for tougher actions. Saudi, Jordanian and Kuwaiti officials similarly expressed worries about threats of environmental disaster in the region.[33] Nevertheless, Tehran's alleged guilt so far has largely been based on its *motivation* rather than actual *involvement* in an impermissible act. The West argues that Iran is sitting on top of 10 percent of the world's petroleum and 15 percent of its natural-gas reserves, and thus needs no nuclear power for decades to come. Iran's leadership routinely rebuts this argument by pointing out that other countries such as the United States, the United Kingdom, Russia and China all possess hydrocarbon resources and yet they all find it profitable to produce atomic energy.[34] They further point out that, at the current consumption rate, oil and gas reserves would soon be exhausted and have to be replaced by nuclear power, in which Iran wishes to be self-sufficient, rather than be dependent on unreliable allies or potential enemies. Yet, even on the *intention* score alone, many analysts find the West's charges based on uncorroborated evidence, questionable intelligence and unauthenticated documents. In the opinion of a seasoned analyst, the evidence collected in the three years since Iran was forced to admit having a secret uranium-enrichment program has been "often circumstantial, usually ambiguous and always incomplete," thus confounding efforts by policymakers, intelligence officials and US allies to reach a confident judgment.[35] Assuming, however, with *The Economist*, that Iran *must* be seeking nuclear weapons because "no one believes otherwise," three questions emerge. *Why* should Iran want to have nuclear weapons to begin with? *Why* should the international community not allow Tehran to join the nuclear club? In *what* time frame can Iran succeed in its pursuit of the forbidden goal? On the question of Iran's motivations, several rationales are offered. First, given widespread and profound discontent among an overwhelming majority of Iranian citizens, the theocratic government may feel understandably paranoid about its own security. A nuclear Iran would strengthen the theocratic oligarchs' sense of invulnerability at home and abroad, and would weaken opponents within and outside the country. While no one thinks the regime would ever use nuclear weapons, once Iran develops a nuclear deterrent, the leadership can more easily ignore international pressure and pursue domestic political repression and human-rights violations with impunity.[36] Second, the possession of nuclear bombs would be considered a hallmark of modernization, giving the country heightened national prestige and clout, thus consolidating its sphere of influence in the region. Third, living in a dangerous neighborhood, surrounded by nuclear powers on all sides and hearing repeated threats from high American and Israeli politicians, a nuclear capability is a credible *deterrent* and a valuable insurance policy against external threats. Indigenous nuclear power might also be regarded as a counterbalance to nuclear-armed Israel and the risks of foreign-inspired separatist movements. Fourth, the Iranian leadership, based on a misperception of the North Korean and Iraqi cases, may believe that an intermediate-range strategic nuclear capability would deter any eventual American or Israeli attacks and thus enable it to assume a bolder and more aggressive foreign policy towards its arch enemies. Fifth, Tehran leaders may believe that the one sure means of bringing Washington to the bargaining table "on an equal-status basis" or at least enjoying the assurances of being treated with greater respect would be to have the bomb; it worked for North Korea. According to an unnamed Pentagon official, the Iranians realize that only by becoming a nuclear state can they defend themselves against the United States.[37] Sixth, as a self-appointed standard bearer of "Islam ruling the world,"[38] the Islamic Republic may resent taking a backseat to Pakistan (which it regards as a relative newcomer on the global scene) and wish to correct a nuclear imbalance. Finally, possession of an atomic bomb would give the theocratic oligarchy entry into the prestigious nuclear club, which, like all exclusive clubs, bestows on members a coveted status far beyond (and largely distinct from) its club's privileges and amenities.[39] The question as to *why* the Islamic Republic should be denied a nuclear-weapons capability,[40] while its neighbors are subject to no such injunctions, has received murkier answers based on some dubious assumptions and certain scare scenarios.[41] The first argument is based on the assertion that a non-democratic and repressive regime defying the world, harboring revolutionary ideals, pursuing regional ambitions, supporting a global terrorist network, and threatening to destroy Israel should not be allowed to have nuclear weapons.[42] Tehran's rulers could use the leverage of the bomb to dominate a large part of the Middle East and Caspian regions, challenging the big powers' interests and clout. A Pew Research Center poll shows that 72 percent of respondents believe that, if Iran were to develop nuclear weapons, it would likely launch attacks on Israel; 62 percent think that Europe and the United States would be the targets.[43] Second, Iran's neighbors would find a nuclear-armed giant a threat to their security and a source of potential blackmail, if not outright aggression. Third, since a nuclear capability would give Iran a distinct military superiority over its rivals—Turkey, Egypt, Saudi Arabia, Syria—it might trigger a new and dangerous arms race in the area. Fourth, a nuclear-armed Iran could advance its aggressive religious or political ambitions thorough various terrorist groups by empowering them with "suitcase bombs." Iran's spiritual leader has already offered to share nuclear technology with Sudan.[44] Fifth, a nuclear Iran could wield a predominant influence on the Organization of the Petroleum Exporting Countries (OPEC) and disrupt maritime traffic in the Persian Gulf. Sixth, and by far the most pointed, a nuclear Iran would represent an "existential threat" to the state of Israel directly with a single shot or through its agents in Lebanon and Palestine.[45] Questioning the validity of objections to a nuclear-powered Iran, however, are a large number of experts who find the threats somewhat exaggerated, if not largely based on hysteria. First, the Islamic Republic's challenge to Washington's interests and power in the region needs no bomb for leverage, as US interests and influence have already been effectively threatened since 1979 through conventional means and via financial support to groups in Lebanon, Saudi Arabia, Iraq, Afghanistan and elsewhere. Second, the chances of the Islamic Republic's engaging in adventurism or naked aggression against its neighbors are far-fetched. The last time Iran started a war was back in 1850 to liberate Herat; its last invasion of another country was in 1738. In the immediate past, even when Afghan Taliban challenged the Tehran government both militarily and ideologically, the clerical leadership showed an astonishing restraint. Third, the possibility of the Iranian nuclear program spawning a Middle East arms race is indeed ominous, but that race started decades ago, and Iran was not the one to launch it. Furthermore, Israel, Pakistan and India are already nuclear powers. Iraq, Afghanistan and the Persian Gulf emirates all enjoy US or North Atlantic Treaty Organization (NATO) presence, alliance or protection and, thus, have no need of a nuclear defensive shield. No Iranian government, no matter how belligerent or stupid, would dare provoke or challenge American or NATO forces. Still further, potential candidates for the race—Egypt, Syria, Saudi Arabia and Turkey—present technical, financial, political and security problems of their own, and their foray into the nuclear bazaar is highly circumstantial.[46] Finally, Iran might hesitate to start a regional nuclear arms race because it would lose its current superiority in conventional weapons. Fourth, there is the straw-man issue of a "bold Iran" engaging in nuclear coercion through the so-called "suitcase bomb."[47] But chemical and biological weapons would be much cheaper to produce, less cumbersome to pack and carry, easier to handle and more devastating in effect. Fifth, Iran's influence on OPEC, whatever it might be, will be neither augmented nor diminished by possession of the bomb, but rather by its own oil-capacity limitations. Last, and most crucial, Washington's concern about the Islamic Republic's posture toward the Jewish state seems to be a bogus argument to neutral observers. The esteemed Israeli military historian Martin van Creveld believes that, "given the balance of forces," it cannot be argued that a nuclear Iran will threaten the United States or even Israel.[48] Since the chances of mutual annihilation loom large in any nuclear first strike, a nuclear Iran would not dare initiate such an attack. Visiting the Natanz centrifuge facility, President Ahmadinejad told the staff, "What enemies fear is not production of an atomic bomb because in today's world atomic weapons are not efficient."[49] The new president may be a political amateur, occasionally making dimwitted statements, but he is neither a fool nor a suicide bomber. Some pundits argue that a Shiite belief in martyrdom, coupled with the Iranian regime's extremist ideology, could render deterrence meaningless.[50] Such people know neither Shiite martyrdom nor the regime leaders' instinct for self-preservation, nor even the mullahs' *bazaari* habit of always looking for the best deal.

Setting these arguments aside and assuming that the Islamic Republic is intent on acquiring nuclear weapons, the next questions would be, *how well* and *how soon* can the regime achieve its goal? Western government analysts, nuclear scientists, UN inspectors and anti-regime activists differ widely in their estimates,[51] according to their own ideological predilections and presuppositions. Accordingly, the country's bomb-making capability ranges from very small to near total, and the time horizon extends from weeks to years. The comparative advantage of nuclear power over other fuel sources also goes from nil to substantial! To reach reasonable estimates on these questions, one has first to separate the time required to master the centrifuge enrichment process from the time needed to actually build a deliverable bomb. They all require a large volume of resources, though exact amounts are unknown, as is the speed at which the task can be pushed ahead with external help. Some nuclear experts believe that Iran—with the knowledge and experience accumulated since the 1950s, a vast nuclear infrastructure built since the late 1980s, advice and assistance acquired from nuclear merchants, and sufficient money and scientific talent at its disposal—should theoretically be able to produce the bomb. However, a number of nuclear scientists question Iran's ability to master the chemistry involved in large-scale conversion. It is even claimed that Iran's "scientific elite" is not advanced enough even to the stage of reverse engineering from other people's know-how.[52] A near consensus, however, exists that the process of nuclear-weapons development from technical capability to actual construction and delivery is no easy task. At present, Tehran claims to be able to enrich uranium by running a small cascade of 164 centrifuges to a level of 3.5 percent, while bomb-grade uranium must be enriched to a level of well beyond 80 percent. On this scale, which many believe to be a bluff, the country supposedly needs to run 1,500 centrifuges continuously for nearly a year to obtain enough enriched material for one bomb.[53] Recent inspections by IAEA technicians reportedly revealed that Iran was encountering many technical or financial difficulties in completing a heavy-water reactor at Arak and a fuel-manufacturing plant at Isfahan.[54] A Russian military chief familiar with the Iran case is quoted saying that Tehran is incapable of producing a nuclear bomb now or in the distant future.[55] On the other hand, a former UN nuclear inspector reportedly believes that Iran has enough black market components in storage to build the 1,500 centrifuges needed for making 45 pounds of highly enriched uranium and one crude weapon.[56] With respect to the time frame, opinions vary even more widely.[57] A 1984 issue of Jane's *Defence Weekly* reportedly predicted that Tehran would have the bomb within two years! Some experts in Israel have been saying firmly every year for more than ten years that Tehran would get the bomb "next year."[58] For the past 15 years, various intelligence agencies have warned that Tehran could build a bomb in three to five years. On more than one occasion during the first half of 2006, John Negroponte, US director of national intelligence, has stated that Tehran does not yet have nuclear weapons and probably will not produce or acquire the necessary fissile materials for the next ten years. A recent estimate points out that Tehran is six to nine months away from mastering the enrichment process and five to ten years from building a bomb.[59] The latest guess is that with no major new technical problems, the task can be accomplished within three years.[60] A report issued in March 2006 by the Institute for Science and International Security also subscribes to the three-year possibility. And if President Ahmadinejad's claim of mid-April 2006 should prove true—that Iran is now testing a P-2 centrifuge for enriching uranium (which would presumably quadruple the capacity of the previously acknowledged P-1 type)—the time span would certainly be shorter.[61] The most intriguing speculation is provided by the IAEA director general, who told *Newsweek* in January 2006 that if the Iranians "have the nuclear material and they have a parallel weaponization program along the way, they are not very far—a few months—from a weapon."[62] The newest estimate brings it down to "only a week or two!"[63]

The brinkmanship game

If it fails to resume voluntary suspension of its nuclear activities and to cooperate fully with the UN inspectors, the Tehran government has been warned by Washington to expect "tough diplomatic actions."[64] Vice President Richard Cheney, addressing the American Israel Public Affairs Committee (AIPAC) on March 7, 2006, spoke of "meaningful consequences" if the regime stayed on its present course.[65] Prime Minister Tony Blair of Great Britain warned Iran about "a serious situation."[66] President Jacques Chirac of France, in a January 19, 2006, televised address, even threatened to use nuclear forces as retaliation against a "terrorist nation's" transgressions. And

Israel's top leaders have portrayed Iran's menace in hyperbolic terms (i.e., "the most serious threat faced by Jews since the Nazi Holocaust"),[67] and vowed that the Jewish state would not tolerate Iran's achieving nuclear independence.[68] Tehran appears not only unshaken by these warnings, but eager for confrontation.[69] Iran's Supreme Leader Ayatollah Khamenei has vowed to pursue Iran's nuclear program in the face of heightened pressure from the international community. "Using nuclear technology," he said, "is a national obligation and a public demand; any going back is the same as losing the country's independence at a very high price." He has further urged Iranians to resist "the enemy's threats" and preserve the nation's "honor and glory."[70] President Ahmadinejad has echoed the same sentiment by saying in a speech to an enthusiastic crowd that "retreating by even an iota in this [nuclear] path is out of the question. We had the revolution in order not to listen [to the West]." And again, "Nuclear technology is not something someone gave us so they can take it back; no one can take it back."[71] In a letter to the UN secretary-general, the Iranian Majlis threatened to force the government to withdraw from the NPT if the United States continued pressuring Tehran to suspend uranium enrichment.[72] Given these and other similarly belligerent positions, the question naturally is, "What next?" Tehran has so far refused to voluntarily suspend uranium enrichment at home or accept a package of Russian incentives, including having the enrichment process carried out jointly on Russian soil. The major nuclear powers, in turn, have dismissed the Majlis speaker's suggestion that Tehran is ready to provide the IAEA with an "objective guarantee" that the Iranian nuclear program is purely for civilian use.[73] Furthermore, Tehran's proposal to have a private international consortium of foreign countries and foreign companies enrich uranium on Iranian soil under IAEA supervision has not received a positive response from anywhere. The face-off has placed Iran's case before the UN Security Council. But the Council's efforts to find a mutually satisfactory solution have come to naught, largely due to distrust among the five major powers and disagreements over the best options. Western powers along with Russia and China have agreed to keep Iran from going nuclear but differ about the means. Policies, tactics and approaches vary considerably, but they are all limited and rather unattractive, ranging from diplomatic negotiations to gradually harsher sanctions and to military action.[74] Sanctions themselves include a vast array of mild to drastic measures with varying impact. Based on past UN actions, possible measures include in order of severity, a Council statement by its president, approved by all 15 members, asking Iran to cease and desist, and a series of resolutions thereafter (to be approved by nine members, including the five with veto power) specifying punishment. These resolutions may involve merely banning travel by Iranian officials, business leaders or nuclear scientists; limiting the number of diplomatic staff in each capital; excluding Iran from international athletic events; forbidding international flights and other means of transportation and communications into or out of Iran; restricting worldwide sales of arms and dual-use high-tech equipment;

barring loans from private international banks or international agencies to Iran; freezing Iran's assets in foreign institutions; banning foreign investment in or transfer of technology to any Iranian economic sector; forbidding all sales of foreign products (including critically needed gasoline) to Iran; embargoing all oil and non-oil exports by Iran; and, finally, expelling the Islamic Republic from all international organizations.

All these sanctions, however, present problems of their own and are a classic example of the double-edged sword. First, although Washington is no longer isolated in its effort to put Iran's case before the Security Council, it is still doubtful whether Russia, China or even some nonaligned countries would agree to stiff economic sanctions against the Islamic Republic. Russia in the past has said that sanctions are in no way the best way to solve the impasse. At a special meeting in Vienna on April 21, 2006, the Russian delegate made it clear that sanctions could be "talked about" only after "concrete facts [confirm] that Iran is not exclusively involved in peaceful nuclear activities."[75] China has also routinely opposed the use of sanctions or similar strong-arm tactics in international disputes.[76] Furthermore, Iran's leverage over most Council members in trade, investment and security areas would make most sanctions perfunctory, impractical or ineffective. The United Kingdom, France and Germany enjoy a lucrative export market of nearly $15 billion in Iran. Russia is a major arms vendor to Iran's defense establishment and is the sole contractor to build Iran's atomic reactor in Bushehr, with scores of Russian scientists in charge. China receives 12 percent of its oil imports from Iran; it has been active in many local development projects (including the Tehran metro) and it has recently signed a $100 billion energy agreement with Tehran.[77] Washington could of course raise its own unilateral sanctions,[78] but as its experience in Iran and some 80 countries so far indicates, these sanctions could easily be thwarted by a shift of trade and investment to other countries at the US companies' peril. Still further, global experiences show that sanctions are likely to hurt ordinary citizens and not be effective in changing the leadership's behavior. Realizing this fact, both American and European officials have repeatedly emphasized that they do not intend to cause hardship and internal suffering to the Iranian public. Aware of the fact that sanctions also run the risk of creating a nationwide backlash similar to the anti-Saddam case, a US State Department official admitted that a heavy-handed sanctions approach would hurt a lot of Iranians "that we do not want to alienate."[79] Finally, short of a total universal sanction on Iran's sales of oil, none of the other economic measures would shake the leadership's resolve or drastically change their behavior. Banned imports can be purchased in the black market. Domestic investments can be financed out of huge oil export receipts and accumulated gold and foreign-exchange reserves. A ban on non-oil exports could hurt carpet weavers and pistachio growers but would not cripple the whole economy and could easily be overcome, given Iran's vast open borders. Only a complete embargo on oil exports (which Iran relies on for 85 percent of its total foreign exchange and more than 70 percent of its annual budget) would make the difference. But, given the near absence of the spare capacity in the global oil supply to make up for the loss of Iranian oil, a large shortage might develop and lead to a disastrous oil-price explosion that no country—least of all, the United States and Israel—could afford for long. And, despite International Energy Agency director Claude Mandel's repeated assurance that the world has enough stocks to replace all of Iran's exports for a year and a half,[80] oil traders speak of $100-a-barrel crude oil in no time if stiff sanctions are imposed. Even the mere mention of a possible ban has in recent weeks sent daily tremors through the New York and London oil-futures markets. For all these reasons, there are great doubts about the vaunted efficacy of sanctions.[81] Some analysts even argue that Iran may win a sanctions war.[82]

Opting for the unthinkable

To paraphrase a celebrated dictum, the military option is sanctions by different means. Bush administration officials have repeatedly quoted the president's declaration that all options, including surgical nuclear strikes, are on the table, but that Washington's strong preference is to deal with the Iranian threat through "effective diplomacy." The military option is backed by the adage that "whoever wishes for peace, let him prepare for war." Needless to say, military intervention, including "surgical" strikes at Iran's nuclear facilities, would at first glance appear to be a viable option for many reasons. It is tailor made for the 2002 Bush doctrine of preemption; it is backed not only by various neoconservative factions but also by some influential politicians in and out of the Bush administration and the US Congress; and it is supported by a surprisingly large number of Americans in several national polls (the *Washington Post*-ABC News, Fox News, *Los Angeles Times*-Bloomberg),[83] although support seems to have varied at different times and in response to differently worded questions.[84] An attack on Iran is also said to give the embattled Bush administration a new story line on Iraq-Iran machinations.[85] There have been suggestions by a number of American neoconservative hawks to denuke Iran with "swift, massive, devastating force that decapitates the regime."[86] It is claimed that this can be done in a single night.[87] Yet this option is the most controversial of all choices. The British, the Chinese and the Russians have all rejected it as impractical because it involves grave drawbacks. To begin with, the Israeli attack on Iraq's facility in 1981 cannot be duplicated and offers no useful paradigm: Iran's 125-odd nuclear facilities (e.g., chemical plants, missile launchers, airfields and small workshops) are partly, if not largely, situated in populated areas or camouflaged from US satellites, and much better protected. The Pentagon has the military capability (attack aircraft, Tomahawk and cruise missiles, B2 Stealth bombers) to knock out Iran's dozen known nuclear sites. Stealth bombers could penetrate Iran's space and suppress air-defense systems relatively easily. Underground facilities could be taken out with bunker buster bombs. But military experts believe it requires hundreds of sorties over weeks of operation. Yet, despite untold civilian casualties, the strikes might not destroy Iran's nuclear capacity, but only set it back by a few years. Nevertheless, ardent supporters of the military option, while conceding that the costs would be high, believe that they would not be as high as the cost of a nuclear Iran.[88] The use of military force by Washington alone, or through a "coalition of the willing" also involves a range of dire consequences. First, it is most likely to face stiff resistance and retaliation from Iranian forces.[89] Tehran has already threatened Washington with a counterpunch, saying, "The US may have the power to cause harm and pain" but it is also vulnerable.[90] Tehran now boasts of having recruited 40,000 volunteer suicide bombers. Iran also possesses thousands of surface-to-air missiles in range of US forces in Iraq. Iranian naval and air forces could attack oil facilities and tankers in the Persian Gulf and choke off oil shipments through the Strait of Hormuz. Iranian navy exercises during April 2006 in the area where new weapons were tested were meant to warn against a naval blockade. Tehran may use its fifth-column assets in Iraq, Lebanon and Afghanistan to destabilize those countries or engage in mischief against US and Israeli targets around the world.[91] The Mahdi army of Moktada Sadr, closely linked to Tehran, has loyal agents in both the Iraqi police and army and can come directly to Iran's support.[92] Lebanese Hizballah possesses thousands of missiles based in Israel's proximity. Military strikes are also likely to alienate not only Washington's European allies, but also even the most moderate and pro-American groups elsewhere. Syria, Saudi Arabia, Bahrain and other Middle East countries with Shiite populations will witness crises and demonstrations, stirring up feelings of resentment, anger and hatred throughout the Muslim world and reinforcing the perception of an anti-Islamic Judeo-Christian conspiracy.[93] The Tehran government will receive a good deal of sympathy and support from the Non-Aligned Movement as well.[94] There is also a presumption—although questioned by some analysts—in which Iranians of all political stripes will rally around the flag and unite behind the current leadership despite their opposition to the theocratic regime.[95] Some analysts even argue that a military strike would be a godsend for the regime as it would create ill-will against the West, enhance the system's authority, and prolong the regime's survival as a vast majority of citizens genuinely support their country's having a domestic nuclear capacity.[96] The move may actually harden Iran's resolve to pursue its nuclear program even more diligently.[97] And there will be charges of aggression in the United Nations, based on a "unilateral, preemptive, illegal and unprovoked assault."[98] Finally, an attack on the Bushehr power plant would run the risk of many civilian casualties in addition to other collateral damage, including an environmental disaster dreaded by all US allies in the Persian Gulf region. A former US national security advisor believes that Washington's war with Iran would be "the end of America's present role in the world."[99] As has been pointed out by many strategic analysts, neither non-universal stiff sanctions nor military strikes short of actual invasion and occupation would be enough to topple the regime.[100] And even if the mullahs were defeated, which foreign government or international organization has the ability or manpower to carry out an extended occupation or to prevent a civil war? Iran of 2006 is vastly different from that of 1941, when it was easily occupied and administered with the help of a cooperating government. In short, the military option is regarded as irrational, lots of pain for not much gain.[101] Yet it should be kept in mind that irrationality has never in history served as insurance against wrongful acts by political daredevils.

A hard nut to crack

Iran's nuclear program has become a vexing international drama at center stage on the global scene. The reasons are not hard to grasp. First, EU-Washington "unity" has been highly effective in converting an opaque foreign-policy matter of no interest to the man in the street in either Iran or the United States into a hot-button domestic issue. The Islamic regime, by underscoring Washington's double standards, hypocrisy and heavy-handed tactics, has been highly successful in galvanizing popular support for Iran's right to enrich uranium at home.[102] In fact, with the exception of respect for Iran's territorial integrity, no other single issue has received such universal backing from Iranian citizens, including diehard opposition groups at home and abroad. In a curious mixture of national pride, anti-colonialism, and standing up to "global arrogance" (a.k.a. Washington), the nuclear program has now become a question of national sovereignty, political independence, and even inalienable rights.[103] The issue is frequently compared with Iran's success in nationalizing its oil in 1951. Western correspondents, analysts and academics visiting Iran and interviewing workers, students and housewives echo the feeling that the United States and the West are trying to keep Iran among an underclass of "nuclear have-nots" in the guise of nonproliferation. Reference is often made to Washington's "strategic hypocrisy" of saying yes to India's nukes and no to Iran's,[104] implying in effect that, if a country somehow manages to build a nuclear bomb despite universal injunctions, it will eventually get away with it.[105] Interestingly enough, both the Non-Aligned Movement and the Organization of the Islamic Conference also fully back Iran's right to nuclear research and development.[106] Second, due to the whipped-up political frenzy in both Tehran and Washington and the consequent mutual distrust, IAEA efforts and EU-led diplomacy so far have failed to find a mutually satisfactory solution. Washington's adamant refusal to negotiate directly with "a regime that is dictatorial in its practice and revolutionary in its aims with an agenda for destabilizing neighbors and the broader Middle East"[107] has further complicated the dispute. The Security Council, in turn, has not been able to agree on any effective measures to induce Iran to compromise, and will probably continue to be deadlocked after the expiration of its deadline. The US threat to invade Iran now has not proved credible, and, with the exception of a small coterie of rabid hawks in and out of the Bush administration, nearly everyone in both liberal and conservative camps finds military intervention a blunt instrument and war with Iran a reckless folly.[108] For all these reasons a number of influential opinion makers in and outside of the US Congress believe that "the best course of action is for Washington to enter direct talks with the Islamic Republic towards a grand bargain."[109] The combination of these factors has enabled Iran to ignore the West's warnings and proceed belligerently with its program. In fact, Iranian officials have hinted that Tehran may respond to international pressure by stopping cooperation with the IAEA, exporting its nuclear technology, hiding its nuclear program, withdrawing from the NPT and even curtailing oil production.[110] The third and most crucial reason for the impasse has been the hidden nature of the sparring partners' true agendas. For both domestic political and ideological reasons that have little to do with the threat,[111] Washington and Tehran have been reluctant to publicize their real demands and unable to meet them. As a result, both governments have engaged in a kabuki dance of dissimulation.

Washington's near obsession with the fate of Iran's nuclear program now, as compared with its blissful unconcern during the 1970s, is clearly the *nature* of the Islamic regime as Israel's archenemy and the principal non-Arab supporter of the groups endangering Israel's security. A simple explanation of Washington's flagrant denigration of the same program today is that Iran is now perceived to be a threat to Israel, while the shah had a close de facto collaboration with the Jewish state.[112] For this crucial reason, there is a minority of pro-Israel groups who will not be satisfied with any solution short of depriving the Tehran government of *any* involvement in nuclear-related work, whether research, engineering or experimentation.[113] As US ambassador to the United Nations John Bolton told *Time*, Iran could defuse international concerns over its nuclear program by following the example of Libya:[114] abandon *all* nuclear activities and curtail its hostility toward Israel. Tehran has its own hidden agenda in this high-stakes game. The leadership's defense of its "inalienable" rights under the NPT, its repeated denials of any nuclear weapons ambitions, its labeling of the IAEA accusations of deception and concealment as lies have resonated with the rank and file. Feigning martyrdom, calling the wider world to its side, invoking the "power of the meek," claiming to be defending not just Iran's rights but also those of other developing countries[115] and reviving Third World laments of the '60s have all been part of a smokescreen to hide the leaders' mortal fear of regime change. Reflecting their distrust, they have on numerous occasions openly argued that, if they submitted to Washington's demand for suspension of uranium enrichment, other excuses would be put on the table. American officials would subsequently raise the issues of the undemocratic structure of the government, violations of human rights, discrimination against women and minorities, absence of religious freedom, support of the Palestinian cause, bankrolling international terrorism, interference in Iraq and Afghanistan, and maybe even teaching nuclear physics at the universities—until Iran ceases hostility toward

Israel and accepts the latter's "right" to exist.[116] Meanwhile, American neocons' open advocacy of regime change, Secretary of State Rice's assertion that Iran is "a menace beyond the nuclear issue,"[117] her $75 million budget request to "promote democracy" in Iran, leaked reports about the Pentagon's war preparations[118] and US Special Forces operations inside Iran's ethnic minorities, full-page ads in support of Israel, and the passage of a stiff sanctions bill by the US House of Representatives in late April 2006, have played into the mullahs' hands. The price of oil has skyrocketed, and sympathy for Iran's case has increased.

Acutely aware of the fact that, despite occasional official denials, Washington's plan for Iran is regime change, the clerical oligarchs have decided to play the high value cards in their hand to thwart it. The faux nuclear card is thus played to obtain the maximum concession: a security guarantee from Washington in the form of a bilateral nonaggression pact (as requested by North Korea) or a similar commitment through other international arrangements. All indications show that Tehran's unpublicized demand, in its formal negotiations with the EU-3 and in informal contacts with Washington from day one, has been a formal security guarantee that would offer the regime immunity against foreign threats. Keeping the West guessing about its nuclear enrichment program has been a ruse to ensure the regime's continuity and survival, even at the expense of Iran's national interest.

Is there a way out?

On April 28, 2006, when the Security Council's 30-day deadline expired, the IAEA's director general, in a sharply worded report, told the Council that, despite the latter's formal request, Iran has accelerated rather than curbed uranium-enrichment activities and has not provided UN inspectors with any new information. As a result, the country's nuclear program continues to be "a matter of concern."[119] The report thus opened the door for a new series of Council debates over how to contain Tehran's nuclear ambitions. The deliberations promise to be lengthy and difficult, due to both parties' intransigence. Iran's leadership has repeatedly said that giving up enrichment is "our red line and we will never cross it."[120] President Bush has said the Iranian government's "intransigence is not acceptable. The Iranians should not have a nuclear weapon, the capacity to make a nuclear weapon, or the knowledge as to how to make a nuclear weapon."[121] These parallels lines will never meet.

The international community now has five theoretical choices, none of which is attractive or satisfactory. The first is "watchful waiting," leaving Tehran to its own devices, ignoring Ahmadinejad's swashbuckling gestures and outrageous statements, letting Iran proceed with industrial uranium enrichment, and trying to contain the program, as in the North Korean case. The second option is to rely on continued world diplomacy i.e., furthering negotiations with the EU-3 and preferably with Washington's participation, returning the Iran file to the atomic-energy agency in Vienna (as requested by

Tehran and preferred by Russia and China) to search for some mutually satisfactory arrangements.[122] The third alternative is for Washington and the EU-3 to invoke Chapter 7 of the UN Charter and lean on Russia and China to come up with certain legally binding and effective sanctions. Fourth, failing to get a vote out of the Security Council, Washington and the EU-3, along with "like-minded" governments, could impose their own sanctions (denying Iran such items as military equipment, dual use technology, and foreign loans and credits). The last option would be "shock and awe," to threaten military intervention, and ultimately engage in armed intervention. Given the fact that no one wants to see Iran develop a nuclear-weapons capability, and considering military action "the worst of worse-case scenarios," the second option i.e., a package of both carrots and sticks, would seem the most promising choice. It involves giving the Tehran regime some credible security assurances, removing or reducing US bilateral sanctions, allowing some limited and supervised form of local enrichment, guaranteeing the supply of nuclear fuel for Iran's power reactors, and offering some tangible incentives to help Iran cope with its acute problems of unemployment and inflation. In exchange, Tehran would agree to a verifiable suspension of any industrial-scale enrichment at home, ratification and implementation of the Additional NPT Protocol, adoption of a noninterference policy in the Arab–Israeli conflict (including withdrawal of support from all anti-Israel groups), and full acceptance of any peace treaty between Israel and the Palestinian Authority.[123] The chances of this package being embraced by either Tehran or Washington are not great. The Ahmadinejad government cannot easily abandon its anti-Israeli clients in the region without losing face at home and credibility in the Islamic world. Nor can the Bush administration afford to give Tehran a non-aggression pact, for an array of domestic political reasons.[124] In all probability, the Iranian strategy from now on will be to play the game and engage in interminable "diplomatic" negotiations with the IAEA in order to gain time while pursuing uranium enrichment and mastering the latest nuclear technology. The Washington-Israel strategy, in turn, would likely involve continued pressure on the international community through increasingly stiff sanctions and other punitive measures to prevent Iran from advancing in the game. Meanwhile, given politicians' almost limitless capacity to take disastrous decisions, military intervention cannot be ruled out. Stupid provocations on the part of the Tehran government or a plausible link between Iran and a terrorist incident on US soil could actually trigger a "surgical" nuclear strike by either Washington or Israel on Iran's facilities.

On May 8, 2006, President Ahmadinejad sent an 18-page letter to President Bush hinting at the possibility of new talks. Regarded as the first direct official contact between the two countries in 27 years,[125] the letter evoked totally different reactions. The Islamic Republic's handful of ardent apologists in the United States and elsewhere praised it as bold, daring, compassionate, shrewd and full of initiatives—opening the door for an entente. Secretary of State Rice, on the other hand, said, "This letter is not the place that one would find an opening to engage on the nuclear issue or anything of that sort."[126] Indeed, the missive was a rambling, poorly drafted, and religion-laced narrative about history and philosophy with no concrete proposals on anything.[127] The Iranian president later proposed direct negotiations with the United States, but Washington stood fast in rejecting direct talks, arguing that there are plenty of channels of communication for Iran to pass information, and that the United States has no intention of making the nuclear dispute a bilateral issue.[128] With the Security Council deadlocked on any concrete and binding resolution, the EU-3, with Washington's approval, again volunteered on May 9 to come up in two weeks with a package of fresh incentives (including affordable energy and greater trade with the West) as well as an implicit threat of sanctions if Tehran refused to accept it.[129] For the moment, all options remain on the table. Those who believe that the Washington-Tehran minuet on nuclear weapons continues because the United States has refused to join the EU in direct talks with the Tehran government, may yet prove their point. The Iranians do not care *who* delivers the goods, just *what* the *package* contains.[130] The only way to resolve the problem effectively is to find a way to satisfy both parties' hidden agendas. Under such an ideal policy, Iran, like many other Islamic states, would abstain from establishing formal diplomatic relations with Israel and would object to the latter's policies towards the Palestinians but would refrain from hostility towards the Jewish state. Israel, in turn, would tone down its hawkish rhetoric towards the Islamic Republic, stop pressuring the US Congress and the EU governments to squeeze Iran, and cease its behind-the-scenes maneuvers to forestall a Washington–Tehran rapprochement.[131]

The key to establishing an entente between Tehran and Washington on all their disputes, including Iran's nuclear challenge, might thus be found in neither Tehran nor Washington, but in Israel's capital. A rapprochement between the new governments of Israel and for the Palestinian Authority, the establishment of an effective central government in Iraq, and improved security conditions in Afghanistan will work in favor of the West in dealing with Tehran—and vice versa. Changes in relations among the United States, Russia and China will also palpably affect the outcome, as may the upcoming elections for Iran's Experts Assembly and the US Congress. In the meantime, Iran's nuclear capability remains front and center on the international stage.

Notes

* First published in *Middle East Policy*, Vol. XIII, No. 2, Summer 2006. Reproduced with permission.

1 "Iran Declares Nuclear Advance," *Washington Post*, April 12, 2006.

2 *Washington Post*, March 11, 2006.

3 For the allegation of Israel's influence on Washington's Iran decision, see John Mearsheimer and Stephen Walt, "The Israel Lobby," available at www.lrb.co.uk/v28/n06, March 21, 2006.

4 *Reuters*, April 29, 2006.
5 "It's Regime Change Again," available at commondreams.org/views, March 13, 2006.
6 *Washington Post*, March 17, 2006.
7 See Dafna Linzer, "Past Arguments Do Not Square with Current Iran Policy," *Washington Post*, March 17, 2005; and Ed Haas, "U.S. Endorsed Iranian Plans ..." *Muckraker Report*, March 6, 2006.
8 For the latest confirmation of this position, see "Iran's Ayatollah Affirms Peaceful Nuclear Plans," *New York Times*, January 19, 2006. See also BBC.Persian.com, March 9 and 13, 2006.
9 "Iran's President—His Own Words," *BBC News*, January 16, 2006.
10 For a full defense of Iran's position, see Javad Zarif, "We Do Not Have a Nuclear Weapons Program," *New York Times*, April 6, 2006.
11 For a brief chronicle of events, see Dafna Linzer, "Strong Leads and Dead Ends in Nuclear Case against Iran," *Washington Post*, February 8, 2006.
12 "Europe to Offer Iran Benefits," *Washington Post*, August 1, 2005.
13 "Iran's Nuclear Policy Requires a Collective Response," *Wall Street Journal*, September 23, 2005.
14 *New York Times*, September 25, 2005.
15 "Atomic Agency Sees Possible Link of Military to Iran Nuclear Work," *New York Times*, February 1, 2006.
16 "Iran's Gift: New Unity in the West," *Washington Post*, February 23, 2006.
17 "China, Russia Join Call for Iran to Suspend Nuclear Program," *Washington Post*, January 14, 2006.
18 "U.S. Compromises on Wording of Iran Nuclear Resolution," *New York Times*, February 4, 2006.
19 "Iranian Threatens Full Production of Nuclear Fuel," *New York Times*, January 23, 2006.
20 "Nuclear Inspections Are Curbed by Iran," *Washington Post*, February 6, 2006.
21 *Washington Post*, February 14, 2006
22 "IAEA: Iran Advancing Uranium Enrichment," *Washington Post*, February 28, 2006.
23 *See Washington Post*, February 28, 2006; and *New York Times*, February 28, 2006.
24 For the details of these stonewalling efforts, see the *Wall Street Journal* editorial, March 1, 2006.
25 See "Security Council Pressures Tehran," *Washington Post*, March 30, 2006.
26 For a sample of these differences see "Russia Warns Against Fast Action on Iran," www.themoscowtimes.com/stories, March 20, 2006; "Envoys Remain Split on Plan Against Iran," *Washington Post*, April 20, 2006; and "Russia Rejects U.S. Appeal on Iran," *Washington Post*, April 22, 2006.
27 *Financial Times*, February 17, 2006.
28 "How We Duped the West," *The Telegraph*, March 5, 2006.
29 Interview with France 2 Televsion, *Washington Post*, February 17, 2006.
30 *Iran Times* (Washington), February 10, 2006.
31 See Jim Hoagland, "Iran's Gift and New Unity in the West," *Washington Post*, February 23, 2006.
32 *New York Times*, January 17, 2006, and January 31, 2006.
33 "Gulf States Join Call for Tougher Action toward Iran," *New York Times*, February 1, 2006; and "Iran's Nukes Concern some Arab Countries," Associated Press, March 22, 2006.
34 For a decidedly sympathetic but poorly evidenced argument about nuclear energy's "profound economic sense" for Iran, see W.O. Beeman, "Warning Signs," *San Jose Mercury News*, February 19, 2006.

35 Dafna Linzer, "Strong Leads and Dead Ends," *Washington Post*, February 5, 2006.
36 For arguments for and against this motive, see Nader Habibi, "Impact of Nuclear Empowerment," available at payvand.com, March 22, 2006.
37 David Ignatius, "An Iran Missile Crisis," *Washington Post*, April 12, 2006.
38 See "Global Jihad," available at www.worldnetdaily.com/news, January 10, 2006.
39 Cf. Mark Helprin, "After Diplomacy Fails," *Washington Post*, April 13, 2006.
40 See J.C. Moore, "Why Shouldn't Iran Have Nuclear Weapons?" *The Independent*, April 30, 2006.
41 See T.G. Carpenter, "Dubious Assumptions about Iran," Foxnews.com, February 8, 2006.
42 "Iran Bomb Scare," *Wall Street Journal*, April 12, 2006. See also ibid. March 20, 2006.
43 info@people-press.org, February 7, 2006.
44 Anne Penketh, "The Big Question," *The Independent*, May 9, 2006.
45 For a sampling of the scenarios, see Fred Kaplan, "Yes, We Should Worry about Iran," *Slate*, March 4, 2006; and "Why the World is Afraid of Iran Nukes," *Indian Express*, February 21, 2006.
46 For an elaboration of these handicaps and other reasons for nonproliferation, see a maverick op-ed by B.R. Posen, "We Can Live with a Nuclear Iran," *New York Times*, February 27, 2006.
47 See *Harvard Gazette*, March 23, 2006.
48 Martin van Creveld, "Knowing How Not to Bomb Iran," available at www. forward.com/articles/7683, April 21, 2006.
49 *Iran Times*, February 24, 2006.
50 See Mark Sappenfield, *Christian Science Monitor*, April 14, 2006; and Dilip Hiro, "It is Not Just Iran's Leaders who Think it Better to Fight and Die than Compromise with America," available at www.telegrah.co.uk/opinion, March 11, 2006.
51 *Iran Times*, February 24, 2006.
52 Cf. sarjoman@notes.cc.sunysb.edu.
53 *Wall Street Journal*, April 13, 2006.
54 *Washington Post*, February 28, 2006.
55 "Iran Incapable of N Arm," *Itar-Tass*, April 15, 2006.
56 abcnews.com, March 25, 2006.
57 For samplings of different estimates, see *Newsweek*, February 13, 2006; RFE/RL, "Iran Report," February 22, 2006; radiofarda, March 7, 2006; timesonline.co.uk, March 9, 2006; *The Guardian*, March 10, 2006; and Agence France-Presse, March 10, 2006.
58 *Iran Times*, February 24, 2006.
59 *Washington Post*, March 23, 2006.
60 "Iran's Nuclear Steps Quicken," *Los Angeles Times*, March 25, 2006.
61 "Iran Claims it's Testing a New Centrifuge," *Associated Press*, April 17, 2006.
62 See "An 'Intolerable' Threat," *Wall Street Journal*, February 3, 2006.
63 Agence France-Presse, March 25, 2006.
64 *The Washington Post*, March 4, 2006.
65 iran-press-service.com, March 7, 2006.
66 *Washington Post*, March 11, 2006.
67 CNN.com, April 24, 2006.
68 CNN.com, April 15, 2006.
69 "Iran's Nuclear Progress," *Washington Post*, April 13, 2006.
70 BBC Persian.com, March 14, 2006.
71 For the sources of all these statements, see *IranMania*, March 14, 21, and 26, 2006.

72 Associated Press, May 7, 2006.
73 *IranMania*, February 19, 2006.
74 See The Congressional Research Service, "Iran: U.S. Concerns and Policy Responses," May 3, 2006.
75 Reuters, April 21, 2006.
76 *New York Times*, January 18, 2006.
77 For a detailed discussion of these factors see F.W. Engdahl, "A High Risk Game of Nuclear Chicken," *Asia Times*, January 31, 2006.
78 See "A Financial Hit on Iran," *Time*, May 1, 2006.
79 *New York Times*, January 20, 2006.
80 Several interviews with French radio stations reported in *Iran Times*, February 24, 2006.
81 Carne Ross, "Could Sanctions Stop Iran," *Washington Post*, March 30, 2006.
82 J.P. Gundzik, "Risky Business," available at http://atimes.com, May 11, 2006.
83 According to a recent poll, 57 percent of Americans favored military intervention to stop Iran building a bomb, *The Times*, February 7, 2006.
84 See Angus Reid Global Scan, *CBS News*, May 8, 2006; and www.zogby.com/news, May 11, 2006.
85 E.S. Clark, "Slouching Towards Tehran," TomPaine.com, May 4, 2006.
86 Mark Steyn, "Facing Down Iran," *City Journal*, Spring 2006. See also Ilan Berman, "Preempting Iran's Ambitions," *Washington Times*, March 3, 2006; and R.M. Gerecht, "To Bomb or Not to Bomb," *Weekly Standard*, April 24, 2006.
87 E.N. Luttwak, "In a Single Night," *Wall Street Journal*, February 9, 2006.
88 Michael Robin,"Nuclear Hostage Crisis," *Wall Street Journal*, April 14, 2006,
89 Supreme Leader Khamenei has already warned that "American interests around the world will be harmed if the United States launches an attack on the Islamic Republic," VOA News, April 26, 2006; and *Washington Post*, April 27, 2006.
90 Molly Moore, "Iran Threatens U.S. with 'Harm and Pain,'" *Washington Post*, March 9, 2006.
91 Richard Clarke and Steven Simon, "Bombs that Would Backfire," *New York Times*, April 16, 2006.
92 "Iraqi Shiite Cleric Pledges to Defend Iran," *Washington Post*, January 24, 2006.
93 Cf. Anwaar Hussain, "Dear Neo-Cons," available at baltimorechronicle.com, February 7, 2006.
94 Polls taken in early 2014 by Aljazeera TV and Zogby International reportedly indicate that a large majority of the population in Moslem countries, e.g., Egypt, Jordan, Lebanon, Morocco, and Saudi Arabia, find Iran's access to nuclear technology in their interest, and are adamantly opposed to any Western restrictions on Iran's pursuit of peaceful nuclear energy. See www.hamshahri.ir, February 22, 2006; and www.emrouz.info, March 17, 2006.
95 For a sample of these views, see Michael Slackman, "Nuclear Dispute Arouses Patriotism among Iranians," *New York Times*, February 5, 2006.
96 Scott Bohlinger," America's Options for Iran," *Asia Times*, March 19, 2006.
97 David Sanger, "Why Not a Strike on Iran," *New York Times*, January 22, 2006.
98 commondreams.org/views, March 4, 2006.
99 *Washington Post*, April 12, 2006.
100 For objections to bombing see E.N. Luttwak, "Three Reasons Not to Bomb Iran," *Commentary*, May 2006.
101 David Isenberg, "What We Know about Iran," available at www.tompaine.com/articles, April 25, 2006.
102 A recent semiofficial poll of nearly 16,000 citizens showed that 76.8 percent back the regime's current nuclear stance. See RFE/RL, *Iran Report*, March 23, 2006. Other polls suggest that more than 80 percent of the public supports Iran's decision to use its full right under the NPT, which is all the government says it has in

mind. See John Danisizewski "Iranians Defend Nuclear Rights," *Los Angeles Times*, March 7, 2006.
103 For a sampling of public sentiments, see a panel discussion at www.radiofarda.com, March 7, 2006.
104 "Good Nukes, Bad Nukes," *Washington Post*, March 1, 2006.
105 See C.A. Robbins, "Explosive Test," *Wall Street Journal*, March 2, 2006. For a similar "double-standard" criticism, see "Iran's Best Friend," *New York Times* editorial, March 5, 2006.
106 *Islamic Republic News Agency*, March 8, 2006; and *IranMania*, March 10, 2006.
107 "Bush Adviser Dismisses Call for Talks with Iran," *IranMania*, April 24, 2006.
108 See two views from opposite camps: Zbigniew Brzezinski, "Been there, Done that," *Los Angeles Times*, April 23, 2006; and Thomas Joscelyn, "Iran War on the West," *Weekly Standard*, April 21, 2006.
109 For a sample, see S.R. Burger, "Talk to Tehran," *Wall Street Journal*, May 8, 2006; Glenn Kessler, "U.S. Under Pressure to Stop Talk to Tehran," *Washington Post*, May 11, 2006.
110 "Iran Hints at Exiting Nuclear Treaty," *Associated Press*, April 24, 2006; and "Iran Raises Stakes," *Washington Post*, April 26, 2006.
111 "The Method Behind Iran's Madness," *Taipei Times*, April 20, 2006.
112 See pacificnews.org/news/view, February 3, 2006.
113 See George Melloan, "Getting Serious about Iran," *Wall Street Journal*, January 17, 2006.
114 *Yahoo! News*, February 19, 2006.
115 President Ahmadinejad's statement at Jakarta, *Washington Post*, May 11, 2006.
116 "Iran Digs In," *IranMania*, March 9, 2006; and "Tehran Stands Firm," RFE/RL, *Iran Report*, March 17, 2006.
117 Associated Press, March 28, 2006.
118 Seymour Hersh, "The Iran Plan," *New Yorker*, April 17, 2006.
119 "Report Sets Stage for Action on Iran," *Washington Post*, April 29, 2006.
120 "Iran's Strategy: Cold War Echo," *New York Times*, April 30, 2006.
121 "U.N. Agency Says Iran Falls Short on Nuclear Data," *New York Times*, April 29 and April 30, 2006.
122 Tehran has already indicated that it would allow UN inspectors full access if the dossier was returned to the IAEA. However, Washington has rejected the offer.
123 For a sample of such proposals, see "Iran," International Crisis Group, February 23, 2006.
124 See Jahangir Amuzegar, "Iran's Nuclear Dilemma," *Middle East Economic Survey*, April 7, 2006.
125 *Washington Post*, May 9, 2006.
126 "No Proposals in Iranian's Letter to Bush," *Washington Post*, May 9, 2006.
127 For a quick look at the letter's main points, see "Will you Not Accept this Invitation?" *Washington Post*, May 10, 2006.
128 See US State Department spokesman, reported by Agence France-Presse, May 22, 2006.
129 "Europeans Work on New Anti-Nuclear Deal for Iran," *Washington Post*, May 10, 2006.
130 Dennis Ross, "A New Strategy on Iran," *Washington Post*, April 30, 2006.
131 See Trita Parsi, "A Modus Vivendi between Jerusalem and Tehran," *Forward Forum*, March 17, 2006.

13 Iran's oil as a blessing and a curse*

In mid-2008—the 100th anniversary of commercial oil discovery in Iran—the country's petroleum deposits, the price of its crude, its foreign exchange reserves, its annual oil export receipts, and its annual trade surplus all set historic records.[1] Iran also possessed the world's second largest reservoir of natural gas. Such an immense fortune is understandably envied by the oil-less developing countries that face the dual problems of insufficient funds for their economic development and rising energy costs. The fortune is also coveted by energy-dependent developed nations that have to pay rising costs for their import needs and face payments deficits. This review intends to argue, however, that natural energy wealth is not always an unmitigated bliss, and that there are costly downsides to such envied endowments.

Iran's magnitude of energy bounty

With more than a century of oil discovery and extraction in its history, Iran is the oldest oil-exporting country in the Persian Gulf region. And with continued discoveries of new oil fields, its current reserves have always exceeded domestic consumption and exports. As a founding member of the Organization of the Petroleum Exporting Countries (OPEC), Iran has also enhanced its intra-group rank from the fourth largest producer in 1960 to the second largest producer in 2008. Iran's current proven oil deposits in situ are estimated to be 520 billion barrels, or about 11.6 percent of the world's known petroleum reserves. At the relatively conservative 24 to 27 percent recovery rate, the country's estimated available reserves are at 138 billion barrels of crude—the world's second largest behind Saudi Arabia. The extraordinary advantage of oil for the Iranian economy—apart from its deposit volume and rising price—is that its extraction cost is low and its sale proceeds contain huge profits. Given the average extraction cost of Iran's various qualities of crude at the well-head to be about $4.35, the $73 per barrel average price of Iranian oil in 2007 would include some $68.65 of pure profit or "value-added."[2]

A similar—and perhaps rosier—picture relates to natural gas. In addition to its vast oil deposits, Iran is also endowed with mammoth reserves of gas. The volume of free and associated natural gas is estimated at about

50.1 trillion cubic meters (tcm) of which 59 percent, or 30 tcm, is considered recoverable—constituting 15.5 percent of the world's reserves and the second largest source after Russia. Furthermore, energy experts believe that Iran still has vast deposits of gas to be discovered and that more than 60 percent of the proven natural gas reserves have not yet been developed.[3] With such immense deposits of oil and gas, Iran is now truly a global energy superpower. Several promising new on-shore and off-shore oil fields, considerable coal deposits, and an ambitious nuclear energy program enhance this status even further.

Sustainability prospects

Threatening this superpower position, however, are a number of formidable, yet surmountable challenges. First, many of Iran's oil fields are old and suffering from a depletion rate of 5 to 10 percent a year because of reservoir damage during the 1980–88 Iran–Iraq war, poor maintenance, and gradual exhaustion.[4] Second, due to the highly subsidized domestic energy prices, Iran has one of the world's highest fuel consumption rates. Because of the inexpensive energy prices inside Iran—often below delivered costs—per capita energy use in Iran is estimated to be 15 times that of Japan, 10 times that of the European Union, and eight times that of the United States.[5] It is also rising at nearly 10 percent a year for gasoline and 6 percent for all fuel products—twice the world's average, and nearly four times the country's rate of population growth. Third, the minimum of $1.8 to $2 billion of new investments a year which are needed to maintain production capacity and make up for reservoir decline, in addition to the $9 to $10 billion a year required to increase production capacity, have been held back by several factors. These include insufficient yearly investment estimated at no more than $3 billion,[6] the reluctance of many major international oil companies to invest in Iran due to the unattractiveness of its "buy-back" contract requirements, US sanctions, and various domestic political impediments.

Fourth, due to increased demand for natural gas from households, factories and automobiles, there have been insufficient supplies for re-injection into aging oil fields to maintain well pressure or supply contracted gas exports. Fifth, gas-guzzling old cars on the roads, inefficient household appliances wasting over 50 percent of thermal energy use, and an estimated 65 percent power transmission losses tend to nullify yearly additions to capacity. Sixth, and finally, some 15 percent of available fuel products are smuggled out to neighboring countries due to their higher prices and more rational foreign exchange rates.

For all these reasons, a recent crop of alarmist forecasts warn that Iran will cease to be an oil exporter by 2012, 2015, or 2020.[7] The nub of these arguments is that, with extravagant energy subsidies, demand for fuel products has been artificially boosted while the Islamic Republic's defiant stand on uranium enrichment—and corresponding UN and US sanctions—have reduced the government's ability to obtain up-to-date technology (including enhanced recovery techniques) in order to increase supply.

Questioning the validity and relevance of these pessimistic projections, however, is the fact that in recent years, for each barrel of crude oil extracted, 1.32 barrels of oil have been added to Iran's total reserves through new discoveries or improved recovery methods.[8] Iran's average daily crude production in mid-2008 stood at 4.1 million barrels, of which nearly 1.5 mb/d (million barrels per day) was exported. Iran's Fourth Economic Development plan (2005–10)—setting targets for public expenditure and investment—calls for an increase in oil production capacity to 5.6 mb/d, and a rise further to 7 mb/d by 2020. Although both goals appear elusive at this time for a variety of financial, economic, and diplomatic reasons, the current average output capacity of 4.3 mb/d could be raised toward the Fourth Plan goal under a proper and rational energy policy, financed by domestic funds. In other words, under a reasonably efficient output maintenance program, and through the pursuit of a rational energy policy, Iran would be assured of a plentiful and fairly cheap supply of oil for decades to come. Even without substantial new oil discoveries, Iran's deposits at the current rate of consumption are projected to last for another 70 years.[9]

A similar scenario looks likely to hold for natural gas. In early 2008, Iran consumed a record 470 million cubic meters of gas a day—all for domestic use. A small 3.5 bcm (billion cubic meters) of gas imported from Turkmenistan for use in the Northern provinces nearly equaled Iran's own 4 bcm gas exports to Turkey.[10] Natural gas provides 60 percent of the country's current use, meeting the needs of 630 cities and nearly 75 percent of the population. Power stations, households and commercial enterprises, and the industrial sector receive roughly similar shares of the total (27–34 percent each), and the balance of 7.5 percent constitutes export and gas injection into the oil fields. It is expected that rising prices and more efficient use will reduce the annual rate of consumption growth from the current 12 percent to about 4 percent in the next 15 years. In 2007, some 8.4 bcm was also still flared due to technical or financial difficulties of collecting them. In the Islamic Republic's "20 Year Perspective" approved by the Majlis (national parliament) and the Supreme Leader, Iran is projected to become the world's third largest natural gas producer by 2024—based on current proven reserves and the potential for finding new fields. Annual production is to rise from 130 bcm in 2007 to 475 bcm by then. According to energy expert Narsi Ghorban, taking into consideration all the potential gas use, Iran could still be a major gas consumer and exporter for most of the 21st century—even with no new gas fields to be discovered.[11] By another estimate, Iran can enjoy 300 years of gas availability under efficient exploitation.[12]

Oil's major blessings

Oil wealth has not only been the mainstay of the Iranian economy, but also the principal source of its economic, technological, and socio-cultural development. This unrequited bounty, making the country the world's fourth largest crude producer and OPEC's second largest petroleum exporter, has enabled the Islamic Republic to wield enormous geopolitical, cultural, and economic clout. While the "oil industry," as such, has by no means the largest share of national product, it is the largest source of the government budget and the main engine of Iran's economic growth. Oil export receipts provide some 59 percent of the 2008–9 budget revenue directly, and nearly 70 percent indirectly through taxes on imports and other activities financed by oil money. Furthermore, foreign exchange earnings from oil are vital to the maintenance of all other economic sectors. Iran's non-energy exports can at best finance only four months of required imports. Agriculture depends on oil-financed imports not only for machinery and "luxury" goods (foreign cars, red meat, and exotic fruits), but also for such staples as wheat, barley, corn, sugar, rice, and potatoes. The national food supply is reportedly dependent on imports—depending on annual rainfall and other conditions—for an estimated 10 to 25 percent of domestic aggregate demand.[13] Iran's industry needs imports of raw materials and semi-processed goods—estimated to be anywhere from 25 to 60 percent of its inputs. And the services sector perennially shows a negative trade balance. The windfalls, breaking a hundred-year record—and rising five times between 1999 and 2007 from $16 billion to more than $79 billion—have given the Islamic regime a unique role in deciding the Middle East's security, stability, and welfare. Also, Iran has adopted an intransigent (boasted as "independent") policy vis-à-vis the West in general and Washington and Jerusalem in particular. In addition to helping the beleaguered Ahmadinejad government to produce a helpful GDP growth, fight spiraling inflation, and fill various economic potholes, the oil bounty has also been instrumental in strengthening the Islamic Republic's global political position. The Tehran government has persistently explained and defended its growing presence and involvements in Iraq, Afghanistan, Lebanon, and the Gaza Strip as constructive, morally justified, and humanitarian—refuting the charges of aggressions, military adventurism, and political offensives as reported in the Western press.[14] However, it is obvious that none of these engagements would have taken place if the Islamic Republic lacked sufficient financial means. Equally impossible would have been Iran's ability to further its nuclear power ambitions—for whatever purpose the development may be.

Another manifestation of Tehran's so-called "independent" foreign policy position, backed by the oil fortune, has been its ability to adopt a clearly hardening position vis-à-vis the European mediators and successfully mitigate the impact of UN and US sanctions. Claiming that the Islamic Republic was engaged in enriching uranium and producing plutonium in order to make nuclear weapons, the UN Security Council, under Washington's leadership, has imposed three rounds of resolutions against Iran between 2006 and 2008—Resolution 1727, Resolution 1747, and Resolution 1803—all targeting the country's most sensitive nuclear activities.[15] The toughest measures in these resolutions include a travel ban on certain Iranian individuals along with the freezing of assets linked to nuclear proliferation, restrictions on the trade of dual-use items involved in weapons development, an embargo on Iranian arms exports, inspections of suspicious and prohibited cargo, and restricting training of Iranian nationals in nuclear activities.

The Islamic regime, in turn, has insisted that its nuclear program is for peaceful generation of energy, within its rights granted by the Non-Proliferation Treaty, and in accordance with Islamic law that prohibits nuclear armament. Tehran's decision to continue its uranium enrichment program, and President Ahmadinejad's boast about tripling the number of nuclear centrifuges,[16] can be traced almost directly to the oil bounty.[17] If Iran lacked the oil money and a lucrative market prospect, it could not rely on the tacit but continued support of two of the UN Security Council's veto-powered members—Russia and China. Beijing's growing energy needs and oil-financed exports to Iran, Moscow's actual and potential ties to the Islamic Republic's arms purchases and ambitious nuclear energy program, and the European Union's increasing interest in Iran's oil (and especially gas reserves) all collectively combined to undermine the prospects for harder-hitting resolutions. The country's expanded nuclear program (and the prospects of additional nuclear reactors besides the current Russian-built Bushehr plant) are all based on oil-financed purchases from abroad. As a cogent editorial has pointed out, sanctions so far imposed on the Tehran government have lacked real economic bite because "all of the key players—except the United States—have strong economic reasons not to put the squeeze on Iran."[18]

Supremely confident of the world's needs for Iranian oil and gas, the Islamic Republic's high officials have scoffed at the UN resolutions and belittled a bag of sanctions unilaterally imposed by Washington on Iran's banking and financial network. Tehran has taken a defiant position toward all the UN resolutions, calling them "legally defective and politically coercive."[19] This unfounded confidence has led President Ahmadinejad and his first deputy to call UN mandates a worthless piece of paper, and the Petroleum Minister termed sanctions as an "old and worn out tool that belongs to the decades of [the] 1950s and 1960s." Citing the presence of 500 companies from 30 countries at Iran's 13th oil, gas, and petrochemical exhibition on 20 April 2008, the minister expressed confidence that the country can withstand current sanctions.[20] The Deputy Oil Minister, confirming that all the world's major commercial banks have officially restricted their transactions with Iran, indicated that these banks are all professionally astute enough to know how to continue business "indirectly."[21] Reports also show that banks in the Persian Gulf region, China, and other parts of Asia have continued their normal transactions, and even filled the gaps left by the reluctance of Western banks.[22]

Curiously enough, despite repeated and vigorous denials by Iranian officials regarding the sanctions' effectiveness, Iran's Minister of Foreign Affairs, in a recent 20-page letter to the UN Secretary-General, reserved the country's "right to resort to legal action to seek redress" for "all the damages they have inflicted."[23] There is no doubt, however, that the restrictive measures so far imposed by the UN—and particularly those imposed by the United States—on Iran[24] have substantially raised foreign trade's transaction costs, restricted access to overseas finance, and disrupted other commercial operations (e.g., merchant marine).[25] Even the January 2008 report by the US Governmental Accountability Office, indicating that Washington's sanctions against Iran have been ineffective since the county has been able to attract $20 billion of foreign investment in its energy sector since 2003,[26] refers only to the (dubious) investment figures and does not address the facts that sanctions have had a visibly negative effect on the Iranian economy.[27] Yet, there is no doubt that rising oil prices have insulated the economy from various sanctions to a large extent.[28]

The oil curse

Offsetting the manifold blessings of the oil wealth is an inherent curse that manifests itself in various economic, political, and socio-cultural arenas. Iran's political economy is the first major casualty. The oil windfall directly and immediately increases monetary resources in the government's hands. And in essentially non-democratic regimes like the Islamic Republic, more money leads directly to greater state power. With larger resources at the government's disposal, the size of the public sector automatically increases, and the free-market private sector is correspondingly reduced. Simultaneously, as the necessity of exacting funds from the public in the form of taxes and levies correspondingly diminishes, the state's discretionary and often arbitrary power increases. Thus, any trend toward a participatory democracy is undermined.

The sheer volume and sudden explosion of unrequited income also creates a thorny allocation problem. A misplaced conviction that the shortage of capital is the main cause of underdevelopment, unemployment, poverty, and other age-old socioeconomic afflictions pushes state planners to follow an expeditious and maximalist approach to spending. Political pressures to spend the manna as fast as possible in order to eradicate scourges of poverty, disease, and deprivation, in turn, results in several unintended yet harmful consequences. This approach inevitably ignores rational cost-benefit analyses of development projects and invariably leads to a good deal of waste, fraud, and corruption.[29]

The Ahmadinejad administration's performance in the last three years vividly attests to the latest manifestation of this phenomenon. From 2005 to 2008, the average annual price of Iranian crude rose from $50.7 per barrel to $92, and within three years, Iran earned $194 billion from exports of oil and another $26 billion from foreign sales of oil products—a combined $220 billion, equal to 16 years of oil receipts from 1988 to 2004. This also meant earning the entire 60 months' projection of oil receipts in the Fourth Plan (2005–10) in only 17 months. By some economists' projections, each $10 increase in the daily price of crude oil, if properly used, should have increased real annual GDP by 1 percent.[30] Yet, Iran's GDP growth rate of 4.8 percent in 2004 rose to 5.7 percent in 2005, 6.3 percent in 2006, and 5.8 percent in 2007—much below that estimation of 9 percent and also short of the 8 percent targeted in the Fourth Development Plan.[31]

At the same time, the government's annual current and development budgets steadily went up by more than 10 percent a year in real terms in tandem with the rising oil prices and mushrooming oil revenues.[32] But due to a highly inefficient use of new income, the massive windfalls did not result in lowering double-digit unemployment or reducing poverty. In fact, plagued by an ineffective and poorly administered tax system, and a non-transparent management of the new wealth, the oil benefits have not been equitably distributed among various social strata. Furthermore, poverty—which by different official estimates still afflicts some 9 to 15 million individuals, or about 13 to 20 percent of the population—has remained intact or even worsened.[33] By a recent estimate, the Gini coefficient of income—a zero to one scale of a country's income distribution, with one signifying totally uneven income distribution—in the three years deteriorated from 0.43 to 0.58.[34] Meanwhile, despite a 50 percent increase in imports (and reportedly turning Iran from a net food exporter to a net food importer)[35] during the period, the official consumer price index which sat at 10.8 percent in August 2005 (when Mr. Ahmadinejad took office) rose to 26 percent in June 2008[36]—resulting in the highest rate in the region and fifth highest in the world.

In a tried-and-true fashion, the Iranian economy thus became afflicted with the so-called Dutch Disease, whereby a doubling of petrodollar-financed imports to $52.6 billion in 2007 (plus a reported $6 billion of smuggled items)[37] failed to stem the inflationary tide. Also, by increasing the share of consumer goods in total annual imports from 12 percent to 20 percent in three years, the influx of petrodollars helped to depress significant segments of domestic industry and agriculture.[38] Instead of trying to cope with this combination of inflation and stagnation in an economically rational manner, however, the statist-oriented Ahmadinejad government took the opposite path. By openly repudiating the efficacy of what he called "decaying capitalist remedies," the president aggravated the government's already daunting task.[39] On the one hand, due to his administration's highly expansionary fiscal and monetary policies, total liquidity increased from 24.6 percent in 2003 to 41.5 percent a year in 2007 (i.e., Rls 650 trillion in 2005 to Rls 1,400 trillion in 2007). A steady double-digit addition to the annual current budgets, on-the-spot approval of ad hoc development projects during the cabinet's nationwide tours, wholesale payments of government employees' delayed salary and pension obligations, generous low-cost loans to young couples for marriage and housing needs, and repeated extractions from the Oil Stabilization Fund to pay for budget deficits all added fuel to the fire.

At the same time, the president bought into the simplistic and irrational belief that high interest rates are the main cause of soaring inflation. Ignoring every economist's warnings, he personally ordered the reductions of banking interest rates from 24 percent to 16 percent first, and then to 12 percent.

Annual inflation subsequently went up from 12 percent to over 19 percent. Despite this evidence, and the experts' argument that interest payments on average accounted for only 5 percent of total cost of goods, the president stubbornly again ordered another cut to 10 percent for some economic sectors in 2008. The unintended consequence of lowering interest rates below inflation rates was to encourage rent-seeking transactions and the diversion of liquidity from the formal to the informal money market in the bazaar, fetching staggering rates of up to 56 percent![40] Not surprisingly, the Central Bank's 15 percent per year long-term bonds (called "participation papers" to conform to Islam's edict against interest) were all subsequently returned for cash as soon as the inflation rate surpassed the interest rate.[41]

The other result of the president's bias was that some of the major economic liberalization policies painstakingly put in place during the Khatami administration—measures such as price decontrol, banking deregulation, trade liberalization, subsidies' proper target orientation, and a hesitant but cautious demarche toward an eventual free-market economy—were thwarted. The impact has been particularly pronounced in the practical neglect of the "privatization" program advocated by the Supreme Leader as a means of combining rapid economic growth with Islamic social justice.[42] Due largely to these reversals, recent World Bank reports on conditions of doing business show Iran's ranking steadily declining from 113 among 175 nations in 2005 to 119 in 2006, 131 in 2007, and 135 in 2008.[43]

Politics and governance have been the second victim of the oil curse. The negative influence of the oil windfall on Iran's internal and external politics is reflected in a movement away from an open society and participatory democracy toward statism and autocracy at home—in addition to a uselessly belligerent position abroad. In the absence of effective constitutional checks and balances, the oil wealth has led to authoritarianism in two inter-related fashions. First, by raising food and fuel subsidies, increasing welfare payments, and providing free or low-cost health and education to the masses—all financed by oil money—the government has been able to buy the rank and file's tacit support of a non-democratic rule. Second, with the oil windfalls large enough to finance an increasing portion of fiscal budget and reduce the need for income and sales taxes to run the government, power-hungry political leaders have developed a penchant for arbitrary rule, often verging on arrogance and occasionally approaching megalomania.

The corrupting influence of the oil bounty on the Iranian polity in the last three years has been reflected by increasing violations of human rights, further encroachments on personal liberties, lack of immunity from unlawful search and seizure, capricious persecution of dissidents, a purge of free-thinking university professors and students, repression of ethnic and religious ministries, tightening up of social restrictions and Islamic moral code, assaults on press freedom,[44] the closure of 22 websites, restricting parliamentary elections, vote tampering, disallowing labor unions, and clinging to an anti-feminist pathology.[45] In the 2008 Index of Economic Freedom, published by the

Heritage Foundation, the Islamic Republic is ranked 151 among 157 rated countries in terms of overall freedoms.[46]

The crucial role of the oil windfall in meeting the government's law and order budgets (i.e., police, national defense, and nuclear ambitions) has left a significant residual for welfare expenditures (e.g., keeping one million *basij*, or paramilitary families, under one or more charitable umbrellas). It has also freed the Ahmadinejad administration from normal public scrutiny and accountability obligations. The Minister of Petroleum has admitted that, by order of the president, he has disregarded a statutory Majlis limit on the import of gasoline in 2007.[47] Mr. Ahmadinejad has also taken a series of ad hoc and arbitrary decisions—disobeying Majlis statutes, making unplanned inroads into the Oil Stabilization Fund, abolishing various specialized national councils (including the former high-powered Money and Credit Council), turning the former Management and Plan Organization into a section of the office of the president, declaring national holidays out of the blue, and doing away with various civil societies.

At the same time, the widely propagandized assertion that any US or Israeli attacks on Iranian nuclear installations would (among other horrifying calamities in the region) raise the price of oil to $200 a barrel—and therefore could not possibly happen—has had another adverse effect. It has emboldened President Ahmadinejad to go on an outlandish verbal rampage, sometimes verging on comical delirium. Thus, addressing a group of clerics in Khorasan province, he called Iran's "self-reliant nuclearization" the "contemporary history's greatest miracle."[48] In another speech in Hamadan city he called Iran "not only the superpower in the region" but "the superpower on the global scene."[49] And in a third harangue, he called Iran "the center of all global happenings" with two divine missions: one, to make Iran "a model of power, progress, and Godliness" for the world; and the other, "to change the whole global direction and management."[50] Then he topped the bravado by adding: "A movement has started for us to occupy ourselves with global responsibilities. God willing, Iran will be the axis of the leadership of this movement."[51] The net effects of these empty and risible statements have made the Islamic Republic increasingly isolated, and brought the country's international credibility to its lowest ebb.

The socio-psychological curse of the oil windfall is the creation of a petroculture that turns hard work into sweet dreams. It undermines the rank and file's self-reliance, creativity, and work ethic—making them increasingly reliant on the state for livelihood and dependent on government dole for welfare. It also diverts business talent and ingenuity from innovation and entrepreneurship to rent-seeking maneuvers and sweetheart deals. This culture, ephemeral and fleeting at first, becomes endemic as time goes by and easy oil receipts increase.

An outstanding manifestation of this mentality is the Iranian population's addiction to low (and often below-cost) prices for public goods and services, and their tacit threat of revolts against any cost/price adjustments. Currently,

Islamic Republic residents enjoy highly subsidized fuel, food, prescription drugs and public services (water, power, telephone, and transport means). The size of the government's direct subsidies, monetary aid, and below-cost sales in the 2008 budget is about $25 billion.[52] Yet, if the value of oil, gas, and fuel products consumed locally is calculated at delivered prices in the Persian Gulf, the notional subsidy would approach $100 billion—out of a GDP of less than $290 billion.[53] Numerous attempts by reform-minded officials since the early 1990s to gradually raise local prices towards international levels have all come to naught. Even a clear legal mandate to this effect in the Fourth Plan (2005–10) law, approved by the sixth Majlis, was countermanded by the seventh as a "new-year gift" to the people! Despite clear and universal recognition that many of these subsidies benefit mostly the top 10 to 20 percent of income earners, repeated attempts to rectify the situation have been blocked by a majority of Majlis deputies worried about their re-election chances.[54] Another clear reflection of this mindset is a propensity to avoid hard work, enjoy leisure, seek shortcuts, and rely on connections rather than creativity. Iranian workers and employees enjoy 25 official holidays a year (compared to the world average of 13.5 days) in addition to weekly Fridays and part of Thursday. This brings the annual workdays to about 220 accompanied by low total factor productivity.[55] The average productivity of the Iranian labor force is variously estimated to have been between 0.9 and 1.9 percent a year—exceeding that of capital productivity—in the last three years.[56] As a result, the 2.2 percent annual increase in total factor productivity targeted in the Fourth Plan has so far been limited to only 1.3 percent.[57]

Influenced by this mentality, even the laudable Islamic tradition of charitable *qar-zol-hassaneh* (QH, whereby affluent income savers volunteer to lend a part of their savings to the poor at zero interest rate) has lost its lofty goal and turned into plain greed. With state commercial banks accepting QH deposits and paying no interest to their depositors—but offering them a chance to participate in various multi-million rial annual bank lotteries—QH funds have increased faster than other long-term interest-bearing deposits. Moreover, they are offered by individuals who are neither rich nor devout, simply in the hope of winning lottery prizes.[58]

The worst aspect of the petroculture is the metamorphosis of the traditional and class-specific corruption into a systemic and institutionalized practice. The multifaceted aspects of this transformation relate to almost all aspects of people's daily life and affect the conduct of nearly all businesses. As is well publicized, no significant transactions between ordinary citizens and public agencies in Iran take place without some illegal or extra-legal payments involved. On the people's part, it covers giving and taking bribes for routine transactions. These include everything, from paying off a poorly paid policeman to fix a ticket all the way to bribing a "revolutionary court" judge to dismiss a case involving a violation of the Islamic moral code.[59] A clear consequence of this conversion is also a change for the worst in the nature and conduct of daily businesses. Here, institutionalized corruption takes a number of different and more sophisticated forms. These range from a special ministerial permit for exclusive imports or exports of certain products;[60] ad hoc changes in import tariffs known beforehand by only a few insiders;[61] sale of products by state enterprises exclusively to certain favored agents at fixed low prices, enabling them to resell them in the free market at higher prices;[62] and gigantic loans made by state banks to influential borrowers who become routinely delinquent in their repayment, with the banks at their virtual mercy.[63]

Where the size of some commercial contracts (for example, the development of domestic oil or gas fields) runs into hundreds of millions or even billions of dollars, the middlemen's commissions, called "success fees," would be neither a pittance, nor embedded in poverty and sheer necessity.[64] Millions of dollars are reportedly paid to well-connected officials facilitating deals. In a piece where the Berlin-based Transparency International ranked the Islamic Republic among the "highly corrupt," a Norwegian official whose oil company was fined for bribery is quoted as euphemistically saying: "There was a clear understanding that companies that are active in Iran are expected to contribute to the Iranian society in one way or another." An Iranian middleman who had facilitated a $1.8 billion oil deal also claims that "doing business in Iran without paying someone is impossible."[65] According to Transparency International's latest report, the Islamic Republic's corruption rank among 179 countries deteriorated from 78 in the year 2003 to 105 in 2006, and 131 in 2007.[66]

Stung by this deteriorating reputation, the Majlis' watchdog Commission 90, invoking the Supreme Leader's eight-point anti-corruption order of 2001, issued a report in early 2008 highlighting the details of 53 of the most significant cases out of a total of 400 confidential files. The report found flagrant wrongdoings by state officials in seven categories: real estate, banking and insurance, industry, oil, education, judiciary, and auto manufacturing.[67] Despite a statute passed by the Majlis in 2006 to identify individual suspects, and against protests from several deputies, the Commission 90 reporter refused to name names, arguing that the head of the judiciary had forbidden such revelations before any conviction by a court.[68] Currently, the debate continues between the president, who blames most of his failures on oil and banking "mafias," and his critics, who ask him to identify these sources.

Some crude realities

Despite its gigantic energy reserves and its privileged position in the region, the Islamic Republic is not in an enviable position. The country's economy is woefully mismanaged: it is not only fraught with thorny problems of double-digit inflation, high unemployment, and sub-par growth, but also vulnerable to unpredictable oil price downfalls and serious universal sanctions. And, ironically enough, its future self-sufficiency in either fuel products or natural gas is questionable. Iran still needs the world markets much more than the latter needs Iran's oil and gas. The world could cope without Iran's energy exports through national strategic reserves, the use of excess capacity in other oil-rich countries, further energy-saving devices, use of alternative sources, and, if need be, higher prices. However, Iran's desperate need for oil export revenues to finance its essential imports (including refined oil products) and pay for ordinary government expenditures disallows even a fairly temporary interruption. Without oil as its lifeblood, Iran's economy would come to a standstill in a very short time.

Undue confidence in large energy reserves as a dominant force has also led the Islamic Republic to defy the international community on the matter of uranium enrichment at its own peril. It has also tempted President Ahmadinejad to engage in such empty boasts as calling Iran "a powerhouse on the global level" capable of providing a "global plan to handle world problems"—thus making the Islamic Republic the subject of worldwide ridicule.[69] Heretical as it may sound, one may wonder whether endowment with more irrigation water and vastly more arable land, instead of oil and gas, would have led to a better social, economic, and political situation for Iran.

Notes

* First published in the *Brown Journal of World Affairs*, Fall/Winter 2008, Volume XV, no. 1. Reproduced with permission.

1 For sources of relevant figures see the British Petroleum Annual Statistical Review, April 14, 2008, available at www.jeslami.com/1387 and www.donya-e-eqtesad.com, August 12, 2008, based on figures published by the Islamic Republic's Central Bank.

2 This compares highly favorably with the World Trade Organization's estimated average added value in manufacturing to be about 5 percent. See www.donya-e-eqtesad.com, April 9, 2008.

3 See "Iran Oil and Gas," *Middle East Economic Digest* 45, no. 5, February 2, 2001.

4 See Stanley Reed, "Surprise: Oil Woes in Iran," *Business Week*, November 30, 2006; Karl Beckman, "The West vs Iran," available at www.antiwar.com, 18 March 2008; and *Middle East Economic Survey*, September 18, 2006.

5 www.sarmayeh.net/, July 25, 2008.

6 See Robin Pagnamenta, "Iran Supply Problems Add to Fears of Oil Hitting $200 a Barrel," Times Online, May 7, 2008, http://business.timesonline.co.uk/tol/business/industry_sectors/natural_resources/ article3882663.ece.

7 See http://emruz.com, December 2, 2007; Roger Stern, "The Iranian Petroleum Crisis," *Proceedings of the National Academy of Sciences*, December 26, 2006.

8 Statement by the Chairman of the National Iranian Oil Company, available at www.hamshahri.net, March 12, 2003; see also the statement by the company's Director of Oil Exploration, ibid., September 22, 2007.

9 Statement by the Minister of Petroleum, available at http://jomhourieslami.com/1386, April 28, 2007.

10 Statement by the Managing Director of Iranian National Gas Company, cited in "Economics of Gas," *Iran Economics*, May 2008.

11 Narsi Ghorban, "Monetizing Gas Reserves: Iran's Options," *Middle East Economic Survey*, November 26, 2001; and "Iran's Future Gas Development and Exports," ibid., February 25, 2008.

12 http://jomhourieslami.com/1386, April 28, 2007.
13 After declaring Iran self-sufficient in wheat production and even readiness for exports in 2006, the government has recently issued a permit for the importation of 2 million tons of wheat in 2008 along with another ton of barley and unspecified quantities of meat, cooking oil, and fruits. See www.jeslami.com/1387, April 16, 2008.
14 See "Countering Iran," editorial, *Washington Post*, April 23, 2008, available at www.washingtonpost.com/wp-dyn/content/article/2008/04/12/AR2008041201848.html.
15 For a glance at the content of these resolutions, see "UN Adds Third Layer to Iran Sanctions," *Washington Post*, March 4, 2008, available at www.washingtonpost.com/wp-dyn/content/article/2008/03/03/AR2008030302816.html.
16 See Nazila Fathi and William J. Broad, "Iran Says it's Installing New Centrifuges," *International Herald Tribune*, April 9, 2008, available at www.iht.com/articles/2008/04/08/africa/09iran.php.
17 Thomas Erdbrink, "Iran Affirms its Defiance on Nuclear Program," *Washington Post*, February 21, 2008.
18 See "Too Easy to Refuse," editorial, *New York Times*, January 28, 2008.
19 See an article on UN Sanctions by Robin Wright and Colum Lynch, "U.N. Imposes New Sanctions on Iran," *Washington Post*, March 4, 2008, available at www.washingtonpost.com/wp-dyn/content/story/2008/03/03/ST2008030303272.html.
20 "Iran to Invest $500b in Hydrocarbon Sector," April 21, 2008, available at http://english.farsnews.com/newstext.php?nn=8702020789.
21 www.radiofarda.com, April 21, 2008.
22 Steven R. Weisman, "U.S. Sanctions Force World Bank to Halt some Iran Aid," *New York Times*, November 5, 2007.
23 See Patrick Worsnip, "Iran Threatens Legal Action over U.N. Sanctions," *International Herald Tribune*, March 27, 2008, available at www.iht.com/articles/reuters/2008/03/26/africa/OUKWD-UK-IRANNUCLEAR-UN.php.
24 Anna Fifield and Javier Blas, "Shell and Repsol Drop Iran Gas Project," *Financial Times*, May 11, 2008, available at www.ft.com/cms/s/0/2428c5c6-1f83-11dd-9216-000077b07658.html?nclick_check=1.
25 The head of an Iranian shipping line reports that due to foreign parties' refusal to carry cargo on Iranian flag ships, he has decided to remove the flag and sail under a "free" flag, see http://emruz.biz, April 24, 2008. See also estimates by an influential Majlis deputy at www.sarmayeh.net, May 18, 2008.
26 http://hamshahrionline.ir, January 16, 2008.
27 "Iran Sanctions Ripple Past Those in Power," *Los Angeles Times*, January 20, 2008.
28 Farnaz Fassihi and Chip Cummins, "Iranians Scheme to Elude Sanctions," *Wall Street Journal*, February 13, 2008.
29 For some examples in the Iranian case see www.jeslami.com/1387, April 12, 2008.
30 Projection by a former head of Iran's Planning and Budget Organization, available at www.hamshahrionline.ir, May 10, 2008.
31 See http://emruz.biz, May 3, 2008. See also *Iran Economics*, Farvardin 1387 (March–April 2008).
32 President Ahmadinejad declares with pride that during two-and-a-half years of his administration some 99,000 new development projects were launched, and 49,000 of them came to fruition. *BBC Monitoring International Reports*, May 6, 2008.
33 See www.payvand.com/news, 3 April 2008. See a special report, and also a statement by a high planning official, available at www.sarmayeh.net, May 5 and 28, 2008.

34 www.hamshahrionline.ir, May 22, 2008.
35 http://emruz.biz, June 29, 2008.
36 www.iran-times.com, May 9, 2008.
37 www.jeslami.com/1387, May 12, 2008.
38 For a detailed description of this situation, see Jahangir Amuzegar, "Iran's Rising New Threats," *Middle East Economic Survey*, January 4, 2008. For a more recent confirmation of this "disease" in the Iranian economy, see www.hamshahrionline.ir/News, April 7, 2008.
39 Speech before a clerical gathering in Hamadan, available at http://emruz.biz, April 24, 2008.
40 www.jeslami.com/1387, May 16, 2008.
41 www.jeslami.com/1387, May 14, 2008. See also criticism by former President Rafsanjani, available at www.radiofarda.com, May 19, 2008.
42 For a report on privatization setbacks see www.hamshahrionline.ir/News, April 14, 2008.
43 www.donya-e-eqtesad.com, May 5, 2008; www.jeslami. com, June 9, 2008.
44 According to a new report, in 2007 Iran banned a media outlet, newspaper, or journal every 36 hours. Twenty-three journalists were arrested and 42 were sentenced in the courts. See "Media Banned Every 36 Hours in Iran," International Journalists' Network, May 10, 2008, available at www.ijnet.org/director.aspx?P=Article&ID=307631&LID=1.
45 For a full text of these infringements see http://emruz.biz, May 18, 2008.
46 Heritage Foundation 2008 Index of Economic Freedom: Iran, available at www.heritage.org/research/features/index/country.cfm?id=Iran. For another account see the 2008 annual report of the Defenders of Human Rights Center, *Iran Times International*, May 23, 2008, available at www.iran-times.com.
47 www.jeslami.com/1387, May 12, 2008.
48 www.donya-e-eqtesad.com, April 11, 2008.
49 http://emruz.biz, April 23, 2008.
50 http://emruz.biz, April 10, 2008.
51 Thomas Erdbrink, "Ahmadinejad Criticized for Saying Long-Ago Imam Mahdi Leads Iran," *Washington Post*, May 8, 2008.
52 www.sarmayeh.net, May 17, 2008.
53 Statements by the Minister of Finance, and Deputy Minister of Petroleum, available at www.donya-e-eqtesad.com, April 6, 2008. For a more detailed discussion of the issue see www.sarmayeh.net, April 29, and May 17, 2008.
54 www.jeslami.com/1387, May 12, 2008.
55 For details see http://emruz.biz, January 7, 2008.
56 See *Iran Economics*, May 2008. See also www.sarmayeh.net, May 23, 2008.
57 www.jeslami.com/1378, June 15, 2008.
58 www.sarmayeh.net, April 26, 2008.
59 These are, in essence, not really bribes, but "taxation without intermediation," a salary supplement directly collected by state employees who are not paid enough by the government.
60 www.donya-e-eqtesad, May 6, 2008.
61 www.donya-e-eqtesad, December 11, 2007.
62 http://jomhourieslami.com/1386, December 12, 2007.
63 www.iran.emrooz.net, May 14, 2008. According to this report, the state banks' nonperforming loans rose from Rls 35,000 billion to Rls 150,000 billion between the end of 2004 and the end of 2007.
64 See the statement by the head of Majlis Research Center, available at www.sarmayeh.net, May 23, 2008.
65 See Kambiz Foroohar, "Rafsanjanis are Iran's Power Brokers for Investors," *Bloomberg Market Stories*, April 21, 2004.

66 Transparency International, *Global Corruption Report 2007* (New York: Cambridge University, Press, 2007).
67 http://emruz.biz, May 30, 2008.
68 www.donya-e-eqtesad, May 30, 2008.
69 See www.iran-times.com, June 13, and July 25, 2008.

14 The Islamic Republic of Iran

Facts and fiction*

Over the last three decades, Iran has been a prominent feature of the world press and global media. Not a week has passed since November 4, 1979—when 52 American diplomats were taken hostage in Tehran—without the clerical government being captured in the international spotlight. The near-daily news about the hostage situation, the Iran–Iraq War, and Washington's Iran–Contra fiasco were followed by reports of alleged terrorist bombings in Lebanon, Saudi Arabia, Argentina and Africa, along with dispatches about assassinations of political dissidents and critics at home and abroad. Later on, attention was focused on political mischief in Iraq and Afghanistan involving US and NATO forces, as well as increasing political repression and human-rights violations at home. Then, reports about clandestine uranium enrichment and nuclear development programs, subsequent UN Security Council sanctions, and other multilateral or unilateral penalties became headline news. And, lately, extensive reports about an alleged terrorist plan to assassinate the Saudi ambassador in Washington, the storming of the British embassy in Tehran by a shadowy group presumably angered by the Cameron government's sanctions on Iran, the downed US Sentinel stealth drone in northeastern Iran, and Tehran's threat to close the straits of Hormuz in case of total embargo on Iran's oil exports have supplied the ravenous international media with continuous, and at times sensational, material.

Despite this nearly ceaseless publicity, however, some fundamental characteristics of the Islamic regime have escaped proper scrutiny and are shrouded in myth. The regime's true political nature, the country's constitutional structure, the power and position of its top leaders, the political challenges it poses to the region and the world, the reasons for its long-term viability in the face of stiff global sanctions, and its ideological influence on the region's political movements remain largely misunderstood and misinterpreted. This brief review attempts to dispel seven of these myths.

(1) The Islamic Republic is one of the Middle East's vibrant democracies, since it holds regular elections for its office holders.

This is not only an exaggeration; it is essentially misleading. The Islamic government has, since its inception in 1979, held regular periodic elections for its major elective offices—the presidency, the Majlis (national assembly), the Assembly of Experts and municipal councils. Supreme Leader Ali Khamenei has called these elections "one of the Islamic regime's main pillars, a symbol of political maturity, and a national pride." But none of these elections can claim to have been a manifestation of real participatory democracy, for several reasons. To begin with, none has been deemed totally free and fair, and every one has been tarnished by reports of fraud and irregularities. Some, like President Ahmadinejad's reelection in 2009, have been widely contested and were followed by massive street demonstrations and popular protests.

Furthermore, none of these elections can pass the test of true popular representation: the people's free choice. By law, candidates for any elective office in Iran must be individually screened and approved before election campaigns by a special 12-member Council of Guardians, a cornerstone of the Islamic Republic. A quintessential qualification for candidacy, among others, is a "demonstrable loyalty" (*eltezam-e amali*) to the concept of rule by an Islamic jurist (*velayat-e faqih*). The Council can, and frequently does, reject candidates' eligibility on this and other vague grounds. Thus, in a Soviet-like procedure, only loyal candidates (*khodi*) are eligible to run, and all others (*geir khodi*) are excluded. In some elections (March 2012, for example), members and affiliates of several political parties, along with 2,700 out of nearly 5,000 registered candidates were not allowed to participate. Majlis candidates (except the incumbents) must also possess a master's degree from a domestic or foreign university. Deputies have no immunity from prosecution and can be hauled before the courts. And, according to a recently passed law, duly elected deputies can be expelled from the assembly during their terms of office if found disloyal to the concept of *velayat-e faqih*.

In addition, democracy is not just a political structure: it has its cultural, social and economic dimensions. A true democracy, in addition to having free and fair elections, requires (a) respect for certain universal values (such as basic civil rights); (b) certain institutions (a free press, active political parties, nongovernmental organizations (NGOs), trade unions, professional associations and similar civil entities); and (c) the rule of law and an independent judiciary as the ultimate guarantors of democratic rule.

The Iranian record on the first prerequisite is clearly dismal. As shown by the ninth consecutive annual censure resolution by the UN General Assembly since 2003 and periodic reports by the United States and other Western countries, Human Rights Watch and Amnesty International, basic human rights are routinely and flagrantly violated by the Islamic Republic. Individual daily lives are strictly regimented; personal freedoms (choice of food, clothing, entertainment and recreation) are all controlled. Dissenting journalists, student activists and defendants' lawyers are arrested on trumped-up charges. False confessions are extracted under torture and presented to Stalinist-type courts to obtain long prison sentences. Members of non-Shia faiths and other minorities are routinely mistreated. Iran's economic-freedom ranking in the 2012 report by Freedom House is 171st out of 179 countries. In political freedom and respect for human rights, it scores seventh, the lowest position on a seven-category scale.

The second prerequisite of a functioning democracy, the vitality of civil society, is also lacking in Iran. The press is censored. The Islamic Republic's ranking in press freedom, according to the 2012 report by the NGO Reporters Without Borders (Reporters sans frontières), is 175th out of 179 listed. The New York-based Committee to Protect Journalists describes Iran as the jailers of the highest numbers of press reporters in the world, with 42 behind bars in December 2011. Radio and television are state monopolies. Connections through the Internet, Facebook, Twitter and other social media are frequently jammed. Political parties are tightly regulated. Trade unions are banned. Lay professional associations are stigmatized. NGOs are selectively allowed to operate.

Third, a competent and independent judiciary, as the ultimate safeguard of democracy, is conspicuous by its absence and is described by its previous chief as "a total ruin." Manned by a group of incompetent and often corrupt political hacks with little or no background in law, the regular and "revolutionary" Islamic courts are charged with the implementation of a seventh-century-type penal code. These courts regularly mete out barbaric penalties (stoning to death, blinding, amputations and public flogging) and the world's highest per capita number of executions. The latest annual report of the World Justice Project, measuring respect for the law and citizens rights, places Iran at the very bottom of the 100 countries observed.

(2) Iran's "Islamic democracy" could be a suitable model for newly triumphal Islamic parties in such countries as Tunisia, Morocco and Egypt.

This is both erroneous and wrong-headed. The Islamic Republic's apologists at home and abroad, feeling self-conscious about the incongruity between their "democratic" system and a typical Western variety, have propagated the fiction that their "Islamic model" is an ideal form of government because it is headed by an eminent theologian—a man of God selected by his peers, who themselves are elected by popular vote.

There are two flaws in this bizarre claim. First, whether or not God's government on earth is superior to man's rule, the term "Islamic democracy" is self-contradictory and oxymoronic. Democracy, as its Greek origin signifies, is rule by the people. Religion can never be a vehicle for democracy. There is no religion based on democratic rule. Islam, like all other religions, is based on faith; democracy is based on a social contract. Democracy is composed of citizens regardless of their faith; Islam is composed of believers regardless of their citizenship. Islamic *sharia* is the reflection of God's rule on earth as prescribed by the Quran. The first and second clauses of Iran's 1979 constitution describe the regime as the manifestation of God's rule on earth. The state is headed by a *vali-e faqih*, who leads the country on behalf of the occult (hidden), twelfth imam. His orders (*hokm-e hokumati*), based on his understanding of Quranic principles, must be obeyed by every citizen, even if opposed by the majority. The people's wishes and votes would be respected only so long as they remain within the *sharia*'s mandates and the *vali*'s edicts. God's incontestable rules can never be remanded by the people's fickle votes, even by a 99 percent majority. A prominent theoretician of the regime claims that the Iranian system should be called the government of "Islamic Justice," a term he claims Ayatollah Khomeini preferred over "Islamic Republic," which he grudgingly accepted only as a matter of expediency.

Second, whether or not the ruler's access to power through popular vote is superior to other selective techniques, the matter does not apply in the case of Iran. True enough, the 86-member Assembly of Experts (all male clerics), which selects the *vali* (Supreme Leader, or *rahbar*) is elected periodically by direct popular vote. But this selection is currently a matter of debate. A recent interpretation by one of the *rahbar*'s own favorite theologians claims that Iran's Supreme Leader is in fact "designated" and "selected" by God himself and only "discovered" by the Islamic theologians of the Assembly of Experts.

In any event, none of the assembly members is actually a free agent; by law they all must first be screened and approved by the 12-member Council of Guardians. The Council itself, however, consists of six theologians appointed by the Supreme Leader, and six lay jurists selected by the Majlis from a list of nominees submitted by the judiciary chief. The chief justice is himself appointed by the Supreme Leader and is naturally expected to select nominees loyal to the *rahbar*. The Majlis deputies, who are supposed to select the council's lay members from among the judiciary chief's nominees, are themselves all screened and approved by the Council of Guardians and loyal to the *rahbar*. Thus, in a near-magical manner, the Supreme Leader appoints himself to the post!

As a further manifestation of this incestuous political process, some members of the Council of Guardians also serve in the Assembly of Experts. Nearly all members of the Assembly are Friday prayer imams appointed by the *rahbar*, or they are the latter's representatives in various public organizations. Another example of the assembly election farce is that, in some precincts, there is only one candidate, no contestant and an outcome that is known beforehand. There is no time limit for the *rahbar*'s tenure. Members of the Assembly of Experts are supposed to supervise his performance and remove him from office in case of incapacity or poor performance. But they usually meet twice a year and routinely issue endorsing proclamations. It is highly doubtful whether the recently triumphant Muslim people of North Africa would crave such a template.

(3) Supreme Leader Seyyed Ali Khamenei is one of the world's last remaining dictators and has unchecked religious and political power over all Iranian affairs.

A popular American magazine not long ago portrayed Iran's Supreme Leader as one of the world's 10 remaining dictators. Another business periodical has recently found him among the world's most powerful leaders. This is not only overweening hyperbole, it is essentially untrue. While some regime-financed clerics and sycophantic bureaucrats may call Ayatollah Khamenei the chosen emissary of the Prophet Mohammad on earth, he is neither a supreme religious authority nor a political dictator. In the unwritten Shiite hierarchy, he is a mid-level clergyman (*hojat-ol Islam*) whose title of "ayatollah" was not acquired through proper clerical procedures (writing a *resale*, or thesis). It was bestowed on him by lay politicians when he was elected Supreme Leader in 1989 after Ayatollah Khomeni's death. He may be regarded as a *marja* (source of emulation) by the poor on the state dole, and he may aspire to be the leader of the Muslim world, but he is generally dismissed by grand ayatollahs in Qom and Najaf as a lightweight. He occasionally issues inconsequential *fatwas* (religious edicts) against wearing ties, teaching music, consuming gold-plated ice-cream or misusing Facebook. But they are generally ridiculed and ignored. He also uses the bully pulpit to issue annual proclamations such as the speedy privatization of state industries, crusades against corruption, efforts toward food self-sufficiency and doubling the national output through an economic *jihad*. But these exhortations have so far remained ignored and unfulfilled.

Within the political hierarchy, he is the titular head of state and commander-in-chief of the armed forces. But Iran does not have one-man rule. And his powers are not unlimited; they are specifically defined by the Islamic Republic's constitution. He is equal to other citizens before the law and can be removed from office in cases of incapacitation or loss of essential qualifications. A clear testimony to his limited power is provided by a speech he delivered in mid-October 2011: "Leaders of Iran's executive branch, the Majlis, and the judiciary, in the fulfillment of their duties, may take certain decisions which the *rahbar* may not like. But the *rahbar* has neither the right nor the power to interfere with those decisions unless the matter involves derailing the Islamic revolution."

As a protector and promoter of the Islamic revolution, he uses all his wits and wisdom in a delicate balancing act by keeping various power centers in tow. Having appointed a veterinarian with no military background as the chairman of the joint chiefs of staff, he maintains a watchful eye on the armed forces. By frequently changing commanders of the regular armed services (without cutting their salaries or perks), he clearly tries to ward off possible challenges from the military. By allowing the Islamic Revolutionary Guard Corps (*pasdaran*) to obtain an increasing chunk of lucrative development projects in no-bid contracts, he is seeking their total loyalty. And, by recruiting thousands of teenage villagers and unemployed vigilantes into an informal militia (the *basij*), he manages to keep street demonstrators subdued.

The most formidable latent challenge to his authority, however, comes from the financially independent grand ayatollahs in Qom, who enjoy vast amounts of public respect and support. They are a potent force that he has been trying to win over, time and time again, by his frequent trips to the city.

As a person, Khamenei is a cautious and calculating man, a master of balancing acts who protects his power and prestige by avoiding involvement in controversial issues and factional politics by appointing special commissions to resolve disputes. In reality, he presides over several political satrapies manned by various oligarchs. In this power-sharing, semi-sanctioned anarchy, tolerated conflicts abound: statutes duly enacted by the Majlis are ignored by the executive branch; decrees passed by the Council of Ministers are found unlawful by the Majlis; the Supreme Audit Court finds gross violations of budgetary appropriations. Yet no one seems to mind. And the show goes on under the *rahbar*'s watchful eyes.

Unlike Machiavelli's ideal prince, Khamenei is neither widely respected nor truly feared. He is routinely obeyed by all because he has convinced other oligarchs that, in any shake-up, they would all come out losers.

(4) President Mahmood Ahmadinejad is a religious fanatic who truly believes in the imminent return of the twelfth Shia imam (*mahdi*), while posing as the main obstacle to a Tehran-Washington détente.

Ahmadinejad has a reputation for delivering crowd-pleasing and combative speeches full of bravado, falsehood and occasional vulgarity. His personal and managerial qualifications for the office may be questioned. But he is neither delusional nor crazy—as many in the West believe. He is a shrewd, street-wise and seasoned politician whose words and gestures, even those deliberately false or misleading, are carefully chosen to achieve specific objectives. He is a self-adulating and authoritarian leader, a demagogue masquerading as a populist, but he is not naïve. He may be the devout Muslim he pretends to be, but he is far from a clergy worshipper. In fact, his "liberal" position on certain hot-button issues—overlooking violations of the Islamic dress code, allowing women to attend sports events, kissing the hands of his old female school teacher, giving interviews to foreign female reporters without full head cover, expressing pride in Iran's pre-Islamic history, and rejecting gender segregation in the Iranian universities—attest to his departures from clerical orthodoxy.

For these reasons, it is widely suspected that his entire twelfth imam scenario is nothing but a clever ruse. It is believed that his expectation of the imam's imminent return, hints about having direct access to him, and claims of benefiting from his daily guidance on government affairs are all masterfully designed to clip the clergy's wings, if not implicitly question the sanctity of the *velayat-e-faqih* itself. For, in a situation where the country's daily public policies are specifically directed and supervised by the occult imam himself, there would hardly be need for a proxy, be it a *vali* or a *rahbar*.

In the matter of hostility toward Washington, too, Ahmadinejad's role is largely misunderstood. His regular anti-capitalist diatribes and grandstanding against the United States may give the impression of a personal anti-Americanism. But this has been merely an act. His oft-quoted bellicose statements about "wiping Israel off the map" and his denial of the Holocaust may have also seemed an obstacle to reconciliation with the United States. This has hardly been the case, however. His verbal assaults on Washington and Tel Aviv are nothing more than a parroting of Ayatollah Khomeini's numerous 1980s sermons; they are not his own constructs. In fact, among Iran's current political leaders, he is probably the most eager closet advocate of resuming diplomatic relations with the Great Satan.

Ahmadinejad's actions in this regard betray his narrative. He is the only president of the Islamic Republic who has congratulated an American president on an election victory. He has written letters to both Presidents George W. Bush and Barack Obama proposing a dialogue. In his annual trips to New York for the UN General Assembly, he has repeatedly asked to meet with US leaders, to no avail. During his last trip, in September 2011, he welcomed the establishment of a hotline between Iranian and American naval units in the Persian Gulf in order to avoid unintended mishaps. And his many suggestions for solving Iran's uranium-enrichment and nuclear-development programs have been the most conciliatory of any Iranian leader. His revered guru, best friend and close relative, Esfandiar Moshai, is rumored to have been making behind-the-scenes contacts everywhere to advance his reconciliation objective. Interestingly enough, the alleged plot to assassinate the Saudi envoy in Washington is rumored to have been hatched by Ahmadinejad's political enemies in order to nullify his pro-American démarche.

The deadlock in Tehran-Washington relations goes far beyond personal grudges or preferences. The enmity toward the United States has been the cornerstone of the Islamic regime's identity, legitimacy and staying power from day one. It has been based on Ayatollah Khomeini's xenophobic posture and opposition to Mohammad Reza Shah, whom he accused of promoting American and Israeli interests. Ayatollah Khamenei's well-guarded leftist tendencies, his unwavering championship of the Palestinian cause (sporting a *kaffieh* in public appearances) and hostility toward the Jewish state (objection to the two-state solution) follow the same line. The *rahbar*'s need for a bogeyman to be blamed for Iran's various setbacks as well as his own numerous failings may also have found hostility toward Washington a perfect ploy.

In addition to this deep-rooted individual hostility, a major force behind continued enmity toward Washington emanates from the ultra-conservative clerical establishment, which sees the resumption of relations as the end of its hegemonic clout. Normal relations with Washington are seen by the obscurantist mullahs as the prelude to the so-called "Western cultural onslaught"—increasing political and social liberalization, rejection of outmoded Islamic moral codes, a welcome adoption of Western democratic institutions and replacement of voodoo by modern science.

Normalization of relations with the United States is resisted by yet another powerful interest group in both the bazaar and the modern economy. Formed during the last 33 years of American absence, the group includes merchants, industrialists, service contractors and others who shifted their trade and business from the United States to China, Russia, East Asia, Latin America and Africa. They are likely to lose to new American rivals. Prominent among potential losers would be the Islamic Revolutionary Guard Corps, which currently enjoys a virtual monopoly in bidding for lucrative projects, and other Guard units widely suspected of being engaged in the increased smuggling of American products.

(5) Global economic sanctions have been to no avail since they have failed to change the regime's behavior or stop its nuclear program.

There is no dispute that, during the long period under sanctions, Iran has not only refused to stop its uranium enrichment program as demanded, but defiantly proceeded to develop more advanced centrifuge capabilities. Furthermore, Tehran has accelerated enrichment of its uranium stockpile to 20 percent and has continued research on nuclear-warhead design. Yet all available evidence shows that increasing economic sanctions, cyber war, a terror campaign and a sabotage program (e.g., the suspicious killing of Iranian scientists, explosions in atomic and ballistic rocket centers, fires in oil and gas pipelines) have not only slowed down Iran's nuclear program, but exerted a heavy toll on the Iranian economy.

Long suffering from certain basic structural problems (gross mismanagement and ineffective leadership), Iran's economy has been further damaged by punitive international measures. Annual economic growth has been slowed and is currently hovering around 2.5–3.0 percent. Official inflation is over 20 percent, and the unemployment rate is in the mid-teens. Private estimates are much higher in both cases. Capital, labor and total-factor productivity are dismally small, in some cases negative. The climate for investment and business is poor, and there is rampant corruption at all levels of the government and in state enterprises, largely intensified by sanctions.

Thus, there is no doubt that the choreographed, multifaceted sanctions by the United Nations, the US Congress, the European Union and other countries—including freezing the assets and banning the travel of hundreds of Iranian individuals and businesses linked to Iran's nuclear program—have had devastating effects. By all evidence, the Islamic Republic today is economically weaker and more chaotic, diplomatically more isolated and altogether more vulnerable than before. After having categorically denied year after year that sanctions were having any effect on the Iranian economy, President Ahmadinejad has recently admitted that sanctions had virtually paralyzed the country's banking system, and called them economic warfare. Scattered private reports point to such variegated sanctions-induced setbacks as a notable decline in daily oil production due to a lack of gas injection; a 20–30 percent increase in import costs due to higher banking, insurance and shipping charges; a shift from higher-quality Western goods to cheaper Chinese substitutes; difficulties in opening letters of credit and transfers of funds in almost all major international banks; virtual stoppage of Western direct investments and technology transfers; the near-impossibility of issuing foreign-exchange bonds in financial markets; and highly disturbing gyrations in the domestic gold and foreign-exchange markets.

The absence of change in the regime's behavior should be thus attributed to three countervailing factors. First, Iran's pursuit of advanced nuclear technologies, as well as its development of various nuclear capabilities, has now become a matter of national sovereignty, scientific achievement and patriotic honor the denial of which is universally considered close to treason—even by the opposition. Second, a number of Islamic, non-aligned, left-leaning and anti-American countries, along with such veto-empowered governments as Russia and China, have refused to abide by tougher Washington and European sanctions and thus eased the burden. Cooperating banks and amenable oil refineries in friendly countries also helped to fill some of the void. Third, large receipts from oil, gas and other exports during the last six years have enabled the regime to finance its annual budget, triple non-oil exports, double imports, and carry out a costly subsidy-reform program, thus lightening the sanctions' effects.

"Crippling" sanctions involving Iran's Central Bank and oil exports have recently been imposed on Iran by the United States and the European Union, avowedly in the hope of building public discontent and compelling the regime to change its nuclear policy. But, as long as the same political and economic realities prevail, little or no palpable change in the government's behavior should be expected. With an estimated $135 billion from oil and non-oil exports in 2011–12, a chest reserve of $120 billion in cash and 907 tons of gold (as reported by the Tehran Chamber of Commerce), Iran has more than enough resources to meet its payment obligations for more than a year. The government has a relatively small and serviceable foreign debt. And Iran can expect a continued positive trade balance as long as crude-oil prices remain above $80 per barrel. Smuggling in and out of the country may also continue to play a significant role in easing the burden. Nevertheless, dark and stormy days for the economy are ahead. Some moderately positive reports about the Iranian economy from the International Monetary Fund and the World Bank in recent months, while clearly attesting to the economy's resilience, also confirm an eighteenth-century sage's dictum that "nations have untold capacity for ruin."

(6) The only way to stop Iran from acquiring the nuclear bomb is to bomb it.

This is a deceptive, futile and dangerous idea backed by some powerful political groups of ultraconservatives in the United States and Israel. The hawks' arguments for a preventive strike are fairly simple, if not very convincing. First, the Islamic Republic is determined to acquire nuclear weapons because (a) all its major neighbors (Russia, Israel, Pakistan and, by proxy, the United States) are already nuclear powers; (b) no country possessing an atomic bomb has ever been attacked; (c) the Tehran government cannot financially afford to match its adversaries in conventional weapons; (d) Tehran has publicly announced its uranium-enrichment capabilities to be up to 20 percent, thus becoming a "virtual" nuclear state; and (e) the November 2011 report by the International Atomic Energy Agency (IAEA) has showed that Tehran is involved in "efforts to master the technology needed for atomic weapons" and is not forthcoming in its various nuclear-development activities.

A nuclear-armed Iran, in the neocon view, should thus not be allowed to proceed: because (1) it would lead to an arms race and nuclear proliferation in the region; (2) it would immensely increase Tehran's prestige in the Middle East, and enable it to use the nuclear umbrella to establish its regional hegemony, forcing smaller countries into its orbit; and (3) it would pose an existential threat to the state of Israel. At the same time, preemptive-strike proponents argue that the US Cold War policy of containment/deterrence vis-à-vis the Soviet Union and China would not stop the Islamic Republic from using its nuclear weapons. Their reasoning: the Iranian regime is shaped by a messianic cult and run by fanatical mullahs who place the highest value on martyrdom and life in the hereafter, thus making annihilation a welcome event!

The flaws in these arguments are many. First, they ignore Tehran's repeated and emphatic denials and *fatwas* issued by Ayatollah Khomeini and other grand ayatollahs against nuclear use. Second, even if Iran were actually engaged in developing a nuclear device, bombing Iran's nuclear facilities would be neither practical nor effective, as several high-ranking American and Israeli authorities have repeatedly pointed out. Iran is not Iraq or Syria with a fixed, open and known nuclear facility and no possibility of retaliation. Bombing multiple Iranian sites near population centers would require many air sorties, causing heavy human casualties and dangerous nuclear fallout. Invading planes could be shot down and their crews taken prisoner. Iran could close the Strait of Hormuz, sending oil prices sky high and damaging the global economy. American and allied ships and installations in the Persian Gulf could be attacked. In short, there could be no "clean and calibrated" air strikes, but a violent and messy affair with untold consequences. New insurgencies in Iraq and Afghanistan could be instigated. An American or Israeli attack on Iranian sites is also bound to trigger a catastrophic regional war involving the Lebanese Hezbollah, Palestinian Hamas, Syria, Saudi Arabia and other Gulf Cooperation Council members.

On top of all these, even the successful bombing of Iran's nuclear facilities with bunker-busting shells might temporarily cripple the nuclear program, but it will not stop it. In fact, it may unify the opposition behind the government and encourage the Tehran regime to redouble its nuclear efforts. Installations may be destroyed, but knowledge cannot be wiped out of scientists' minds.

Third, and most significant, the Iranian clergy's alleged character traits are grossly misunderstood. The concept of the "hereafter-fixated mullahs" is a complete fiction. A cursory look at the ruling clergy's mode of living in Iran—multiple wives, spacious living quarters, luxury cars, foreign bank accounts, sumptuous wedding and anniversary parties for their offspring—attests to their love for life and fear of death. Shiite clerics in Iran may reject certain aspects of Western culture, but they are hardly suicidal.

In many experts' views, a deterrence policy is probably the most cost-effective way to deal with the situation.

(7) Iran's massive pro-democracy demonstrations of 2009—the Green Movement—have been the main inspiration for the uprisings in the Arab world, the so-called Arab Spring.

This connection seems highly far-fetched, for several reasons. First, the lapse of time between Tehran's June 2009 street demonstrations and the first spark in the Tunisian uprising in December 2010 makes the events too distant from one another to be correlated. Second, the nature of the riots, the protesters' demands and the dynamics of the discourse have been vastly different in the two cases. In Tunisia, as in Egypt, Libya, Syria, Bahrain and Yemen, grievances were about dictatorial regimes that had resulted in mass unemployment, high inflation, rampant corruption and rising poverty. In Iran, the complaints focused solely on the rigged presidential elections and "lost votes." Similarly, the demonstrators' demand in the Arab world was straightforward: the ouster of the long-ruling dictators. In Iran, there was no demand for regime change or the Supreme Leader's dismissal. Third, the Arab uprisings were generally leaderless and sprang almost spontaneously from the frustrated, aggrieved and unemployed youth seeking a better material life. In Iran, the "Green Movement" was backed by two aging former officials and solid members of the Islamic Regime's *nomenklatura* who were deeply and personally involved in some of the regime's questionable deeds. These "opposition" leaders did not push for the theocracy's downfall. They wanted, in fact, to go back to Ayatollah Khomeini's "golden era," his "true teachings" and a strict observance of Iran's Islamic constitution.

The much later demonstrations in Iran during 2010—which involved faint chants against the *rahbar* and scattered stifled demands for Khamenei's ouster—have themselves, ironically, been influenced by the Arab Spring, rather than the reverse. The new anti-*rahbar* cries started *after* Ben Ali's ouster in Tunisia and Mubarak's in Egypt.

Avoidable pitfalls

The distorted picture that these myths present goes beyond mere abstractions. The myth of a popularly elected government in Iran and the fiction of an "Islamic democracy" propagated by the regime's mouthpieces around the world have enabled the Islamic Republic, one of the world's most notorious misogynist regimes, to gain a seat at the UN Commission on the Status of Women, the principal world body dedicated exclusively to gender equality.

The exaggerated notion about Ayatollah Khamenei's absolute power and unique prestige has deflected attention from the fact that, since the end of the Iran–Iraq War, Iran has been steadily moving from a theocratic oligarchy toward a quasi-military dictatorship in which the top brass, masquerading as devout Muslims, enjoy not only increasing political clout but also growing financial power—with dire consequences for the country and the region.

The myth about President Ahmadinejad being responsible for the Tehran–Washington rupture has camouflaged the real stumbling blocks. The reason Ayatollah Khamenei and other top political leaders have been reluctant to engage in a serious dialogue with Washington is not essentially a clash of personalities or hostility toward a grand bargain, but simply a matter of profound mistrust. In March 2010 Ayatollah Khamenei rejected President Obama's "extended hand" (of friendship) by calling it a "steel hand inside a velvet glove." Rightly or not, Iran's political leaders are convinced that Washington's ultimate objective regarding Iran is "regime change," and that all the talk about nuclear weapons or human-rights abuses is sheer political subterfuge. A recent newspaper report, attributed to an unnamed Washington official, indicates that the sanctions are designed to create enough popular discontent to force a change. Thus, unless and until the Iranian leaders are disabused of this notion, there will be no gesture of reconciliation from the Iranian side. At the same time, given the current make-up of the US Congress and the domination of US politics by special-interest pressure groups, Tehran's overt and unrelenting hostility toward the state of Israel, as well as its undisguised opposition to the two-state solution, will prevent Washington from considering any genuine détente with Tehran.

The illusion about the futility of sanctions has played into the hands of those who advocate "neutralizing" the Iranian nuclear threat rather than containing it. Ignoring the devastating effects of sanctions and coercive measures on ordinary Iranian citizens—consequences explicitly claimed to be unintended by the Obama administration—American and Israeli hardliners are emboldened to propose yet stiffer and more coercive measures.

The fiction concerning Iran's nuclear ambitions has complicated Iran's normal relations with its neighbors and the international community at large. It has led the hawks to get ahead of the facts and overplay the significance of the Islamic Republic's drive for nuclear technology by falsely claiming that the latest IAEA report finds Tehran on the threshold of having a nuclear bomb. And the preposterous notion about the mullahs' craving for martyrdom and defiance of mutual annihilation has likewise prompted the warmongers to push for early preventive strikes.

Finally, the false notion about the Arab Spring's emanating from Iran's Green Movement has enabled the Islamic Republic's propaganda machine to portray the North African uprisings as a "great Islamic awakening," a "struggle against the West," and a "revival of Islamic rule." In truth, none of these movements has showed any similarity to Iran's 1979 revolution. There have been no "death to America" or "death to Israel" slogans, no burning of the American flag, and no demands for an Islamic government. In their general yearning for freedom, democracy and respect for human rights, there has been a clear rejection of an Iranian-type Islamic rule. Interestingly enough, in the UN General Assembly votes on Iran's 2011 human-rights violations, Tunisia and Libya voted against the Islamic Republic, and Egypt abstained.

A clearer understanding of these myths may not end the West's Iranian conundrum, but it might lead to less swashbuckling and more effective ways of dealing with it.

Note

* First published in *Middle East Policy*, Spring 2012, Volume XIX, No. 1. Reproduced with permission.

15 Iran's economy facing a challenging year*

In mid-February 2013, some 43 Iranian academic economists sent a long, open letter to President Ahmadinejad, warning him about the gravity of the country's current economic crisis, and asking him to reconsider his ongoing socio-economic policies in order to forestall national upheavals. The letter noted that, given the unprecedented large oil export receipts during 2005–12, the economy was expected to experience faster growth, lower inflation, reduced unemployment and improved welfare. Yet, due to the administration's misconceived idealism and its non-professional and ad hoc approach to economic realities, the nation was suffering from the double scourges of both high prices and massive unemployment.

This warning letter closely echoed a similar missive addressed to the president six years earlier by some 60 like-minded Iranian economists alarmed by the corrosive effects of Iran's ongoing "stagflation"—a combination of high inflation and protracted unemployment called the "Dutch disease." In both letters, the groups called attention to the country's major economic woes in detail, analyzed their causes and made a number of professional recommendations. There was neither an acknowledgment nor any reaction to the letters by the chief executive.

Thorough and well-reasoned as the economists' last letter is, its references to the broad-based and far-reaching economic sanctions by the UN, the EU and the US are peripheral and non-focused. Iran's current grave economic crisis seems to be almost exclusively blamed on the government's incompetence and mismanagement, while the crippling effects of sanctions on the country's international trade and payments are not sufficiently emphasized. No amount of incompetence and mismanagement would have resulted in the current malaise if the oil export embargo and payment restrictions had not been in place.

Troubling signs

The economists' letter seems to hint that after the Nowruz celebrations and the exhaustion of the cash bonus, the country might be in for a rough ride. Current visible signs indeed seem to indicate that the Persian New Year

(March 2013–March 2014) is likely to witness—apart from unforeseen political crises related to the June 2013 presidential election or other events—a combination of anemic growth, double-digit inflation, near record unemployment, multiple exchange rates, a banking system in trouble and the fate of the fiscal budget (including the second phase of the Subsidies Reform Program) in limbo. By some pessimistic estimates, the coming year promises to be the most worrisome twelve months since 1994. The one dimly bright spot on the horizon is the possibility of a compromise with the P5+1 group (the five permanent members of the UN Security Council—China, France, Russia, the UK and the US—plus Germany) on the nuclear issue—leading to the relaxation of economic sanctions, and new opportunities for investment and growth. An improvement in the non-oil trade might be another blessing.

A brief look at the anticipated behavior of these basic indicators shows the gravity of the country's economic problems in the remaining months of the current administration and the first months of the new government to be elected in June 2013.

The new year's gross domestic product (GDP) growth is variously estimated to be in low single digits due to a combination of factors: (a) a drastic 50% fall in oil export earnings; (b) considerably reduced domestic and foreign investments; (c) a deteriorating business climate caused by open quarrels among the top political leaders; (d) lower volumes of capital goods imports due to foreign exchange shortages; (e) increasing bankruptcies and factory closings as the legacy of poorly managed subsidy reforms; (f) difficulties in conducting international business because of escalating sanctions; and (g) reduced appropriation of development funds in the proposed 2013–14 fiscal budget—the sharpest in the last eight years. The lowest growth projection is by the IMF at a mere 0.8%. The highest figure, forecast by private analysts, is in the low single digits.

Continuing double-digit inflation is the second challenge. Endemic to Iran's post-revolution economy, inflation has been generally caused by: (a) a steady increase in production costs on the part of mushrooming and highly inefficient state enterprises; (b) stagnant productivity of labor, capital, and management; and (c) steady increases in government expenditure, accompanied by perpetual budget deficits. In the 34 years since the revolution, Iran has had only four years of officially balanced budgets. The more recent price hikes, however, are rooted in the Ahmadinejad administration's monetary and welfare policies, ie: (a) massive monetary assistance to the so-called "quick returns" enterprises (absorbing some IR430 trillion in bank loans) with disastrous results (50% closed down within two years); (b) profligate investments in the low-cost housing project (*Maskan-e-Mehr*) with no palpable effects on urban housing prices; (c) spot allocation of funds to ad hoc local "development" ventures demanded by the welcoming crowds during the president's nationwide tours; and (d) selection of non-professional contractors to undertake gigantic construction projects. As a result, total liquidity has increased from IR1,640 trillion in 2007 to IR4,780 trillion in 2013—or nearly 300%.

Ironically enough, both rising and falling world prices of crude oil (as the lifeblood of the Iranian economy) have contributed to rising inflation, either through undertaking expansive fiscal measures or resulting from budget deficits financed by the Central Bank of Iran (CBI)'s printing press.

The most recent and sudden surge in consumer prices, however, is clearly attributable to the drastic plunge in the free market value of the rial—from about \$1 = IR12,000 in December 2011 to about \$1 = IR34,000 in recent days. The national currency, which had been distinctly overvalued for years and in desperate need of adjustment, lost its exchange parity overnight once the fresh embargo on Iran's oil exports and restrictions on the CBI's operations were announced by the EU and Washington in late 2011 (MEES, August 6, 2012).

Due to the continued tightening of economic sanctions, the increase in the consumer price index (CPI) is now officially expected to surpass 31% by April 2013—the highest in the region, the fourth highest in the world, and Iran's own highest in the last 17 years. Private estimates go as far as 50%. A maverick US economist puts it at over 100%. In the months to come, the expenditure of the Nowruz bonus, and continued budget shortfalls, are expected to add at least 6–7% to the current official figure.

Unemployment, particularly among educated youth, will continue to be a vexing problem for the government in the coming year—due in part to anemic GDP growth, and increased entrants to the labor market. Despite President Ahmadinejad's repeated promises during his tours in 2006, 2008, and 2010 to end unemployment within a year, the total number is currently estimated to surpass 3mn—even with the practice of considering two hours of work during a week as employment. The latest official numbers show a national jobless rate of 13.5%—with those for 15–24-year-olds reaching 25.5%. For women, the rate is even higher. By private estimates, the national jobless rate is currently no less than 20%—the highest in the last 30 years and among 17 similarly ranked countries. The government's repeated claims to have created more than a million jobs each year in the past five years have been summarily dismissed by private analysts as incompatible with anemic (or even negative) GDP growth during the period. The combination of inflation and unemployment figures—the so-called "misery index"—is now 43.7%, up from 23.6% in 2005. Ironically enough, a factor contributing to higher unemployment has been a phenomenon called multi-jobs occupation. According to official labor statistics, some 25–35% of workers under the Labor Law are "double-job" employees. Similarly, some 60% of public sector "managers" reportedly have two or more jobs.

The current national exchange rate system is in chaos, and in need of a clear policy. Currently, there are three rates in place—an official "reference" rate of \$1 = IR12,260 applying to the foreign currency supplied by the CBI for imports of "essential" goods and services. Then there is the "free market" rate, ranging from \$1 = IR30,000–IR40,000 with no restrictions or regulation for purchase and sales. And then there is an officially administered "transaction" rate that is determined daily, some 20% below each day's free market rate—appropriated for "semi-essential" items. With the list of "essential" items frequently changed by the Transaction Center, the perils of perpetual uncertainty and the opportunities for rent-seeking activities abound. Thus, while doctors, nurses, and health officials loudly complain about the dearth of life-saving drugs due to the exchange shortage, fleets of imported luxury cars roam the streets of Tehran.

Although nearly all responsible officials talk about the desirability of a return to a single rate, the goal has so far proven elusive. There is no agreement among senior officials regarding the single "equilibrium" rate. While President Ahmadinejad believes that the current "reference" rate of $1 = IR12,260 is the right one, and should be adopted as such, the Minister of Trade and Industry asks the public to "forget about the US dollar at 10,000 rials, and get used to 40,000."

The banking system is also expected to experience a rough ride in the coming months. All state and private banks—while technically modern, electronically equipped, and normally functioning well—present several problems of their own. Apart from being under universal economic sanctions and badly constrained in their routine international transactions, they suffer from massive debt to the CBI, enormous non-performing loans and a troubling number of bounced checks. The banking system debt to the CBI now stands at IR540 trillion—up by 42% in one year. The system's non-performing assets are estimated to have reached IR800 trillion—up by 36% in one year—and an alarming 18% of total system assets. The number of bounced checks has been steadily rising every year in the last five years and now exceeds IR370 trillion, or nearly 5% of all checks issued.

Finally, in the coming year Iran is expected to face a difficult and painful fiscal situation. The proposed budget for 1392 (2013–14), recently presented to the Majlis for ratification, faces an uncertain fate in the coming weeks. The budget proposal calls for expenditure to rise by nearly IR7,300 trillion ($590bn at the official rate) or some 29% over the previous year. Current expenditures are to rise by some 20%, while development outlays are to decline by 4%. While the draft budget's assumptions regarding Iran's reduced daily oil export volume, the average price of Iranian crude and total foreign exchange available to the treasury are fairly realistically estimated, there are no guarantees that they will materialize as projected.

A controversial and troubling aspect of the proposed budget is the section dealing with the resumption of the second phase of the Subsidies Reform Program (MEES, December 14, 2012). Irrespective of the acceptability of the proposed figures to the Majlis once it begins to discuss the budget in the next few weeks, the fate of the second phase seems in peril at this juncture. A majority of the Majlis deputies (including the powerful Speaker), backed by the Iran Chamber of Commerce and Industry and most private economists, are against an early resumption of the program's second phase. Given high and rising inflation, the harsh and escalating economic sanctions and the forthcoming presidential elections in June 2013, they believe that the second phase should be postponed until 2014. Private analysts, concerned economists and many legislators also believe that, given the program's less than satisfactory performance in the first phase, its time horizon, scope of operation, sources of finance and methods of welfare compensation should be totally reexamined, and adjusted.

The president, rejecting the negative evaluation of the program and its alleged negative impact on liquidity and inflation, has adamantly opposed any postponement proposal, arguing that some 30% of the program's objectives have been fully achieved in the first phase and the rest could be accomplished through a "shock therapy" operation in a final second phase. At the second anniversary of the program in December 2012, he said he wished the naysayers (read: Majlis deputies) would have let him implement the whole program in a single year (instead of five) because the "high-minded" people of Iran were ready for such "shock therapy." And now, he again asks the Majlis to let him finish the whole price adjustments during the last few months of his administration.

Meanwhile, the president continues to claim that the immediate total energy price adjustment is the "key to curing Iran's current economic malaise"—without saying how. In a series of statements during a long speech in the Majlis in January 2013 and a televised dialogue with viewers later, he expanded on his unorthodox and somewhat mystifying salvation theory. Ignoring all evidence to the contrary, he said the early resumption of the second phase was "the only way to bypass and surmount the nefarious aspects of the universal economic sanctions"—without elaborating on the causative links. In yet another perplexing statement during the late February 2013 TV program, he claimed that the resumption of the second phase would be "the best way to reduce the share of oil export receipts in the national budget and the national economy"—again without elaborating on the process involved.

Given the short period left of his lame-duck administration, and the rial's recent plunge making domestic energy price adjustments to the Persian Gulf levels several times more difficult, it does not look like he will have the chance to prove his points.

Self-inflicted wounds

Of the thorny economic problems which Iran is going to face in the coming year, independent of sanctions, almost all are self-induced. They are rooted in a wrong-headed populist strategy of combating endemic inflation by hoodoo remedies. Faced with protracted double-digit price rises caused by perennial budget deficits and excess spending, President Ahmadinejad decided early in his administration to combat this demand-caused economic disequilibrium by focusing on the supply side. Thus, instead of trying to raise revenues or reduce wasteful expenditures, he chose a crowd-pleasing, short-term economic policy of controlling costs—with scant regard for its harmful long-term implications. To keep household and business expenses in check, the government proceeded to hold three vital cost factors—the exchange rate, interest rates and the basic energy prices—in check through government diktats. The outcome has been a near disaster in all three areas.

The short-sighted policy of keeping the exchange rate artificially overvalued in order to hold import costs down led to a number of troublesome consequences such as: (a) reducing domestic producers' ability to compete with foreign suppliers; (b) bringing down domestic production capacity of import-competing industries by some 30–40%; (c) idling thousands of workers with each additional billion dollar of imports; (d) worsening Iran's non-oil trade balance; and (d) giving a hefty subsidy to foreign farmers and manufacturers The overvalued exchange rate also resulted in increased national dependence on the world economy (even for essential food items). Thus, with the imposition of new tough sanctions on Iran's oil exports and its Central Bank operations announced in late 2011, the long-dormant pressure on the rial blew up and the current era of exchange instability ensued.

The government's extensive interest rate regulation must take its share of the blame. Holding interest rates on saving deposits below the inflation rate and keeping bank charges on commercial and investment loans below free-market levels in the bazaar have inflicted immeasurable damage to the economy. Low (and negative) returns on deposits have discouraged savings and parsimony, stifled productive investments had led savers to move their funds from bank accounts to other outlets such as real estate, precious metals and US dollars. Losing savings deposits has led the banks to borrow steadily from the CBI for their voluntary as well as state-mandated loans. Government dictated loans to favored, but money-losing, projects have been a main cause of the banks' non-performing assets. Sizeable differences between mandated bank interest rates and the rates prevailing in the bazaar, combined with the small penalty for late repayments of loans, have induced some well-connected businessmen to borrow money from the state banks at rates in the low 20s, lend the borrowed sum in the bazaar at percentage rates in the 30s, and postpone repayments of the loans for years at an annual penalty of only 6%! Poor and unprofessional assessments of borrowers' proposed projects and the concentration of bank loans on a few selected mega borrowers have been other causes of the banking system's problems. Nearly 80% of the total bank loans are now reportedly in the hands of less than 12% of active businessman. In the absence of real banking system reforms in the coming year, the situation is likely to get worse—particularly if the sanctions are not removed.

Finally, keeping energy prices artificially down for years has resulted in profligate energy consumption, the continuation of energy inefficiencies, the rise of energy-intensive industries vulnerable to external shocks, a growing need for energy imports, intolerable air pollution and a clear rise in energy smuggling to neighboring countries.

Light at the end of the tunnel?

The past Persian year has been described by the CBI governor as "the most difficult" economic year since the 1979 revolution. Yet if the full effects of the harsh and tightening sanctions are allowed to continue or even worsen, the coming months will be just as difficult, if not more so. By everyone's admission, the broad-based and crippling sanctions have so far failed to impact the Islamic Republic's nuclear policy and programs. And they have not produced the popular unrest and street riots to force the government's hand that those imposing the sanctions had hoped for. The Tehran government has not surrendered to the West's demands and has continued the pursuit of its chosen path. But, continually escalating sanctions are beginning to bite hard, and have taken a very heavy toll on Iran's middle and working classes, who have seen their purchasing power steadily reduced, their savings depleted and their jobs in jeopardy. In a recent interview with German broadcaster Deutsche Welle, the Tehran Chamber of Commerce president openly admitted that the middle and lower strata in Iran now face great difficulties in meeting their five essential needs—food, housing, clothing, healthcare, and education.

Whether or not Tehran's intransigence in the pursuit of its controversial nuclear program is worth so much pain and suffering for the Iranian people is an intriguing question. In the absence of a credible nationwide referendum, it would be hard to know the people's true feelings about the policy. With the exception of the Islamic Republic's leaders themselves, whose answer is accurately predictable, there can be only guesses regarding the feelings of others. In general, there is no doubt that the country's politically conscious citizens must all be proud of their country's advances in nuclear technology. There is also no doubt that a small but influential group of conservative and xenophobic hardliners continues to insist that Iran will never abandon its current defiant stance and continued hostility toward the West. Likewise, the scientists and engineers currently engaged in nuclear research might be thought to resent being denied their scientific rights. Active smugglers and organized crime groups that now thrive on sanctions may also be found to support the status quo. From another perspective, a minority of upper-class *nouveaux riches*—those who reportedly live in $10mn penthouses "above the clouds," enjoy their $250 dinners at the Milad Tower's restaurant, purchase their $20,000 outfits at the Giorgio Armani boutique and drive their imported Porsches and Maseratis—may be found not to care one way or the other about the government's inflexible position.

A secret poll conducted among the country's middle and lower strata, however, might indeed show that an overwhelming majority of respondents would be willing to go easy on the nuclear issue, a phenomenon that has absolutely no effect on their daily life, in order to receive some relief, which has everything to do with it.

A possible respite

Iran's fundamental economic woes are not all caused by sanctions, and they are not going to go away if sanctions are removed. Yet no relief from the current economic malaise would be imaginable without some relaxation of these tightening restrictions. Optimism recently expressed by both parties to the Almaty negotiations, and the conciliatory remarks by Iran's Supreme Leader in his Nowruz speech in Meshed, offer a glimmer of hope that there might indeed be some light at the end of the tunnel for Iran's suffering population. The possibility of a new government—economically savvy, politically seasoned and diplomatically adept—being elected in the June 2013 presidential election can only add to this optimism.

Note

* First published in the *Middle East Economic Survey*, April 5, 2013. Reproduced with permission.

Index